Praise for

The Magic of Flowers

I have been using herbs and essential oils for years, but The Magic of Flowers *has expanded my horizons in ways I never could have anticipated. This book is a unique and powerful approach to working with nature's most beautiful plants, written in a simple and evocative style. Tess Whitehurst doesn't just write about flowers—she translates their messages into words anyone can understand. This is the only flower magic book you'll ever need.*

DEBORAH BLAKE,
AUTHOR OF *EVERYDAY WITCH BOOK OF RITUALS*

The Magic of Flowers *by Tess Whitehurst is one of those rare books that I wish had been written years ago. While I've worked with flowers before in flower essences and in medicinal tinctures, I've only added a few to my magical practices up to now—but that definitely changed after reading* The Magic of Flowers! *Wonderfully researched, easy to read, and full of spells that reach beyond the simple "101" of many books, this book has found a permanent place on my "most used" reference shelf!*

KRIS BRADLEY,
AUTHOR OF *CONFESSIONS OF A PAGAN SOCCER MOM*
AND *MRS. B.'S GUIDE TO HOUSEHOLD WITCHERY*

Thorough, deep, and multifaceted, The Magic of Flowers *is a must for any healer or magical practitioner's shelf. Whitehurst has a keen understanding of flower energies, which she conveys directly to the reader through her words. She has gathered wisdom from her own experience as well as through research. The book is more than an encyclopedia, though, as it also teaches the reader to work with flowers directly for beauty, health, healing, and magic.*

CLEA DANAAN,
AUTHOR OF *SACRED LAND*
AND *LIVING EARTH DEVOTIONAL*

Tess Whitehurst is an intuitive counselor, energy worker, feng shui consultant, speaker, and author of *Magical Housekeeping, The Good Energy Book,* and *The Art of Bliss*. She has appeared on the Bravo TV show *Flipping Out,* and her writing has been featured in *Writer's Digest*, *Whole Life Times Magazine*, and online at the Huffington Post and Lemondrop.com. She lives in Venice, California.

Visit her online at www.tesswhitehurst.com.

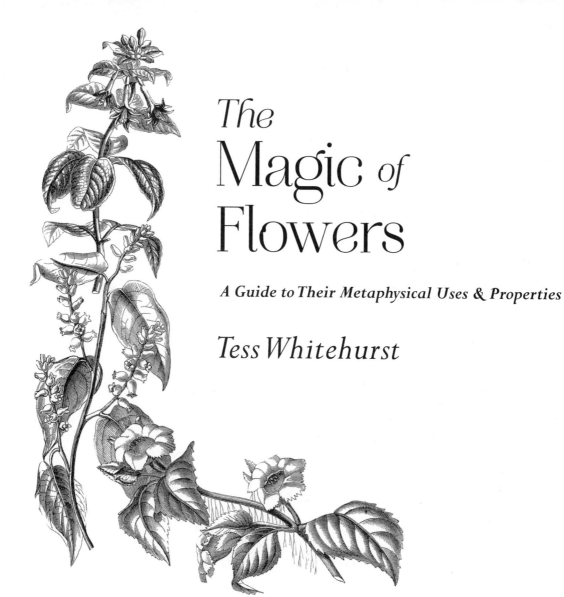

The
Magic of
Flowers

A Guide to Their Metaphysical Uses & Properties

Tess Whitehurst

Llewellyn Publications
WOODBURY, MINNESOTA

FIRST EDITION
Second Printing, 2014

Book design and edit by Rebecca Zins
Cover design by Adrienne Zimiga
Cover illustration: Cheryl Chalmers/The July Group
Interior decorative illustrations from *1167 Decorative Cuts CD-ROM and Book* (Dover, 2007),
Classic Floral Designs (Dover, 2010), *Old-Fashioned Floral Designs CD-ROM and Book* (Dover, 1999),
and *Traditional Floral Designs* (Dover, 2003)

Llewellyn Publications is a registered trademark of Llewellyn Worldwide Ltd.

Library of Congress Cataloging-in-Publication Data

Whitehurst, Tess, 1977–
 The magic of flowers : a guide to their metaphysical uses & properties / Tess Whitehurst.—First edition.
    pages   cm
 Includes bibliographical references and index.
 ISBN 978-0-7387-3194-0
 1. Flowers—Miscellanea. I. Title.
 SB405.W55 2013
 581—dc23
                                                                                    2013005160

Llewellyn Publications
A Division of Llewellyn Worldwide Ltd.
2143 Wooddale Drive
Woodbury, MN 55125-2989
www.llewellyn.com
Printed in the United States of America

Contents

Introduction

I have always wanted a book like this on my shelf: a useful, practical reference guide to the magic of flowers. As a matter of fact, I've pined for it for years! After years of working with floral aromas and flower essences, after countless lovely moments in quiet contemplation with living blossoms, and after I wrote and published two magic-related books and innumerable magic-related articles, it finally occurred to me: "Hey, *I* could write that book!"

And I have so enjoyed it! First of all, I had a good excuse to make regular trips to a local botanical garden. As if that weren't enough, once I got there, I spent exquisite quality time with the flowers, tuning in to their unique vibrations and taking notes on wisdom they wanted to share. Then, as I wrote each entry, I ferreted out and studied existing literature about the blossom's magical and traditional uses. Sometimes I found a lot of information about a flower, and sometimes I found little or none. But whenever I found information— for example, the flower's meaning in the Victorian language of flowers, the mythical origin of the flower's name, or a traditional folk charm employing the blossom—I found that it resonated very deeply with the wisdom I had received from the blossoms themselves.

At first this felt uncanny and even miraculous, but in time I came to feel that it was the most natural thing in the world. What I mean is, once you enter into the realm of flower magic, you begin to recognize the energetic signatures of blossoms in the same way you can recognize whether a person is happy or sad, or in the same way you can hear what someone is trying to say if you just quiet down and listen. Flowers, after all, give one the feeling that they are closer to the etheric realm of pure energy than the tangible, physical realm. And dwelling as they do on the border between seen and unseen, they allow us to see beyond the veil of duality and into the heart of truth. So, naturally, sensitive flower enthusiasts from all time periods and all cultures, when tuning in to the wisdom and magical signature of a blossom, would pick up on similar aspects.

To frame this concept a different way, consider that songs are geometrical patterns that convey emotion and vibration in a universally recognized way. In fact, a 2008 study at the Max Planck Institute for Human Cognitive and Brain Sciences has effectively demonstrated that people are frequently able to identify the emotions in songs from cultures that they are all but completely unfamiliar with. Similarly, each flower possesses what might be seen as its own unique, recognizable energetic signature, though everyone's experience of the flower will naturally be somewhat different based on his or her emotional makeup and current life situation.

With this in mind, it is my intention for this book to be a window into this subtle and whimsical—yet very real—realm of flower magic. Then you may have your own direct, transcendent experiences with these mystical beings, who can serve as therapists, healers, and emissaries of the Divine.

An Orientation to Flower Magic (Read This First)

A flower is a manifestation of divine beauty and wisdom. And while each flower's vibration is unique, what it expresses is universal: it is available to all of us and is already a part of us. Flower magic, then, might be defined as employing a flower as a focal point for our intention or as a window into our own divine aspect in order to affect a desired positive change. While simply spending time with a flower can provide an infusion of nourishment and spiritual sustenance, flower magic can take many additional forms. So, while you'll find that each flower entry contains targeted suggestions for a variety of healing and manifestation purposes, this section will introduce the primary magical methods discussed in this book and establish a basic framework for your own flower magic practice.

Proximity

The simplest form of flower magic is proximity: bringing a flower or bouquet into your home, giving a flower as a gift, or even spending time in a place where the flower is growing. While this type of magic can work whether you are conscious of it or not, it becomes greatly enhanced when you're aware of a flower's magical properties and when you consciously employ the flower for a particular magical purpose.

Here are some loose guidelines to help you maximize the power of proximity:

- If you gather a flower, gather her with consciousness, compassion, and respect. In other words, first tune in to her energy and let her know what you would like help with. Then, gently ask her if it's okay to gather her. When and if you intuitively feel that it is—if you feel a positive, open, relaxed feeling in your body and mind rather than a closed or tense one—follow your inner guidance about how to best gather the blossom. You might also like to leave something near the base of the plant(s) as payment for the blossom(s), such as a small amount of blessed water, a bit of wine or ale, a crystal, or a coin.

- If the flower is growing near your home or workspace, take a moment to consciously employ the flower's assistance (see "Quiet Contemplation" on the following page).

- If you purchase a flower or bouquet (at a flower shop, for example), do your best to obtain flower(s) that are ethically and sustainably grown and harvested. Also, take a moment with the blossoms: relax your mind as you gaze at them. Then conjure up the feeling of your magical intention, believing and knowing in your heart that, in the space beyond time, it is already present in your life experience: it is already true. See pictures and feel feelings related to the manifestation of your intention. Then, from a feeling place (not a thinking one), consciously send the energy of this intention into the blossoms.

Quiet Contemplation

The second most basic method of flower magic is sitting in quiet contemplation with a living, growing blossom. In addition to providing a relaxing and uplifting meditation, this can offer a very potent infusion of wisdom, guidance, and healing. To do this, sit or stand comfortably near the living flowering plant with your spine straight. Become aware of your breath and consciously relax your body. When you feel centered, begin to gaze at the blossom; as you do so, relax more and more deeply. Continue to gaze at the blossom until you feel so engrossed in the moment that you have entered a slightly altered state. You will find that this is very easy and that there is no need to try too hard—it is simply a matter of focus, such as when you are reading a novel and you get swept away into the landscape of the book. Once this shift occurs, gently bring whatever situation or concern you would like help with to mind and present it silently to the flower. Open your heart to the wisdom you receive. You may like to have a notebook handy to jot down anything you may want to remember, but this is unnecessary, as the wisdom will be conveyed to you on many levels, not just on an intellectual one.

During this time you might also consciously converse with the flower, asking her for further, active assistance with your magical intention.

Care

While caring for a flower is always a magical act, you can choose to imbue the pastime with a laser-focused magical intention. For example, perhaps your goal is to manifest a love relationship. You might choose a flower that represents romantic love, such as a tulip, and bring one or more tulips into your yard. As you plant and care for them, you might conjure up the feelings you associate with an ideal romantic relationship, knowing that the time and energy you invest in caring for the plant are fueling your manifestation efforts and creating a space in your life for the relationship to appear. You might also consciously enlist the tulip's help with drawing this desired love into your life.

Rituals and Charms

If you already have a magical practice and feel comfortable with spellcraft (i.e., crafting your own rituals and charms), you can incorporate these blossoms into your magic in ways that intuitively feel right to you. Or, if you are new to magic, you will find numerous simple yet effective rituals and charms embedded within the flower entries. Just be sure to relax your body and mind before you begin and to fuel your efforts with belief, visualization, and strong, clear intention setting.

Aromatherapy and Essential Oils

A lovely, sensual way to employ the magic of flowers is through the potently fragrant, highly concentrated essential oil of a blossom. Not all blossoms are available in essential oil form, but the entries in this book will alert you to the ones that are available and also provide suggestions for how to employ them.

Some basic methods of employing aromatherapy and essential oils in flower magic include:

- Diffusing the essential oil with a commercially available essence diffuser or oil burner.

- Adding the essential oil to a carrier oil (such as jojoba or sweet almond) and anointing yourself with it. However, everyone's skin and every essential oil is different: for example, some people can wear lavender oil "neat," or undiluted, while some with extremely sensitive skin may not even be able to handle it diluted. Generally, essential oils should be sufficiently diluted before they're applied to the skin. Also, some oils are irritating to almost everyone, so do your homework.

- Adding the essential oil to a mister of spring water or rose water, shaking it, and misting a person or space. (You will find rose water in a number of mist recipes throughout the book. This is often employed because it possesses a delicious fragrance as well as a very pure and loving vibration. Rose water can be purchased online and at most health food stores.)

- Anointing objects or charms.

Flower Essences

Working with a flower essence—a homeopathic form of medicine formulated and popularized by natural-health pioneer Dr. Edward Bach—is a delicate yet powerful method of flower magic. A whole other thing entirely than essential oil (although they sound similar and can both be found in tiny bottles), a flower essence is essentially the vibration and subtle wisdom of a flower in water, along with some sort of vibration-preserving ingredient such as brandy. These can be purchased on the Web or in health food or metaphysical supply stores from a number of reputable companies: Bach Flower Essences, Alaskan Essences, FES Essences, and Star Essences, to name a few. (With so many flower essence companies in existence, I have found that virtually every blossom you can imagine is available somewhere on the Internet. When ordering online you will just want to be sure that you feel confident in the integrity of the website and the ordering process.) Or, if you're a do-it-yourself type, you may also make your own. It is a bit involved, so you might like to take a class or check out a book on the subject, although you'll find basic instructions in appendix A.

Magically speaking, flower essences are the closest thing to the actual living blossoms themselves and hold the purest essence of a flower's unique wisdom and healing abilities. They work on both energetic and emotional levels, and merge with our personal energy or the energy of a space to create positive shifts in our aura, mindset, and holistic well-being.

Flower essences can be employed in several ways, including:

- Taking two to four drops under the tongue or in water as needed for a specific purpose or on a regular basis (say once or twice per day) until you feel that you have sufficiently assimilated the flower's wisdom and healing properties.
- Adding twenty to forty drops to one's bath water.
- Adding two to ten drops to misters of rose water or spring water and misting a person or space.

Where flower essences are concerned, you will notice that I often specify a range of drops rather than a set number. This is because—in addition to the fact that different flower essences will possess different levels of concentration—working with flower essences is something of an intuitive science. In other words, there *is* wiggle room, so feel free to follow your intuition when it comes to exact amounts.

Affinity

An interesting and revealing practice—and one from which much healing and wisdom can be gleaned—is simply being alert to the blossoms that you seem to gravitate toward or have a noticeable affinity for at any given time. For example, perhaps you're visiting a botanical garden, florist, or nursery, and you discover a blossom that you just can't get enough of. This means that there is something about that flower's energy that you are craving. As such, spending time in quiet contemplation with that flower or bringing that flower into your home or yard will have a special power for you and will be particularly energetically nourishing.

Similarly, if you find yourself in a place where flower essences and essential oils are sold, you may find yourself particularly drawn to a certain fragrance or vibration. Be assured that this, also, is significant in some way.

In either case, whether or not you consciously discover why you are gravitating toward a certain flower (which can be a useful diagnostic tool in itself), spending time near that flower (or that flower essence or aroma) and incorporating it into your flower magic practice will very likely provide the type of energetic infusion that you will most benefit from at this time.

A Few Words about Correspondences

At the end of each flower entry, you'll find a small section called "magical correspondences." Correspondences are the planet(s), element(s), and gender(s) that each flower's vibration is similar to or in alignment with. The purpose of providing these is to help you get a feeling for the flower's energy, as well as to assist you with the timing and planning of your magical workings. For example, if a flower that you're using in your magic is in alignment with the element of Air, you might like to plan your ritual for a time when the moon is in an Air sign: Gemini, Libra, or Aquarius. Or if a flower is in alignment with the Moon, you could coincide your magic with a Monday (the day of the week ruled by the Moon) or a time when the Moon is in the sign of Cancer. The gender has to do with whether the flower has more of a yin nature (soft, receptive, feminine) or a yang nature (active, projective, masculine).

These correspondences are not set in stone, as everyone's experience of a plant will be different. (Indeed, some of them are in agreement with traditional wisdom, and others I discerned on my own.) Additionally, it is unnecessary to feel limited or constrained by them. For example, if you feel inspired to work with a moon flower on a Sunday (the day of the week ruled by the Sun), please do.

If you do feel moved to plan your magic according to the correspondences, however, you might find it useful to check the correspondences charts in the appendices.

A Cautionary Note

Please be mindful that many flowers, including many of the flowers in this book, are toxic to humans and domestic animals. When prepared correctly, flower essences are not toxic, as they contain the vibration of a plant rather than actual plant matter. Still, if you choose to make your own, please be very careful. Also, *never confuse essential oils and flower essences.* Essential oils are highly concentrated and made of the plant, while flower essences are made of brandy and water. *Essential oils are never to be taken internally and can even be extremely irritating to the skin.*

Author's Notes

Obviously every flower on this list will not necessarily grow in your area, so just work with the ones that do, as there will almost certainly be at least one that fits with your magical intention. Or, if you read about a flower that you have a burning desire to employ and it doesn't happen to grow in your area, you might find a commercially available flower essence online or at a health food store or metaphysical supply shop.

Also, although I wanted to write about every flower in existence, for practical purposes I wrote about eighty of them. And while I tried to cover all the old standby flowers (daisy, lily, tulip, rose, and so on), as well as a good selection of the more obscure varieties, I apologize if I left out your favorite or one that grows in abundance in your neighborhood! However, it is my intention to point you in the direction of engaging in your own flower communication practice and discovering your own portal into the magical properties and uses of our friends in the floral realm. In other words, if you want to know about the magical properties of a flower that isn't included in this book, just ask her yourself!

Finally, you will notice that a number of times throughout the text, after I have recommended gathering one or more blossoms for the purpose of a ritual or charm, I suggest that you place a silver dollar or shiny dime near the base of a plant as an offering and token of thanks. This is because, in my experience, many plant spirits (also known as elementals, faeries, or devas) really enjoy receiving shiny silver objects that are denominations of human money. I don't pretend to understand exactly why this is the case, but this is the message that I've received. There are other ways to offer a thank-you token, such as by pouring out a small libation of ale or blessed water. Also, if you're worried that a child or passerby might find the coin and pocket it, don't be. The plant spirit is just interested in the essence of the coin and your gesture of offering it, not in hoarding it for an extended period of time.

Oh—and if you don't see a particular flower, be sure to check the index in case it's listed under an alternate name.

The Flowers

The moment you become aware of a
plant's emanation of stillness and peace,
that plant becomes your teacher.

ECKHART TOLLE

African Daisy

frican daisy's cool receptivity is perfectly balanced by her deep well-spring of magical power. Luckily, she has the ability to awaken this same exquisite balance in the hearts of those with whom she comes into contact.

While there are a number of flowers commonly referred to as African daisies, this entry pertains to the varieties that fall under the closely related genera *Osteospermum* and *Dimorphotheca*.

Magical Uses

Divine Alignment

Like the energy center at the top of the head known as the crown chakra, African daisies are like doorways or portals between our everyday, illusory consciousness and the eternal realm of the Divine. So spending time in quiet contemplation with one or more of them can help open up your crown chakra and connect you with the nourishing flow that is your alignment with God/Goddess/All That Is. Other ways to employ her magic include incorporating her into a ritual or placing her on your altar; employing the flower essence; or adding forty drops of the essence to your bath water, along with one cup of sea salt, lighting a purple or white candle, and soaking for at least forty minutes.

Energy Healing

Whether or not we've formally studied energy-healing practices, our bodies are lightning rods, our thoughts are electrical impulses, and our feelings have resonance. As such, we all have the ability to channel divine healing energy through our hands and through our thoughts, feelings, and intentions. African daisy can help with these endeavors by facilitating the flow of divine energy through our bodies and conscious awareness, and helping us direct it in ways that bring healing.

So if you're studying any sort of healing modality (including not just pure energy work, such as reiki, but also things like acupuncture, massage, psychology, or even Western medicine), you might like to add African daisy essence to your water once per day. Employing the essence under your tongue provides a nourishing boost to your healing abilities and personal energy field.

Energetic Fine-Tuning

Like the famed wizard and beneficent ascended master Merlin, African daisy specializes in alchemy and energetic fine-tuning. So if you're already feeling energetically clear and would just like to fine-tune your vibes and help them stay balanced in an ideal way, try misting yourself and your surrounding energy field with rose water into which you've added eight to ten drops African daisy essence. (This might be helpful after a ritual or a yoga class or when you've just undergone a major life change and you'd like to facilitate the ideal restructuring of your energetic equilibrium.) You might also use this same mist potion to mist your home or workspace after performing a clearing to harmonize the energies and hold the new vibrational tone in place. And, if you're an energy healer, you might like to mist your clients and friends with this potion to seal their healing at the end of their session.

Magical Power

Worried that your magical power isn't what it should be? Pshaw—you're powerful beyond comprehension! Still, because many of us came into awareness of magic later in life, because we dwell in a culture that doesn't exactly embrace the subtle realms, and because most of us could love and value ourselves a whole lot more than we presently do, we can sometimes feel a little unsure about our magical power. Plus, in order to wield it effectively, we need to sense it, believe in it, and have confidence in ourselves. What's more, we need clarity and a strong ability to focus our intentions. African daisy can help with all of these things, which is how she helps us align with and intensify our magical power. If this is your intention, try taking African daisy essence under the tongue every morning and every night until your magical faculties come sufficiently into focus. You might also try creating the following amulet.

MAGICAL BOOSTER AMULET

On a Monday, tune in to an African daisy blossom and have a silent heart-to-heart with her: let her know your intention to come into alignment with, and have confidence in, your magical power. Then let her know that you're going to gather her; wait for an inner okay before you do. (In other words, after tuning in to the flower and requesting a blossom, wait until you feel comfortable and positive in your body and mind. If you don't receive the okay, come back a different day and try again or try another blossom.) After gently snipping the blossom, leave a shiny dime or silver dollar as a gesture of thanks. Dry the blossom on your altar. While she's drying, sew or otherwise acquire a small lavender drawstring bag that can be worn around your neck (perhaps with the drawstring made long enough to be a necklace). On a full moon night, after the moon has risen, add the blossom to the bag, along with a small moonstone and a small white quartz. Burn white sage smoke around the bag. Hold it in your open, cupped hands and say:

> *By light and blossom of brightest moon*
> *I boost my magic and boost my mood*
> *By ancient stone and crystals cool*
> *My sacred power I now exude.*

Anoint it with jasmine and lemon essential oils. Wear it around your neck. Anoint with the oils again to refresh the magic as desired.

Mystique

Perhaps you're interested in performing magic to surround yourself in an aura of mystique—you know, like as an interesting variation on a more straightforward beauty ritual or a spell to make you irresistible at a party. Here's an example of a mystique-conjuring practice employing African daisy.

Veil of Mystique Mist Potion

In a mister of well water (or spring water in a pinch), add four drops African daisy essence, ten drops ylang ylang essential oil, and five drops neroli essential oil. Shake well. Mist your entire body and aura to surround yourself in a veil of beauty and mystique.

Psychic Abilities

African daisy's alignment with the subtle realms makes her a great ally for those who would like to boost their psychic and intuitive powers. For this purpose, try adding African daisy essence to your drinking water. Also, please note that water itself is a potent psychic ability enhancer, so it's ideal to drink a good amount of it every day for this reason and many others.

The previous page's magical booster amulet will also help with this intention.

Protection

By aligning us with the Divine; strengthening our energetic field; and shoring up our magical power, confidence, healing abilities, and awareness of the subtle realms, African daisy can be a powerfully protective ally. She can especially help those of us who get frightened because we feel that there are possibly dangerous invisible forces that are beyond our awareness and therefore out of our control. If this sounds like the kind of protection you're looking for, try planting African daisies in your yard or employing the flower essence.

Magical Correspondences

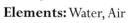

Elements: Water, Air
Gender: Female
Planets: Moon, Uranus

Agapanthus

lthough she is often called the lily of the Nile, agapanthus actually hails from South Africa, not Egypt. Still, the moniker is highly appropriate, especially since her energy is so in alignment with the beloved and awe-inspiring goddess of goddesses Isis. Elegant, intelligent, wise, and utterly self-mastered, the beautiful agapanthus can help us find our confidence, live our destiny, and be the reigning queen (or king) of our own life experience.

Magical Uses

Authority

Anytime we find ourselves in a position of authority, it is important to accept the mission and fully inhabit our role as an authority figure. Not because we are superior (because we aren't) but because this way, not only will we enjoy our position more, but we will also be more effective at reaching our goals and helping others to be happy and shine.

This is an important part of what agapanthus has to teach. Her mere vibration can help uncover our own inherent comfort with roles of authority. In fact, you'll notice that all of her other magical properties lend themselves to this goal quite nicely.

For this purpose, I suggest any or all of the following:

- plant her in your yard
- imbibe the flower essence

- spend time in quiet contemplation with her, and mentally ask her for help and guidance regarding your specific situation

Confidence

Agapanthus teaches the kind of confidence that arises from true self-esteem combined with high standards and an attitude of excellence. If this is something you could use a little more of, you might employ the flower essence, plant agapanthus around the outside of your home, or perform the following ritual. (Incidentally, you can use this same ritual for any of the magical uses listed in this section—just substitute the desired quality in place of "confidence.")

....

SIMPLE CONFIDENCE INFUSION RITUAL

Visit a blossoming agapanthus. Sit or stand comfortably, and relax your mind. As you gaze at her, connect with her energy and sense her quiet, intense confidence. Request that she share this with you. Then, when you feel her say yes, open your heart and mind to allow this energy to flow into your being. When this feels complete, thank her by pouring a bottle of clean water around her roots.

Elegance

All of agapanthus's magical qualities combined equal elegance. So if elegance is a quality you're craving, or if you'd like to magically pour it on thick for a particular interview or event, agapanthus can help. You might employ the essence by creating the following potion so that you can exude an aura of elegance.

....

AURA OF ELEGANCE LOTION POTION

Start with eight to twelve ounces of a cruelty-free body lotion or body oil. Magically speaking, the only thing that matters about the fragrance is that it says "elegance" to you, so either create your own fragrance blend and add it to the lotion/oil or choose one already fragranced to your liking. Then simply add four drops agapanthus essence, shake well, and apply liberally after showering or bathing. Be aware that this will have a very powerful effect, so I recommend lighting a candle, relaxing, and breathing deeply for at least five minutes after applying to steady your energy and align with the vibration of agapanthus in the most ideal way.

Excellence

Agapanthus energy is like an Ivy League college, a five-star restaurant, an A-list celebrity, an elite team of NASA scientists, or a classic Aston Martin in perfect condition. In other words, her standards don't stop at "pretty good" or even "great" but soar all the way up to "top of the line." So if excellence is a goal of yours in any arena, you might like to get agapanthus on the payroll. For example, you might try:

- spiking the punch (or other beverage) at a business meeting with six to ten drops of agapanthus essence and saying a quick blessing before the meeting to craftily give everyone's standards an excellence infusion (alternatively, you might add three to six drops to a mister of spring water and mist the room before everyone arrives)

- planting agapanthus around your home or business

- adding the essence to your drinking water until you feel you've sufficiently assimilated the excellence vibe

- imbibing the essence before a job interview, test, public presentation, etc.

- spending time with a blossoming agapanthus (see previous page's simple confidence infusion ritual)

Intelligence

We are all highly intelligent; it's just a matter of finding the things we love and the areas where we excel. Once we do, focus and hard work become blessings rather than curses, and we can often have fun even as we move through the trials and tribulations along our beautiful life path. When we find ourselves in the midst of such a trial or tribulation—say, a particularly difficult college class or a challenging situation at work—we can lend momentum to our success by employing agapathus's magical ability to enhance and fortify our natural intelligence. For this purpose, try employing the essence, spending time in quiet contemplation with a blossom, or planting agapanthus around your home or business.

Intuition and Inner Knowing

There is the kind of eerily accurate intuition that comes from the watery, otherworldly realm of the spirit. There is also the kind of spot-on intuition that comes from a vast storehouse of knowledge and finely honed mental processes. And then there is the kind of intuition that takes it to the next level by combining both. This, my friends, is the brand of top-shelf intuition we are talking about when agapanthus is involved. If you are a spy, an intuitive counselor, a parent, or really a problem solver of any kind (and who isn't?), you might want to take her energy for a spin: employ the essence, plant her around your office, or spend some time connecting with her vibe (as in the infusion ritual).

Knowledge of Our Own Divinity

This particular life experience seems to be characterized by two ways of perceiving: the true way of perceiving and the illusory way of perceiving. The true way is that we are all one with the Divine. The illusory way is that we are all separate from each other and everything else. When we perceive exclusively in the illusory way, we can hold ourselves back from living our greatness by asking things like "Who do I think I am to be healing people (or doing any number of things my soul really wants to do)?" or "What is the point of painting pictures anyway? Why should I care?" But when we also have an awareness of our divine nature, we can allow our gifts to flow through us without getting attached to the idea that the "little me" did them or wants to do them. We can perceive that a little human with little human flaws can allow divine inspiration and beauty to flow through him or her in order to benefit the world. We don't have to wait until we are perfect or superhuman to do what our heart is urging us to do, and once we do it, we don't have to feel like we are superior to everyone else. We can hold both awarenesses at once—the illusory one and the true one—and, as such, our gifts can blossom forth and bless the world. This is just one more aspect of agapanthus's message!

To become even more deeply aware of your own divine, eternal nature as it flows through your temporary, illusory nature, try employing the essence or spending time in quiet contemplation with a blossoming plant.

Self-Mastery

Self-mastery is the ability to consistently manage our thoughts, process our feelings, and care for our body in ways that benefit us and help us grow. Considering all the aforementioned facets of agapanthus's wisdom, is it any wonder she can help us with this? She helps us to love ourselves as we are and recognize our strengths as we work toward our goals and strive for ever-greater levels of excellence. For this reason, she might be a great ally to help with keeping your New Year's resolutions or initiating any self-improvement endeavor.

Magical Correspondences

Elements: Air, Water
Gender: Female
Planets: Jupiter, Saturn

Alyssum

As a child, after reading *The Secret Garden* by Frances Hodgson Burnett, I asked my mom if I could have a little garden outside our apartment complex. When the apartment owner said yes, one of the first flowers I brought in was alyssum, both white ("Carpet of Snow") and purple ("Violet Queen"). Her etheric, faery-like beauty and sugary scent, combined with her heartiness and ease of growth, made her a simultaneously practical and magical choice. Now when I see her growing, it's like running into an indescribably dear old friend.

Magical Uses

Comfort

You'll find that the energy and wisdom of alyssum is very similar to the sweet, cozy, nourishing feeling of being around the archetypal comforting grandmotherly figure. For example, imagine your heart is broken and you go to your (archetypal) grandmother's house crying. (I say "archetypal" because obviously we don't all have that type of grandma. But we can still imagine.) She gives you her shoulder to cry on until your sobs subside. Then she goes to the kitchen and makes you some chamomile tea. As you drink it, she places a homemade afghan around your shoulders. Even though your heart is aching, you suddenly feel so loved and cared for that it was almost worth the heartbreak.

This type of comfort can also be helpful in situations such as the following:

- staying in the hospital

- healing from a serious or long-term condition
- moving away to college
- moving to a new town or city
- long-term stress of any kind
- healing from abuse
- healing from low self-esteem or a lack of self-love
- major life changes

To receive alyssum's comforting benefits, try imbibing the essence, planting alyssum near your home in pots or flowerbeds, or employing her in rituals and charms designed for the purpose.

Gentleness

Similarly, if you find that you've been experiencing harshness of any kind due to inner or outer situations, alyssum can help. This might include things like:

- harsh work environments
- feeling a lot of anger, violence, greed, or resentment or spending time with people who emanate those emotions
- city environments or places with a large concentration of people
- frequent loud or jarring noises
- being around people or animals in pain
- spending time near large freeways or wide roads with a lot of traffic

The suggestions in the "comfort" section will also work for this purpose.

Grounding

When we use words such as *all over the place*, *overwhelmed*, *frazzled*, *spacey*, or *on edge* to describe how we feel, it usually means we're not grounded. In other words, our personal energy is not anchored in the earth in a healthy, safe, nourishing, and balanced way. Alyssum can help with this by bringing us down to earth, reminding us what's really important (love and the present moment), and soothing our stress-abused nerves. In other words, she reminds us to send our roots into the nourishing sweetness of the now.

For this purpose, again, see the suggestions in the "comfort" section or create a charm such as the following.

ANCHORING CHARM
Place four fresh alyssum blossoms and an iron pyrite on a piece of green cotton fabric. Tie closed with hemp twine and anoint with patchouli and a little jasmine, neroli, or rose essential oils. Pin inside your clothes to keep you grounded in the sweetness of the here and now. Re-anoint as necessary to keep the scent fresh.

Healing and Immunity

Alyssum's comforting and grounding abilities allow her to help soothe away the stress and worry that can keep our immune system from functioning at its best. In this way she can support healing and immunity. For this purpose, take the essence or add it to your bath water. Fresh blossoms in water next to the bed of a healing person can also confer these benefits.

Keeping the Peace

Traditionally, alyssum is perhaps most known for her magical ability to banish anger and help establish peace. If disputes or discord seem to be the norm, or if teamwork and group harmony are crucial, you might want to sneak a few drops of alyssum essence in everyone's food, juice, water supply, etc. Alternatively, you might completely cover and surround a picture of the concerned parties with fresh alyssum blossoms, or you might make the following mist potion.

"Keep the Peace" Mist Potion

Place nine drops alyssum essence into a mister of rose water, along with about five drops each patchouli and neroli essential oils. Close the lid and shake. Mist the space in which you'd like to establish peace. If they'll let you, mist any parties that are especially beset by anger or discord.

Staying True to Oneself

In one way or another, we are all artists. And despite those who may try to convince us otherwise, it's important for us to remain true to our personal vision, not only regarding our creative projects but also regarding our lives. Of course, this doesn't mean that we can't learn from other people or receive helpful feedback from them, but it does mean that we must be the ultimate decision makers when it comes to what we are going to say, be, do, decide, and create. Alyssum can help us to know the difference between false ideas of who we "should be" and who we really are.

This can help with things like:

- business meetings and dealings
- parties and networking events
- high school, junior high, college, and other situations involving peer pressure
- times when we are trying to "find ourselves" or define ourselves

Try employing the essence before and during these types of situations.

Magical Correspondences

Element: Earth
Gender: Female
Planets: Venus, Saturn

Amaryllidaceae (Clivia and Amaryllis Belladonna)

*N*ative to South Africa, amaryllidaceae—strikingly beautiful members of the amaryllis family—share a hippie-like freedom and a variety of wisdom just trippy and mind-expanding enough to be reminiscent of hallucinogens.

Magical Uses

Creativity and Playfulness

Inland from Malibu and west of the San Fernando Valley, there is a decidedly hippie enclave of Los Angeles known as Topanga Canyon. The residents are so rebellious and unique, in fact, that year after year, they refuse to be incorporated by the city so that they can continue to exist without street lamps or subsidized electricity. Last spring and summer, I noticed the exotic, pink-blossomed belladonna amaryllis wildly sprinkling Topanga's weedy hillbilly landscape, flagrantly exerting her freedom and liberation for anyone who cared to notice.

The orange or yellow clivia, though I seem to notice her thriving in more cultivated landscapes throughout the city, possesses the same creative, playful wisdom as her wilder "naked lady" sister. Both can help us to:

- get in touch with our creativity
- be more playful
- have more fun

- express our uniqueness

- sow our wild oats

- assert our individuality

- connect with the realm of the Divine, from which
  all true creativity springs

For any of these purposes, try employing her in rituals, taking the essence, or spending time with a blossom.

Crown Chakra Opening

In order to conform to cultural norms and exist in our society in a functional way, we often have to close our crown chakra to some extent—or, in other words, significantly shut down the part of us that knows we are eternal and one with the Divine. You might say that hallucinogens help with this by re-opening our crown chakra and connecting us once again with the truth of our divine connection and eternal nature. However, this hallucinating state is not sustainable if we want to continue to participate in society as we know it, which is why most of us don't desire to consume hallucinogens daily. What *is* desirable to most of us, however, is to be conscious of the divine, eternal realm while still having one foot in the "common dream," a.k.a. society, so that we can be inspired and divinely connected while continuing to do things like pay our electricity bills and make friendly small talk with our mothers-in-law. And amaryllidaceae is great for this!

You can facilitate this intention by employing the essence or spending time with the flowers themselves. You might also like to add seven drops of the flower essence to a mister of rose water, along with seven drops ylang ylang essential oil and an apophyllite crystal for a crown chakra–opening mist potion.

Joy

When you consider how miraculous and unfathomable this life experience really is, joy seems much more natural than indifference or depression. Still, sometimes we can forget the natural causes for joy that are within us and all around us. And amaryllidaceae is an expert at reminding us by bringing us back to our senses and awakening us to the magic of life. So, to refresh the joy that is your natural state, try employing amaryllidaceae in any way mentioned above.

Self-Acceptance

Have you ever been to a hippie gathering of any kind? I have. Something that's stayed with me is seeing older women and women who may normally be considered "overweight" walk around with nothing but sandals on, luxuriating in their own beauty. And, similarly, I've enjoyed observing women with no makeup on with such deep levels of self-acceptance that you can't help but marvel at their unique natural beauty that shines forth from within. This is the type of radical self-acceptance that clivia, naked lady, and amaryllidaceae in general can help us achieve. (She's a hippie chick, what can I say?) For this purpose, spend time in quiet contemplation with her, take the essence, or add the essence to a body lotion.

Magical Correspondences

Element: Water

Gender: Female

Planet: Neptune

*A*ccording to legend, Fortuna, the Roman goddess of women and luck, in her incarnation as Fortuna Virgo, the patron of newly menstruating maidens, once sprinkled stardust like seeds across the earth. And from each grain of stardust, an aster grew: quite a fitting genesis for a flower with such an ethereal beauty and considerable array of magical powers.

Magical Uses

Astrological Wisdom

The Hermetic precept and beloved magical proverb "As above, so below" applies to the interweaving of form and spirit, seen and unseen, known and unknown. Perhaps more literally, it applies to the connection between what takes place in the heavens and what takes place here on earth in our little human lives (i.e., the art and science of astrology).

And if astrological wisdom is one of your preferred methods of peering through the veil and walking between the worlds, aster can help deepen your current understanding and support you as you undertake further study. For this purpose, you might plant aster in your yard, strike up a personal relationship with her, take the essence, or create the following mist potion and mist your space and yourself before doing things like studying astrology books, casting charts, working with clients, writing astrology-related articles, and so on.

Astrologer's Mojo Mist Potion

Place a glass bowl of spring water in the light of the full moon. Add an apophyllite crystal (that has been cleansed in running water for at least two minutes) and float four fresh aster blossoms on top. Allow the bowl to sit undisturbed in moonlight for one to two hours. Then fill a tiny dropper bottle half full with water from the bowl. Fill it the rest of the way with brandy and close the lid. Pour the remaining water, blossoms, and crystal out near the base of a tree. Add thirteen drops of the essence to a mister of rose water. Shake before using. (Feel free to use the same essence later to make additional batches.)

Beginnings

According to Gretchen Scoble and Ann Field in *The Meaning of Flowers*, "Asters speak of the tiny beginnings from which all great things proceed." Indeed, when we are at the beginning of a project or an undertaking, she can help bless our efforts and fortify our staying power by reminding us of the beauty and necessity of beginnings, as in Lao Tzu's oft-quoted proverb, "The journey of a thousand miles begins beneath one's feet."

So if you're launching a business, beginning a college career, buying your first house, or engaging in some other sort of beginning, you might like to employ the essence. As an added bonus for times like these, she also helps open doorways and smooth transitions (see page 36). You might also like to add a few drops of aster essence to the punch bowl or champagne bottles to bless a new endeavor and get everyone involved off on a similarly positive vibrational foot.

Cleansing and Detoxifying

With powerful connections to both the neutralizing earth and the perspective-enhancing cosmos, aster can help support our detoxification efforts, whether they're physical, emotional, spiritual, environmental, or any combination of the four. For example:

- Plant aster in your yard to help neutralize and clear negativity and emotional toxins from the home.

- Add aster essence to your water to support physical detoxification and weight loss.

- Add aster essence to rose water and mist yourself and your space to cleanse challenging energetic patterns such as earthbound entities or psychic cords.

- Add aster essence to your bath water to support any form of personal detoxification.

- Add three drops aster essence, a squeeze of fresh lemon juice, and twenty drops milk thistle tincture to a juice drink or smoothie made with leafy greens, carrots, and sprouts as a holistic hangover cure (and also be sure to drink lots of water).

Connection to the Divine or Cosmic Realm

One of aster's main energetic dynamics has to do with opening doors between realms, times, and perceptions. And one of the doors she's especially adept at opening for us is the doorway between the so-called mundane or everyday and the realm of the magical/infinite/Divine. In truth, there are no separations, but because our current reality is characterized by the *illusion* of separation, it can be helpful to have a little assistance weaving a doorway between the magical and the mundane, the divine and the everyday, to remind us that everything is magical, everything is divine, and we are one with all of it.

If you'd like to begin to see everything as magical—to be awake to the magic of life— you might like to take aster essence daily or plant her around your home. You might also consider employing her to help you get into that magical zone before and during your magical workings. For example:

RITUAL WINE

Add four drops aster essence to a wine glass or chalice of red wine and drink before and during your magical rituals.

MAGICAL PREP MIST

Add fourteen drops aster essence to a mister of spring water, along with four drops thyme and three drops rosemary essential oils. Shake and mist the space before working magic.

Doorways and Transitions

Transitions and doorways of all kinds can be smoothed and enhanced with aster's energy. For example, aster can help with transitions from:

- the womb to the world
- childhood to puberty
- puberty to adulthood
- one job to another
- being in a relationship to not being in a relationship or vice versa
- one home to another
- one living situation to another
- one season to another (i.e., she can help support our immune system and inner equilibrium during seasonal changes)
- sleeping to waking
- waking to sleeping
- this life to the next

For any of these purposes (or others), you might like to employ the flower essence or fresh flowers in any way you feel guided.

Gentleness

Anytime a softening of energy is desired in order to create a kinder, gentler vibe, aster can help. Try planting her around the space, bringing in some fresh blossoms, or adding five to ten drops of the essence to rose water and misting the space. If you're interested in soothing your own personal energy, try employing the essence or spending time in contemplation with some flowers.

Psychic Abilities

Counselors of any kind, other guidance-oriented professionals, and anyone who wants to enhance his or her intuitive mojo may want to keep fresh asters in the room or plant them outdoors near the entrance or around the home or office. You might also mist the room with rose water or spring water into which you've added two to four drops of aster essence, or hang a charm in the room. Create the charm by placing dried aster blossoms and a labradorite crystal in a piece of lavender cotton and tying it shut with a black or indigo ribbon.

Protection

Planted around the home, aster is an excellent protector from harsh, negative energies. She can also be helpful if you find that you must traverse an energetically challenging situation, either once or on a regular basis. For example, if you work in a place with harsh and often negative energy or if you have to visit a part of town that always seems to leave you feeling drained, you might imbibe the essence regularly. This will surround and infuse you with a lavender-blue aura of cool, gentle, and effervescent energy.

Traditionally, in European folk magic, aster blossoms were considered to be like watchful and protective eyes that would recognize and prohibit negative energies and entities from passing. To employ this aspect of aster's magic, plant asters near the entrance to your home, tune in to them, and silently request their assistance.

Romantic Love with Spiritual Overtones

Whether or not we yearn for a partner of a particular faith, I think it's safe to say that when we yearn for a romantic partner, we yearn for a partner with whom we feel some sort of spiritual or magical connection. And since like attracts like, aster's romantic and spiritual energy helps us get into the energy that attracts this kind of partner. As such, she can be a great addition to any magical endeavor performed for the purpose of attracting a magical and spiritual love, such as the following love altar.

LOVE ALTAR TO MANIFEST A SPIRITUAL ROMANCE

Spread a white cloth or flowy, warm-colored scarf on a table or shelf. Add a bouquet of asters, two lepidolite crystals, an incense holder with a stick or cone of vanilla incense, and two red votive candles (placed side by side on a saucer, candle holder, or small plate). Light the candles and incense. Stand in front of the altar, place your right hand on your heart and your left hand over it, close your eyes, breathe deeply, and consciously relax your muscles. Feel yourself being swept up in the type of romance you'd like to manifest, but please do not visualize anyone specific. Feel and visualize you and this partner simultaneously connected to your earthy sensuality and bathed in otherworldly starlight. When this visualization or feeling seems to reach a crescendo, open your eyes and hold your open palms toward the altar. Say:

Beloved divine partner, star of love, I summon you!
As you are seeking me, I am seeking you!
I give thanks that we are now united.
I welcome you into my life with open arms,
a loving heart, and a warm spirit.
I welcome you.

Safely allow the candles to burn all the way down (snuffing and relighting as necessary). Add fresh sticks of incense as desired. When the asters no longer appear fresh, release them in a moving body of water or place them near the base of a tree.

Support for Teen Girls and Newly Menstruating Maidens

As aster is an expert in transitions and femininity, and as she is sacred to Fortuna Virgo (by some accounts the patron goddess of newly menstruating maidens), she can be an excellent ally for girls experiencing their first moon cycles. For example, you might give a bouquet of asters as a gift to a newly menstruating maiden, or, if you are performing a simple ritual to honor her, you might decorate with fresh asters. Mothers of newly menstruating maidens might honor their daughter's transition with a small glass of red wine or a cup of red raspberry leaf tea (both of which can help soothe cramps) containing two to three drops of aster essence.

Magical Correspondences

Elements: Water, Air
Gender: Female
Planet: Venus

Baby Blue Eyes

his gentle sky-blue flower's official botanical name is *Nemophilia*. *Nemo* means "glade" and *philia* means "love"—and judging from her often self-chosen locations along her native West Coast (particularly meadows and open spaces), baby blue eyes does appear to love a good glade.

I've found that baby blue eyes is one of the foremost floral experts on healing the inner child, soothing our inner dialogue, and restoring our natural ability to enter into healthy, lasting, trust-filled romantic relationships.

Magical Uses

Freedom from Past Hurts

Baby blue eyes powerfully embodies and radiates the energy of innocence. She can help us to rise above old hurts and any accompanying challenging patterns and to return to our original whole, wonder-filled emotional state. This frees us up to experience what is now rather than projecting what was onto the present through fear or negative expectations.

For this reason, she can be an excellent ally when you're ready to put the painful past behind you and step into a joyful, liberated present. For this purpose, try quiet contemplation, ritual work, and employing the flower essence.

Gentleness with Oneself

In *You Can Heal Your Life*, author Louise Hay writes: "Each one of us has a three-year-old child within us, and we often spend most of our lives yelling at the kid in ourselves. Then we wonder why our lives don't work."

When we are ready to stop berating and speaking harshly to ourselves and our inner children so that we can begin to live happily, experience success as a matter of course, and naturally express the fullness of our potential, baby blue eyes can help. For this purpose, I suggest adding the flower essence to your drinking water until gentler, more positive inner dialogue begins to take hold. Quiet contemplation with the blossom would also be helpful, as would the following charm.

SELF-GENTLENESS CHARM

On the new moon or the day before the new moon, light a white or off-white soy candle near a mirror into which you can comfortably gaze. Add one fresh baby blue eyes blossom (gathered gently and lovingly) and an angelite crystal (that has been cleansed in running water and sage smoke) to a small blue flannel bag. Tie closed with a small length of blue ribbon or hemp twine. Hold it against your heart with both hands, sit comfortably in front of the mirror, and lovingly look into your eyes. Say something like:

> *(Your name), I love you very much. I apologize for treating you harshly in the past,*
> *and I now vow to do my very best to begin to treat you with the compassion and honor*
> *you deserve. Since this is a new habit, it might take a little bit of time, so*
> *whenever I notice I have strayed, with forgiveness I will bring myself back*
> *to a kind inner dialogue. With caring perseverance, in time, I know*
> *I will turn the tide and create a new habit of tender, loving self-regard.*

Until new habits are established, wear the charm close to your heart day and night (employing a safety pin if necessary), and touch it whenever you need a little extra support.

Healing the Inner Child

As baby blue eyes helps us to heal our inner child, this frees us up to enjoy playfulness, wonder, whimsy, and inspired creativity. For this purpose, you might try any of the above suggestions (including the self-gentleness charm) or the following mist potion.

....

MIST POTION TO HEAL THE INNER CHILD

Add four drops baby blue eyes essence and four drops neroli essential oil to a mister of rose water and shake to blend. Mist your entire aura upon awakening and before going to sleep for up to one month. You can also mist your personal space or workspace to enhance inner child healing and creativity.

Letting Go

Sometimes we stifle our own emotional healing process through a habit of holding on to "old stuff." For example, perhaps we underwent a particular challenge in our childhood and we've always held on to an idea that our life would have been perfect or our potential would have been expressed if only it weren't for that one thing. Or sometimes, without realizing it, we might hold on to an old hurt because it represents a certain label that our ego has latched on to, such as "incest victim" or "adult child of an alcoholic." In other words, on some level, we think, "But that's *who I am*. If I weren't that, who would I be?" (To clarify, I'm not saying those things didn't happen, I'm just saying they're not *who you are*. They're just things that happened, and they don't need to continue to have power over your present or future.)

Sometimes these dynamics can even spill over into the physical realm, as in the case of someone with chronic pain or fatigue as a result of so many old, unreleased emotional hurts or in the case of someone who unwittingly holds a medical diagnosis in place because on some level she defines herself by it.

Baby blue eyes can help us loosen the grip on any or all of these conditions so that we can surrender them to the Universe (God/dess) for healing and transmutation, and so that we can move on and be free.

For help with letting go of a long-standing hurt, issue, label, or condition, starting the day after the full moon, begin adding baby blue eyes essence to your drinking water. Continue through one complete moon cycle. Additionally, you might perform the following ritual.

A Ritual Bath for Letting Go

During the waning moon, light a blue candle and draw a bath. Add one cup sea salt, one-fourth cup baking soda, one-fourth cup Epsom salts, forty drops baby blue eyes essence, and six drops ylang ylang or lavender essential oil (whichever smells better to you or feels right for the purpose). Hold your hands over the water and say: "Great Goddess, please infuse this water with vibrations of healing, purification, and release." Visualize very bright white light coming down from above, entering the crown of your head and going through your heart, arms, and hands and into the water. Soak for at least forty minutes, being sure to drink lots of water as you do.

Natural Beauty and Wildness

When we connect with our wildness and the natural beauty of the physical world, our true beauty can shine forth from within. And when we treat ourselves with gentleness and love and let go of what is no longer serving us, we begin to recognize our own unique beauty, which also allows it to radiate out into the world for others to see and enjoy.

To amplify and revel in your own natural beauty, try adding baby blue eyes essence to your drinking water. Before drinking, hold the glass or bottle in both hands and say a simple blessing, such as "Great Goddess, please infuse this water with vibrations of wildness, natural beauty, and love."

Relationship Healing

If you think about all the aspects of baby blue eyes' wisdom presented in this section, you'll realize that they all add up to releasing baggage and, in the process (if you so desire), clearing the way for a healthy, beautiful romantic relationship. Not only that, but because she helps us clear out old stuff from our past, she can also help us heal challenging relationships with other important people in our life, such as parents, siblings, and friends.

To soothe and unravel old hurts and clear the way for more ideal relationships of all kinds, try any of the above suggestions that resonate with you or incorporate baby blue eyes into rituals designed for that purpose.

Trust

First and foremost, real trust starts with trust in the Divine: trust in the underlying order and perfection of All That Is. Once we have that level of trust, trusting individual people and situations becomes much easier and more natural. And when we find ourselves involved in something that truly isn't right for us, we trust our own intuition enough to extricate ourselves from it. So, in general, we don't have to have that free-floating feeling of fear and mistrust of other people, ourselves, or the way things are.

By helping us heal and release old hurts, love what is, and revel in our own wildness and natural beauty, baby blue eyes helps us to establish this kind of sure-footedness and all-encompassing trust. To employ her help with this, I suggest employing the essence or spending time with a blossom.

Magical Correspondences

Elements: Water, Air
Gender: Female
Planet: Venus

Bird of Paradise

*A*ccording to authors Gretchen Scoble and Ann Field in *The Meaning of Flowers*, "The extraordinary tropical bloom of the bird of paradise suggests that something *strange and wonderful* is about to occur." And you'll likely find that a mere passing glimpse of this exotic beauty can be a window into arcane alchemical wisdom and the invisible, whimsical reality that shapes and animates all things.

Magical Uses

Awareness of the Interconnectedness of Life

The fact that a bird who shares this flower's unique color combination pollinates him—and that the blossom itself is ideally constructed to accommodate the bird—is an appropriate metaphor (and actual representation) of the flower's unique vibrational message: that all of life is interconnected and interwoven into one giant organism, and that the entire universe is one interconnected, unified field of energy. Magically working with bird of paradise blossoms can open us up to this awareness, which has a wealth of benefits, including:

- an increased feeling of meaning in one's life
- motivation to make a positive difference in the world
- inspiration
- creativity

- joy
- goodwill toward other creatures and the planet

Quiet contemplation, ritual work, or working with the flower essence are all great ways to employ the flower for this use.

Awareness of Invisible Reality

In the same vein as the previous section, bird of paradise can help us become aware of the invisible reality that underlies, animates, and connects all things. For example, if you've ever seen the artwork of Alex Grey, you've likely noticed that even though his images don't depict everyday reality in the usual sense, they still seem familiar—like you're aware on some level of the inner mechanisms they depict. This is because they take the invisible reality (which we can all sense to some degree) and make it visible to our everyday eyes. Bird of paradise can help us sense this invisible reality in an even deeper and more conscious way. For this purpose, try any of the previous suggestions.

Intuition and Insight

Naturally, since bird of paradise helps us perceive the interconnectedness of all things and the subtle invisible reality, he also helps us see and understand the inner workings of things in highly useful ways and manners that might be accurately described as intuitive and insightful (although it should be noted that bird of paradise gifts us with a form of intuition that's more thought-based and less feeling-based). This can be especially helpful for those times when you have a burning desire to understand a particular mechanism or phenomenon, or when you'd like to be able to clearly and dispassionately see the patterns at work before making a big decision.

To receive these benefits, try spending time in quiet contemplation with a blossoming bird of paradise. Once you've tuned in and aligned with his vibration, silently present everything you know about the issue or situation in a detached, almost mathematical way. Then, on an internal level, explore the patterns at work in the issue or situation. Take your time, and look both backward and forward in time as you feel guided.

Mathematical Prowess

When I say that bird of paradise can share the gift of mathematical prowess, I don't just mean he can help us ace our calculus class (although he can). I also mean that he can help artists, architects, musicians, dancers, investors, computer programmers, and anyone else whose work (or play or finances) can benefit from an infusion of mathematical structure, precision, and insight.

Try connecting with the wisdom of the blossom and consciously aligning with his vibration. Then set the intention to consciously direct this alignment into whatever aspect of your life would most benefit from it.

Protection

Because bird of paradise helps us to align with our intuition, the inner patterns at work in any given situation, and the invisible reality, he can be an especially protective magical ally for those of us who are prone to free-floating anxiety and fear, especially when coupled with an unsettling feeling of being overwhelmed with life, mired in muddled thinking, or out of control in our life or environment. He settles our minds, clears our thoughts, and helps us feel that we are more than equal to any situation that may arise. Receive these benefits by spending time in quiet contemplation with a blossom or employing the flower essence regularly until your inner disarray is replaced with a feeling of calm self-mastery.

Sacred Geometry

For those whose magical practice tends to veer toward the alchemical and sacred geometrical side, the previous sections may have helped you correctly surmise that bird of paradise is a wonderful floral ally for you. He can also help you enhance your expertise when it comes to other geometry-heavy magical modalities such as feng shui and hexwork (from the pow-wow tradition).

Walking Between the Worlds

Consider this flower's name: bird of paradise. Birds have been associated with omens and divine messages all over the world since time immemorial. And paradise—well, that's another name for the realm of heaven, or the divine realm. And since bird of paradise is a plant firmly rooted in planet Earth, you might think of him as a bridge between the realms of form and spirit, visible and invisible, physical and metaphysical. Hence, he can help us be in the physical world while staying aware of the invisible aspects that shape it and weave it all together. In this way, we can consciously and masterfully co-create our destiny through a partnership with the interconnectedness of All That Is.

Magical Correspondences

Elements: Air, Fire
Gender: Male
Planet: Mercury

Black-Eyed Susan

For a summer flower so evocative of sunshine and brightness, black-eyed Susan can sure seem a little spooky. Just as the peak of summer heralds the reaping time and the quickly approaching dark half of the year, her sunny disposition has a dark side and reminds us to integrate all points along the wheel of life and death.

While there are a number of flowers known as black-eyed Susans, this entry focuses on the one most commonly known by that name, specifically *Rudbeckia hirta*.

Magical Uses

Cleansing and Releasing

Black-eyed Susan's unique wisdom and healing vibration can help aggressively clear away what is no longer serving you on the emotional plane. What I mean by "aggressively" is that the dynamic isn't exactly gentle and gradual: it's more like an energetic purgative of nonphysical (i.e., emotional and spiritual) toxins, which can cause some upsets as our lives shift to meet our newly cleansed outlook and mental state. While this may be ideal in some cases, in others it may not be, so tune in to your intuition to be sure. For this purpose, try employing the flower essence or just spending time with some blossoming plants. To help clear and shift your energy in a quicker and more efficient way, you might also add a single drop of her essence to another essence as an activator.

Grounding

Black-eyed Susan can help us stay grounded, calm, and energetically healthy, especially when we feel beset by harsh or challenging environments or situations. For example, if you've recently started a new job that involves heartbreaking aspects such as violence, illness, or death, black-eyed Susan can help you to look any and all situations in the face while staying effective, calmly energized, and deeply connected to your intuition and guidance. For this or similar purposes, try employing the essence or misting yourself with spring water containing ten to twenty drops lavender or geranium essential oil and two to four drops black-eyed Susan essence.

Integration

Just as none of us are always happy or always sad, we each contain many dimensions and aspects of both light and dark. And if we've been feeling lopsided in either direction or unable to integrate our bright and shadowy aspects for any reason, black-eyed Susan can help. She steadies us energetically and shows us that even seeming opposites can coexist harmoniously with one another in our psyches, relationships, and environments.

For this purpose, try adding a drop of black-eyed Susan essence to any other essence or essence blend. To encourage grounding and integrating energy, add two to four drops of the essence and one cup sea salt to your bath water or add four drops to a mister of spring water, along with ten to fifteen drops vetiver essential oil.

Mediumship, or Connecting with Transitioned Loved Ones

If you're a medium or if you intend to become a medium, black-eyed Susan can enhance your powers by helping you to see through the veil and shine light into the seeming darkness of the otherworld. Similarly, if you feel drawn to connect with a loved one who has transitioned to the other side, black-eyed Susan might be a good ally to enlist. For either purpose, spend time in quiet contemplation with the blossoming plant, allowing yourself to receive a silent, wordless lesson on the dynamics of mediumship and peering beyond the veil. Alternatively or instead, imbibe the essence before endeavoring to connect with the otherworld in any way or before bed if you'd like to connect in your dreams.

Magical Correspondences

Element: Earth
Gender: Female
Planet: Pluto

Bleeding Heart

This tender little blossoming valentine (introduced to the Western world from China via the nineteenth-century botanist Robert Fortune) can be a potent magical ally when it comes to matters of the heart and emotions. So potent, in fact, that I do not recommend snipping the flowers or incorporating entire bleeding heart blossoms in your magic (unless you're using them to create a flower essence), as this can be too much and is more likely to throw situations out of balance than to remedy them. On the other hand, provided you take care that the situation is appropriate (see below for guidance), simply employing the flower's vibration—perhaps by working with the flower essence or spending time in proximity to a blossoming plant—will be more conducive to your magical success.

Magical Uses

Beauty in Pain

Feeling the fullness of one's emotions is a beautiful thing, whether those emotions are so-called positive emotions or so-called negative ones. It's the lack of feeling—or, more accurately, suppressed feeling—that lends itself to depression, annoyance, and boredom. And when we encounter the emotional pain of heartbreak or grief, feeling it as fully and freely as possible allows us to more quickly process it and release it. What's more, when we surrender to our pain, we can see the beauty in it even in the midst of it, and as a result we can more easily transmute it into joy and artistic inspiration. Bleeding heart helps us do this.

For this purpose, you might imbibe the essence once per day for at least one full moon cycle. Other ways to employ bleeding heart's magic for this purpose include:

- bringing one or more bleeding heart plants into your yard and lovingly caring for them
- adding twenty to thirty drops bleeding heart essence to your bath water, along with at least one cup sea salt, and soaking for at least forty minutes
- creating the mist potion for opening the pathways of the heart (see below)

Emotional Availability

Deep and abiding relationships depend on the emotional availability of everyone involved. When your magical intention is to open the pathways of the heart and to enhance receptiveness and vulnerability, bleeding heart may be the magical ingredient for you. She can also be helpful for relationship counselors or for increasing heart-centered connectedness within any group or partnership. For example, you might create the following potion and mist a space before or during any situation that might benefit from this aspect of bleeding heart's wisdom.

....

MIST POTION FOR OPENING THE PATHWAYS OF THE HEART

Add nine or twelve drops bleeding heart essence to a mister of rose water, along with ten drops lavender and five drops rose geranium essential oils. Shake gently before use.

Healing Depression

Often, depression occurs when we suppress negative emotions and consequently find ourselves in a stagnant emotional state. As previously mentioned, bleeding heart can get these emotions flowing by helping us feel—and even find blessings in—these painful emotions. This energetic dynamic is important to be aware of when employing bleeding heart for the purpose of healing depression as, at first, when we begin to feel our feelings, things can seem to be getting worse. So if you choose to work with bleeding heart to heal your depression or someone else's, the best strategy is to consciously surrender to your feelings as much as you can without fighting or judging them. You might like to simultaneously employ emotionally soothing flowers into your magic, such as lavender essential oil or essence, rose water, neroli essential oil, rose geranium essential oil, and citrus blossom essence (to name a few).

For this purpose, try any of the previous suggestions or work with the essence or the living, blossoming plant as you feel guided.

Attracting Love

Traditionally, bleeding heart has been magically employed to draw a love relationship. However, this can be very potent and have lasting consequences, so be very careful how and when you do this. For example, under no circumstances should bleeding heart be employed in love-drawing spells or rituals that target a specific person. Rather, if you feel 100 percent ready to draw a lasting, meaningful, emotional relationship into your life (which is a very serious thing, make no mistake), you might try the following ritual.

LOVE-DRAWING RITUAL

Lovingly care for a blossoming bleeding heart plant in your yard or outdoor pot. Every Friday during the waxing moon, cleanse a shiny dime in sage smoke or sunlight. Approach the plant. While holding the dime against your heart with your right hand and placing your left hand over it, have a silent conversation with the plant, employing her assistance in drawing a beautiful romantic relationship into your life. Express gratitude for this eventuality, then place the dime near the flower's base as an offering. Repeat until your wish has been granted.

Magical Correspondences

Element: Water
Gender: Female
Planet: Venus

....

The Flowers 55

Bougainvillea

As a flower enthusiast living in Los Angeles, I am compelled to include the bougainvillea, a South American and Polynesian native who generously splashes her vibrant color all over this town. Interestingly, however, her colorful aspect doesn't come from her flower: rather, it's the tiny little five-pointed butter-colored blooms at the center of the brightly colored leaves that are often mistaken for her petals.

While it's been said that her leaves and flowers are sometimes employed in Mexican folk medicine to treat congestion and skin conditions, there is very little information about this available to the layperson at this time, and I don't have any personal experience with it, so I don't recommend trying it at home unless you are a sufficiently knowledgeable herbalist or are under the guidance of one.

Magical Uses

Beauty

Of all of bougainvillea's many magical aspects, her powers of beautification are her signature. For example, she can be employed for beautifying purposes in the following ways:

- Plant her around the front of your house or near your front gate to infuse your life with beautiful moments and your lifestyle with beautiful elegance. (Be sure you're in the right kind of climate and that she gets plenty of sun and not too much water, especially if she's in a pot.)

- Spend time in quiet contemplation with a blossoming bougainvillea to absorb her beautifying energy and to align with your inner beauty so that it may shine outward and enhance your outer beauty even more abundantly.

- Add two drops bougainvillea essence to a bottle of witch hazel and use it as a facial toner to enhance your attractiveness.

- Add six drops bougainvillea essence to a mister of rose water and mist your entire body and aura to enhance your attractiveness and charm.

Cleansing

Like the sunlight that she loves so much, bougainvillea can help purify and evaporate lingering toxins in our mind, body, and spirit so that our personal energy field and lifestyle begin to be characterized by a simple, clean aesthetic. Similarly, she helps us strip away the extras (clutter, limiting beliefs, undesired commitments, old hurts and emotional stuff) so that we can feel energized, efficient, and streamlined.

For this purpose, cultivate or care for bougainvilleas, spend time in quiet contemplation with a blossoming bougainvillea, or imbibe the essence regularly, starting at the full moon and continuing throughout an entire moon cycle.

Radiance

Consider bougainvillea's tiny, unassuming blossom and the way she doesn't let that stop her from being the star of the show in any given garden. Similarly, bougainvillea can help us be ourselves and shine our light in a gorgeous, fabulous, unabashed way. This can be helpful for anytime we want to step into the limelight or just be seen and appreciated in a positive way. For example, she can magically support us through things like auditioning, feeling comfortable in social situations, starting new careers or businesses, or promoting ourselves or our work. To receive these benefits, take the essence before any situation during which you'd like to shine your light. Or if you'd generally just like to increase your radiance and comfort with taking center stage, take the essence twice per day for one moon cycle, starting at the new moon. You also might like to incorporate her into rituals or potions designed for the purpose, such as the following potion.

RADIANCE POTION

Over ice, fill a glass so that it's two parts orange juice and one part sparkling water. (If appropriate and desirable, you may want to leave room for a shot of vodka.) Lightly chop a clean, organic red rose petal and add to the glass, along with six drops bougainvillea essence. Hold it in both hands and say:

I am a star! I shine brightly,
and I gracefully attract attention, adoration, and respect.

Drink completely before any situation during which you'd like to shine. (This is a powerful one, so watch out! Be sure to balance out your radiance with subtlety and humility so that you leave a lastingly positive impression. And if you went the vodka route, perhaps be mindful of the booze consumption from here on out!)

Passion

Like the heat on the tropical islands where she thrives, bougainvillea lends herself to passion. This can be helpful in a number of ways, including:

- refreshing the passion in a relationship
- inspiring passion in others (toward you or a cause)
- renewing your passion for a project or cause
- discovering where your passion lies and pursuing a passion-filled career

For any of these purposes, take two to three drops of the essence twice per day, spend time with a blossoming bougainvillea, incorporate her into rituals or charms designed for the purpose, or surround yourself with live bougainvillea plants (in your yard or on your patio).

Magical Correspondences

Element: Fire
Gender: Female
Planet: Venus

Calla Lily

The unified, pure white petal of the calla lily is like a pristine flow of divine energy or an otherworldly white flame. Exotic yet simple, delicate yet strong, the calla lily truly lives up to her designated meaning according to the language of the flowers, which is "magnificent beauty."

Magical Uses

Divine Connection and Opening the Crown Chakra

Calla lily remembers the truth of our oneness with All That Is. She can help us remember to dwell in this truth and to break through the illusion of separation. To glean some of her wisdom, employ the essence, bring her into your yard, or spend a little quiet time with the flower.

Peace

No matter what the scale, calla lily can help with our magical objectives related to establishing peace. For example, if two or more of your children don't get along, you might put a single drop of calla lily essence in their breakfast every morning until some semblance of peace prevails. Or you might try creating the following mist for bringing peace to your household and nurturing your prayers and spiritual petitions.

Peace Mist

Place eight drops calla lily essence in a mister of rose water and shake. Hold it in both hands and visualize a sphere of very bright white light filling and completely surrounding the bottle. Think or say the word *peace*, and direct the energy of the word into the bottle. For peace in the home, mist the interior of the space daily until harmony is established. To send peaceful energy to the world, place a small globe or map of the world on your altar and mist it as you pray for and visualize peace.

Peaceful Transitions

Because of her magical ability to remind us of our fundamental innocence and our connection with the Divine, calla lily can be excellent with helping loved ones transition from this life into the next. Placed by the bedside, she can help ease the fear of death by releasing feelings of guilt, bringing peace to the heart, and fortifying the inner connection to the realm of the Divine. It can also be helpful to place a bouquet or two near a casket before burial or to place a bouquet on top of the casket for burial. In general, rituals designed to help ease the soul's transition to the realm of light can benefit from the incorporation of calla lily.

Saintliness

Do you have what it takes to be a saint? Absolutely. Saints were people, too, with faults and imperfections, just like you and me. And, just like you and me, they were also one with the Divine. To embrace our own saintliness, all we need to do is recognize the truth of our oneness and the illusory nature of our separation, and to act out of that recognition.

If you're craving connection with your inner saint, spend some time with calla lily, take the essence, or add it to your bath.

Sleep

Calla lily helps us release fears and worries and slip into sleep peacefully. Try taking three drops calla lily essence under the tongue before bed or drinking the following sleep potion.

SLEEP POTION

Place equal parts dried valerian root, dried chamomile, and dried lavender blossoms in a tea infuser. Boil water, pour a mug's worth over the herbs, and steep for ten minutes. Strain, add three drops calla lily essence, sweeten to taste, and drink before bed.

Soothing Grief

Because of the divine connection and deep peace she provides, along with a generous helping of time, calla lily can give us the perspective and soothing energy we need to help heal our grief over the loss of a loved one or a broken heart. To help soothe your grief with calla lilies, employ them in your garden, in rituals, or as a flower essence. A calla lily bouquet is also an excellent choice as a gift to someone who is grieving.

True Innocence

Have you made mistakes? Sure, we all have. Do you feel fundamentally unworthy of the good things in life? At one time or another, we've all been there too. But the truth is, we're all doing the very best we can at the moment. Not only that, but at our cores, we're all as innocent as the day we were born. As such, just like babies, we're completely forgivable, lovable, and worthy of every good thing life has to offer.

If you're ready to relieve yourself of the burden of guilt (which truly isn't doing anyone any good) or if you feel weighed down by deep-seated feelings of dirtiness or unworthiness, calla lily can help you return to your childlike purity and innocence. She also can help you remember that you are as deserving and as valuable as a newborn child.

Magical Correspondences

Element: Water

Gender: Female

Planet: Venus

Camellia

While her beauty is legendary, camellia is not one for basking in the limelight. In fact, the essence of her wisdom is the true confidence that comes from humility and vulnerability, the organic energy that comes from doing what you love and loving what you do, and the simple joy that comes from working contentedly behind the scenes.

Magical Uses

Alignment with the Divine Feminine

Camellia blossoms—especially the pink and white varieties—bring connection and alignment with the Divine Mother and the feminine aspects of the Divine. They teach by example that softness, gentleness, and feminine beauty do not preclude power, confidence, and strength.

Camellia blossoms often naturally fall to the earth while they are still in the height of their beauty. These naturally fallen blossoms are ideal additions to an altar honoring Quan Yin, Mother Mary, White Tara, Parvati, or another gentle, nurturing aspect of the Divine Feminine.

Authenticity and Decision Making

When you express the sincerest truth of who you are, you bring the greatest possible measure of grace and healing to the world. While those you admire can provide clues to unraveling the mystery of your life direction and life path, you are totally unique, and no amount of imitation can ultimately deliver you to your destiny.

If we choose to quietly tune in and listen to camellia's wisdom, she wordlessly whispers exactly the encouragement we need to trust ourselves and our visions so that we can make effective life decisions and follow the paths that our heart most wants to travel.

For this purpose, you might take the essence or perform the following ritual.

RITUAL TO TAP INTO YOUR HEART'S WISDOM

If you're at an important fork in the road or you're just not sure which direction to take, visit a blossoming camellia bush. Sit or stand comfortably, relax your body, take some deep breaths, and quietly observe the camellia. Simply be present with the moment: listen to the sounds of nature around you and let the beauty of the flowers infuse your consciousness with a deep sense of wordless calm. After a while, have a conversation with the plant out loud but in a quiet voice. (If this feels awkward because people might see you, it will work just as well to have the conversation silently.) Tell her all about the situation and exactly what you're feeling and thinking about it. Explain what you see as your options and the main concerns you have about which direction to take. Get it all out.

Then relax again, just as you did before. Feel all your worries being swept up and transmuted by the divine energy connected with the plant. Quiet your mind again and let go of the situation, fully surrendering once more the present moment. Finally, after a time, gaze directly at a blossom and focus on the physical location of your heart chakra in the center of your chest. Put your right hand over your heart and your left hand over your right. Take a deep breath and bring your mind gently back to the situation at hand. Say (or think):

"Heart, which way do you want to go? Heart, what do you want to do?" Then calmly, without any anxiety or panic, allow the clear wisdom of your heart to come through. Know that whether a concrete answer arises at that very moment or not, you have created the necessary shift; your answer certainly will appear at the perfect time and in the perfect way. Pay attention to your dreams and daydreams, and follow the guidance you receive.

Energy

When we're aligned with our authentic self and focused on our divine life mission, we feel a natural, sustainable energy buzz. As such, a side effect of working with camellia is increased energy, both mental and physical. If you feel fatigued and you suspect the cause is that you're trying to force yourself to do things that are not in alignment with your authentic self, you might take the essence regularly until your direction shifts and your natural energy returns.

Interestingly, this aspect of camellia's magic is mirrored in the way tea—a product of *Camellia sinensis* (a close relative of the popular flowering garden plant)—naturally infuses us with energy and focus.

Friendship

Just as tea is popularly associated with old friends and rituals of welcome and hospitality, camellia herself possesses the same energy as a true friend. As such, she can be helpful when you want to draw or maintain true friendships or to gain insight into a friendship. You might bring naturally fallen blossoms into your home, arrange them around the edge of a plate, and write a friendship-related wish or desire on a piece of paper as if it had already come true. For example, you might write any of the following:

- I have many wonderful friendships.
- I strike up wonderful new friendships easily and effortlessly.

- I know just what to do about my friendship with _____.
- I see the truth of _____'s heart and understand where our friendship truly stands.

Once you've written your intention, fold the paper, being sure to fold it toward yourself each time. Then place the folded paper in the middle of the plate of camellia blossoms, place a candle on top, and light the candle. Burn at intervals (extinguishing when you leave the house or can't attend to fire safety for any reason) until it burns all the way down or until the blossoms fade, whichever feels right. Then return the blossoms to the base of a tree. Keep the candle to burn for other purposes later or dispose of the stub. Put the paper at the bottom of a dresser drawer, and then recycle, bury, or burn it when your intentions have manifested in the physical world.

Humility and True Confidence

Although they share the same root cause, there are two main ways that insecurity manifests. One is feeling inferior to others, and the other is feeling superior to others. Usually, insecurity manifests in both ways and changes depending on the situation.

While we inevitably will be better than others at some things and in some ways, at other things and in other ways, others inevitably will be better than us. But the truth is that no one is ultimately better or worse than anyone else. We are all just different: we have different strengths and different challenges. In fact, if you look deeply, you'll discover that the idea that there is any sort of value differentiation in human beings is entirely an illusion, with absolutely no basis in anything at all. It is just a useless cultural idea that most of us have adopted somewhere along the way—perhaps in preschool or kindergarten. And whenever we spend time believing in this idea, it is a complete waste of energy that we could be spending on something actually useful and valid, such as creating art, putting our dreams into action, petting the dog, or hugging our partner.

What's more, when we choose not to believe in the illusion that we are better or worse than anyone else, we epitomize humility, and true confidence arises.

And so if you find that you feel inferior or superior to others—i.e., you are in need of humility or true confidence—you might ask camellia for help, as she's an expert in this area. Spend time with her, tend to her, or take the essence.

Receptivity

Sometimes we may feel that in order to get the things we want in life, we have to struggle and demand and force, and as a result we constantly project energy and effort out into the world. The trouble with this is that life is about balance, and in order to be open to receiving the divine gifts that the universe has in store for us, we must balance our constant *doing* with simple *being*. In other words, it is nearly impossible to receive a gift with a clenched fist; with an open and relaxed palm, however, it is the easiest and most natural thing in the world.

Camellia can help open us up to prosperity by helping us symbolically unclench our fists through quieting our minds, opening our hearts, and creating the space in life for blessings to flow. She also teaches us to gratefully accept help as it's offered to us, in all its many forms, from beings in both seen and unseen realms.

True Prosperity

As a result of all the magical uses cited previously—receptivity, being in alignment with our authenticity and most ideal life path, true confidence, and alignment with the divine feminine—camellia aligns us with true prosperity: not simply having a lot of money and resources but living a life that is satisfying on all levels, receiving and being in the flow of divine blessings in all forms.

Interestingly, in the nineteenth century, camellias were considered status symbols because they were so expensive.

Magical Correspondences

Element: Earth
Gender: Female
Planets: Jupiter, Moon

Carnation

As the child of a funeral chapel family, I can say with every confidence that if anthropologists from the future were to study the funeral customs of today's Western world, they would say that carnations were inextricably intertwined with death and the grieving process. Having spent as much time as I did at work with my dad, I cannot smell a carnation and not think of a funeral. Indeed, in my experience, bouquets and arrangements gifted for the proceedings were more often than not made up primarily of this beautiful, sweet-and-spicy scented blossom.

Although I am fairly certain that most grievers don't choose carnations with the flower's magical properties in mind, carnation has been traditionally associated with death and rebirth, or—as in the case of traditional Christian-themed art—resurrection. Also, many suspect (as I do) that the name *carnation* is, like the related words *incarnation* and *reincarnation*, aligned with the human cycle of birth, life, death, and rebirth, as well as the sensual and emotional aspects of dwelling in this physical realm.

Magical Uses

Beauty

Carnation's sensual, spicy sweetness and his bright and vibrant countenance lend themselves to magical workings performed for the purpose of increasing one's physical beauty. For this purpose, try taking the essence or adding it to a bath. You might also sleep with carnations near your bedside, add carnation blossoms or petals to your bath water, incorporate carnation into spells or charms designed for the purpose, or add four to six drops carnation essence to a mister of rose water, misting yourself as desired.

Heart Healing

Carnation resonates with the energy of the heart, and his bright, vigorous magic can help rebuild the heart's energy field after grief or heartbreak. (Perhaps this is another underlying reason why carnation is so generously incorporated into modern funeral proceedings.) For this purpose, try spending time in quiet contemplation with carnation, planting him in your yard, bringing him into your space, giving him as a gift, incorporating him into spells or rituals, or taking the essence.

Love

Carnation's affinity for the heart and for the sensuality of this present life experience, as well as his sweet and spicy scent, all lend themselves to his magical ability to enhance, conjure, or magnetize romantic love. In fact, carnation essence is a potent addition to traditional love potions—you know, the kind that you secretly dose someone with to make him or her fall madly in love with you; tempting, isn't it? But don't do it! You don't want to mess with anyone's free will.

What, you're not dissuaded? You still want to try it? Well, okay, here's an example of a potion that—by honoring free will and only enhancing what is already there—will be relatively karmically safe for everyone concerned. You can secretly dose your partner, your date, or whomever you like. But please, for your own sake: only give this potion to one person at a time, and make sure that person is not romantically attached to someone else. Also, only employ it only when you really, really can't help yourself, and definitely do not use it more than once per moon cycle.

Love Potion

On a Friday when the moon is waxing, ideally when the moon is in Libra or Taurus, fill a tiny dropper bottle (perhaps one ounce) half full of brandy. Add three drops vanilla extract, six drops carnation essence, and three drops garnet elixir (this is a gem essence and is available online and at some metaphysical supply stores—I like Alaskan Essence's Rhodolite Garnet, but there are many). Fill the bottle the rest of the way with food-grade rose water. Hold it in both hands and whisper:

If love for me you truly feel
If your desire is really real
These feelings I do now ignite!
All inhibitions fall away
And you go under love's fair sway
Throughout this dear enchanted night!

The night after creating the potion, sleep with the bottle under your pillow. Then, at a future date, add two to three drops to the object of your affection's beverage. The potion will stay potent for up to six months. Please be aware that this potion is designed only to work to enhance someone's existing feelings, not to conjure up feelings that aren't there. But, either way, your endeavors won't be wasted—if there are no feelings to enhance, at least you'll know, right?

Other ways to employ carnation for love purposes include working him into charms or rituals, giving him as a gift, or adding the flower or flower essence to your bath water.

Perspective

Carnation's alignment with the cycle of death and rebirth makes him an excellent ally when taking the long view is of the essence. For example, sometimes we can get so caught up in a drama or an ambition that we forget the big picture and lose sight of the things that really matter. This is why carnation can be a great addition to essence mixtures, charms, baths, or mist potions formulated for worry or stress, and why it's a good idea to bring him into your garden or space when you want to take a step back and remember to enjoy the process of life.

Rebirth

Like most of the symbols associated with ancient Egypt's funerary rites, carnation (as a symbol of modern-day funerary rites) is a symbol not only of death and life, but also of rebirth and new beginnings. He is a reminder—like new blossoms in the spring taking different forms but retaining the same essence—that our soul naturally seeks to be reborn again and again into this physical world. Similarly, when we seek rebirth in any area of our present life, carnation will gladly lend his magical support. Consider incorporating carnation into rituals or charms designed for this purpose, trying any of the previous suggestions or employing him as your intuition dictates.

Vigor and Longevity

Far from being a delicate flower, carnation exudes the energies of heartiness and strength. Taking the essence under the tongue, spending time with carnations, or bringing a bouquet of carnations into your space can lend potency to one's energy field, and, as a result, instantly boost overall health and well-being. In fact, author Scott Cunningham suggests placing a bouquet of carnations near the bed to help speed a person's healing process. Similarly, taking the essence regularly can help boost vigor and longevity. You might also incorporate carnation into spells or rituals designed for the purpose.

Magical Correspondences

Element: Fire

Gender: Male

Planets: Saturn, Jupiter

Chamomile

This soft, feathery-leaved member of the daisy family has a sweet scent that is evocative of apples, bananas, or vanilla. Chamomile's main magical or energetic properties may be described as soothing and smoothing. With such a gentle positivity and sunshiny perspective, he can help turn the tides on negativity and harshness of all varieties while aligning us with our most ideal energetic flow.

When working with chamomile, please be mindful that some people are allergic to the daisy family.

Magical Uses

Animal Support

Chamomile flower essence is an amazing all-purpose tonic for cats and dogs. A single drop added to their water supply can help soothe stress, heal challenging behaviors, support healing and overall wellness, comfort them during transitions, and establish peace between multiple animals.

Breaking Curses and Spells

I know that to some of us, a curse may appear to be an old-fashioned or even imaginary concept, but it actually describes something very real. However, it's nothing to panic about: regardless of how it got there, you might think of a curse as simply an undesirable pattern that's stuck in the energetic matrix in the same way the chorus of a song can get stuck in your head. And because chamomile smooths out the harsh edges and aligns everything with a sunny positivity, it can be helpful for eradicating curses, unwanted spells, and any other similarly challenging patterns.

For this purpose, try sprinkling the dried herb or misting whoever or whatever may be holding the curse or challenging pattern with chilled chamomile tea or spring water into which you've added ten to fifteen drops chamomile essential oil. This can also be helpful when it's your intention to change the energetic momentum of a home or business (after a challenging period, for example). To break a love spell, try the following ritual.

"BREAK A LOVE SPELL" RITUAL

During the waning moon on a Saturday, Sunday, or Tuesday, ceremoniously and mindfully eat nine pistachios, spinning once in a counterclockwise direction after swallowing each one. Next, visualize very bright golden-white light surrounding and filling a glass or bottle of at least twenty ounces of spring water, then drink it all at once. Finish by anointing your forehead, throat, heart, belly, and the palm of each hand with chamomile essential oil (if you have sensitive skin, dilute appropriately with a carrier oil or substitute chamomile tea).

Healing and Protecting Children

Gentle chamomile is an extremely helpful flower when it comes to supporting and healing children (and our own inner child, who can generally be treated therapeutically in the same way as actual children). For example, in his book *Encyclopedia of Herbal Medicine*, Andrew Chevallier recommends adding an infusion of chamomile (chamomile tea) to bath water to "relax fractious and overtired children, or adding five drops of essential oil of chamomile to twenty ml of a carrier oil to create a diaper rash treatment."

If your child (or inner child) feels unsafe in her bedroom, before bedtime, you might diffuse the essential oil or mist the room with spring water into which you've added equal parts lavender, peppermint, and chamomile essential oils.

Chamomile tea or an herbal tea containing chamomile (such as Sleepytime, Celestial Seasoning's famous relaxing blend) can help soothe bedtime fears and nightmares while promoting deep, restful sleep.

You might also like to plant the flower in your yard, add one to two drops of the flower essence to your child's food or beverage once daily, or incorporate the dried or fresh flower or essential oil into any sort of ritual or charm designed for the purpose of protecting and healing your child or inner child.

Peace and Harmony

As you might expect, chamomile's soothing, cooling, balancing energy heartily lends itself to promoting peace and harmony within individuals, couples, groups, situations, and spaces. For this purpose, you might try:

- diffusing the essential oil
- misting the space with a water or rose water blend containing the essential oil or flower essence
- serving or drinking chamomile tea
- taking the essence
- growing the flower in your yard
- adding the dried or fresh herb or essential oil to your bath water
- sprinkling the dried herb around the perimeter of a lot or the outside of a home or business
- bringing in one or more bouquets of the fresh flowers
- attaching a small sachet of the dried herb to the inside of your clothes, near your heart

- incorporating the essential oil or dried herb into rituals or charms designed for the purpose of promoting peace and harmony

Positivity

When we choose to look at life in a positive light rather than a negative one, our whole experience can change in an instant from one of struggle to one of joy. And, especially when our inner dialogue or current life situation seems to be characterized by tension and harshness, chamomile can help with this. For this purpose, try any of the suggestions from the previous section.

Prosperity

Author Scott Cunningham recommends chamomile flower for prosperity rituals and mixtures, and he mentions that gamblers employed the tea as a hand wash to help ensure success. This makes sense from an energetic perspective, as chamomile aligns us with our most ideal life flow, which always includes a generous supply of blessings.

To shift into a more positive and prosperous mindset, you might employ any of the suggestions from the "peace and harmony" section. And, for a variation on the gambler's hand wash theme, you might create the following money-drawing lotion potion.

....

Lotion Potion for Prosperity and Luck

On a Thursday or Sunday during the waxing moon, place five to ten drops chamomile essential oil in pretty jar. (Optional: enhance the scent by adding drops of vanilla and/or jasmine essential oils as well.) Fill the jar the rest of the way with unscented lotion. Close the lid and shake well to blend. When this is complete, place the closed jar in the center of a small green or red plate, and surround the jar with nine pieces of citrine quartz (which have been cleansed beforehand in running water, sunlight, and white sage smoke). Take some deep breaths, and feel centered and connected to the earth. Then hold your open palms toward the jar and visualize sparkly gold light entering the crown of your head and going down to your heart, down your arms, and out through the palms of your hands and into the jar. Say:

I am always in the right place at the right time.
I am in divine flow.
I am a fountain of divine prosperity.
All doors are open to me now.

Leave the jar arrangement on your altar or in a special place, and rub the lotion into your hands daily before work or any situation during which you'd like to experience increased prosperity and luck.

Sleep

It's possible that chamomile is best known as a gentle, safe, non-habit-forming sleep aid. Indeed, I was first introduced to him when my mom gave me a cup of Celestial Seasoning's Sleepytime tea when I was a nervous little six-year-old girl who couldn't seem to get to sleep.

For relief of occasional sleep challenges, try drinking a cup of chamomile tea before bed. For chronic insomnia, try drinking a chamomile blend containing valerian root (such as Sleepytime Extra) before bed, while also taking the essence regularly. (Also remember to exercise often and not to overdo the caffeine, as these are rules one and two when it comes to getting a good night's sleep.)

Soothing

As mentioned above, chamomile's main energetic action may be described as soothing, and this action takes place in both physical and metaphysical realms. As a matter of fact, according to aromatherapist Gabriel Mojay, in Eastern medicine chamomile is employed to help smooth the flow of chi, or life-force energy, and to clear heat and reduce inflammation. Magically and medicinally speaking, chamomile can be employed to help soothe:

- digestion

- eye strain

- bladder and urinary tract ailments

- tension and stress

- pain

- skin ailments

- premenstrual and menstrual challenges

- cramps and spasms

- irritability

- anger

- discord

- harsh vibrations

- grief

Magical Correspondences

Element: Water
Gender: Male
Planets: Sun, Moon

Cherry Blossom

A favorite flower in Japan, cherry blossom's pure and positive vibration can help uplift our mood, align us with the Divine, draw romance, and powerfully enhance our mental, physical, and spiritual well-being.

Magical Uses

Divine Love

Within us is a divine spark of consciousness, and the more we acknowledge and tune in to this spark, the happier we are and the more everything seems to work in our lives. What's more, we begin to notice that the entire visible world is alive with the same divine energy—and that, as such, we are one with everything, and everything is on our side. From this awareness, we realize that the trees, the sky, water, air, our clothing, our food, our friends, strangers, our homes, the ground beneath our feet, and even seeming challenges that may come our way are all conspiring to shower blessings upon us. We feel grateful for everything in our lives, and everything in our lives feels grateful for us. In other words, our lives are defined by divine love, which we constantly emanate, embody, and receive.

Because cherry blossoms emanate the energy of divine love in an uncommonly pure and potent way, they can be magically employed to remind us of this love. This lifts our spirits and establishes the energetic atmosphere that will bring greater harmony and blessings into every area of our lives. For this purpose, employ the flower in a ritual, spend time with her, or take the essence.

Forgiveness

No matter how wronged or slighted we may have felt in the past, holding on to grudges, grievances, and old hurts is always an energy drain and holds us back from experiencing joy and the fullness of our power. So if it's early spring and you're ready to forgive a person, group of people, or situation, you might perform the following ritual.

FORGIVENESS RITUAL

Put some shears or scissors in a basket or grocery bag, along with a bottle of water, a pen, and a journal or notebook. You might also want to bring a folding chair or a little blanket or towel to sit on.

Visit a blossoming cherry tree. Sit comfortably. Relax and take some deep breaths as you quiet your mind and tune in to the energy of the blossoms. When you feel ready, write out what you're ready to release. Tell the story that has caused you to hold on to unforgiveness and anger, and don't censor yourself. Tell it with all the emotion the story currently holds for you. Get nasty. Call people names if you want. Then describe in detail how it feels to hold on to this situation and how it affects your life. For example, it likely leads to feelings of disempowerment and exhaustion, and perhaps you also find that you feel suspicious and untrusting of people who have nothing to do with the situation at all.

Now take a leap of imagination and envision how it would feel if you were able to let go of the situation—to let it be what it is but not to fight with it anymore: to accept it, begin to heal it, and be free. You don't have to actually forgive yet, just imagine what it would feel like if you did, then describe that in your journal as well. When this feels complete, tune in to the blossoms again and silently communicate everything you have just discovered about your feelings concerning the situation. Explain that you're ready to forgive and move on, and ask the blossoms to help you. Hold the bottle of water in both hands and say a prayer of blessing in any way that feels right to you, then pour it around the base of the tree. Then, with the shears, lovingly gather five- to six-inch lengths of seven blossoming branches. Thank the tree profusely, place the branches in the basket or bag, and go home. Once home, dissolve one-half cup sea salt in a warm bath and float the blossoms on top. Soak for at least forty minutes.

Gentleness

If things have been feeling a bit harsh lately at work or if your relationship or home life has been beset by irritability and snappishness, cherry blossoms can help soften things up. Bring bouquets into your home and/or take the essence.

HEART AND CROWN CHAKRA ALIGNMENT

Each chakra represents its own constellation of life aspects, yet the chakra system is holistic: each chakra affects and interacts with every other chakra. When the heart chakra (at your sternum) and crown chakra (at the top of your head) are both balanced, activated, and aligned with each other, we powerfully radiate and receive the energy of divine love. Additionally, we live from our hearts and follow our divine guidance, which helps align us with our most ideal life path. Cherry blossoms enhance and vitalize each chakra individually and together.

To garner these benefits, take the essence and play some soft, relaxing music. Lie flat on your back with your arms by your sides, palms upon the floor, bed, or yoga mat. Place one small stem of cherry blossoms at the top of your head, one on your heart, and one in each of your palms. Close your eyes, take some deep breaths, and relax deeply for at least twenty minutes.

Remembering One's Primal Innocence

Mistakes? Sure, you've made them—we all have. But no matter what you think you've done or not done, the truth is that you are, and always have been, *doing the very best you can*. Life is confusing. We can't expect ourselves to do it perfectly, and mistakes are actually an indispensable aspect of the learning process.

What's more, the past is dissolved as completely as if it never happened at all. There is only the present. There only ever has been the present. The past and the future are illusions, or simply ways of communicating about what we remember or foresee.

With these things in mind, cherry blossom would like to remind you that the truth of your being is 100 percent innocent *right now*: as innocent as a newborn baby, puppy, or kitten. You are completely forgiven for everything you've ever thought, said, done, and not done.

If you need help remembering this, spend time with the flower, take the essence or add it to your bath, or incorporate cherry blossoms into a ritual.

Romance

The romance that cherry blossom brings into our lives is not your everyday type of romance. If you're looking for a light spring fling or some amusing but not too serious romantic adventures, cherry blossom is probably not the love-drawing flower for you.

But if, on the other hand, you're ready for a keeper—for someone with whom you don't just have a physical connection but also a spiritual and emotional one—cherry blossom just might be the flower to choose for your magical workings.

In *Cunningham's Encyclopedia of Magical Herbs*, author Scott Cunningham describes a simple Japanese cherry blossom love spell: to draw love, "tie a single strand of your hair to a blossoming cherry tree."

Weight Loss

Because cherry blossoms provide spiritual nourishment as well as self-forgiveness and self-love, they can be employed to help heal the emotional causes of overeating or eating in an unhealthy way. To employ cherry blossoms for this purpose, simply take two drops of cherry blossom essence under the tongue three times per day.

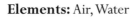

Magical Correspondences

Elements: Air, Water

Gender: Female

Planet: Venus

Cherry Plum

 or such a small and delicate-looking tree and blossom, cherry plum has a whole lot of pep. Like a tough but fair coach who cares passionately about not only our performance on the field, but also our true happiness and overall well-being, she riles us up, fills us with energy and joy, and pushes us out of our comfort zones, inspiring us to step into our power and claim our heart's desires. Magically speaking, she gets things moving: our energy, our endeavors, and our lives.

And here's some great news: cherry plum is one of Edward Bach's thirty-eight flower essence remedies. So, if you'd like to experience her magical benefits and you don't happen to have a blossoming tree nearby, you can almost definitely pick up a bottle of her essence at your local health food store.

Magical Uses

Agelessness, Timeless Beauty

When our aura, or energetic field (the sphere of energy/light that occupies the same space as our bodies and extends out from us in all directions), is strong and clear, our beauty increases rather than decreases over time. An invisible yet palpable light shines from our hearts and eyes, and our mere presence has a healing effect on everyone we meet. The magic of cherry plum blossoms lends itself to agelessness and timeless beauty by healing, brightening, and fortifying our personal radiance.

TIMELESS BEAUTY TONIC

On the morning of a new moon, place four drops of cherry plum essence in a wine glass of sparkling mineral water. Hold the glass in both hands and visualize very bright white light filling the water and extending out in all directions like a miniature sunrise. Think or say the word *radiance*, and direct the energy of the word into the water. Then drink. Repeat every morning until the next new moon.

Chakra Healing and Clearing

Every once in a while, it might come to your attention that one or more of your chakras (which are invisible wheels of light that are part of your energy field) are blocked or in some way imbalanced. If this is the case, in addition to any other healing work you're doing or undergoing, such as reiki or yoga, you can work with the energy of cherry plum blossoms to help unblock and balance your chakras in exactly the way that is most needed. If you don't have a blossoming cherry plum tree nearby, take one to two drops of the essence or place directly onto the skin near the chakra area itself three times per day, until the block or imbalance feels resolved. But if you do have a blossoming cherry plum tree nearby, you might try the following.

....

CHAKRA HEALING SESSION

Obtain a white quartz crystal point, cleanse it with sunlight or white sage smoke, and visit a blossoming cherry plum tree on a sunny day. Sit or squat near the trunk. After tuning in to the tree, hold the crystal in both hands and say or think, "Beautiful cherry plum tree, I've brought you this gift in the hopes that you'll help me heal my chakra(s)." Place the crystal at the base of the trunk. Then place both your hands on the trunk and explain (silently or aloud) what you'd like help with as if you're talking to a therapist or trusted friend. If you know the emotional issues attached to the chakra imbalance, talk them out as best you can. Then lie down on your back on the earth beneath the blossoming branches. (You might bring a blanket or towel if you're concerned about getting dirty or wet.) Relax as deeply as you can, breathe, and allow the energy of the cherry plum blossoms to thoroughly heal your chakra(s) and emotions. Notice any inner guidance, thoughts, images, and impressions that you receive. Allow yourself to feel any feelings that may come up. When your healing feels complete, touch the trunk again, say a heartfelt thank you, then go on your way.

Circulation, Digestion, and Physical Healing

As I mentioned, cherry plum blossoms get things moving. As such, if blood circulation, lymphatic circulation, or digestion are issues for you, you might support your other healing endeavors by taking the essence or spending time with the flower.

And, because good digestion and good circulation support general health and help heal a whole host of physical maladies and emotional challenges, either of the previous remedies can help support healing of all varieties.

Courage

Things can start to feel stagnant, depressing, or just plain boring when we're terrified of moving forward or afraid of our own power. If you need a dose of courage to take initiative, move out of your comfort zone, or move toward realizing your dreams, cherry plum can help.

....

COURAGE SHOT

Anytime you'd like an extra dose of courage, fill a shot glass with pomegranate juice and add four drops cherry plum essence. Cradle the shot glass in your open left palm and place your right hand under your left. Visualize a shower of very bright golden-white light coming down from above, filling and encompassing the shot glass and your hands. Call upon the energy of divine courage, direct that energy into the liquid, then drink. Visualize/imagine/feel the energy of courage lighting up your entire body and aura from the inside. You might repeat daily until you feel you've internalized the courage, or just do a shot anytime you could use a boost.

Determination and Following Through

Need the energy to get started and follow through with a business project, an art project, or even something as simple as clearing the clutter out of your garage? Cherry plum might be just the ticket. You might spend time near a blossoming tree to receive an etheric pep talk or simply take the essence. The cherry plum and pomegranate courage shot would also be great for this purpose.

Inspiration, Passion, and Joy

If you feel depressed, listless, passionless, or joyless, it could be that all you need is to get your energy moving in the right direction—which, as you've probably learned by now, is cherry plum's specialty. Any of the previous remedies can help restore your inspiration and passion for life.

Removing Energetic Blocks

See previous sections.

Strength

You might employ the wisdom and magic of cherry plum if you'd like to get your strength back physically, mentally, spiritually, or emotionally. For this purpose, see the previous ideas and remedies.

Success

Cherry plum is also great for blessing any new project or endeavor with the energy of success. For this purpose, a sprig from the blossoming tree—when removed with love and respect and exchanged for the gift of a crystal or a bottle of wine, champagne, or ale poured out near the base of the tree—may be placed over the threshold of a new business, in the area where a new project is born, or near a symbol representing the project or endeavor. Before you remove the branch, be sure to discuss the endeavor with the tree and explain what you'd like help with and the outcome you seek, then thank her profusely.

Magical Correspondences

Element: Fire
Gender: Female
Planet: Mars

Chrysanthemum

hrysanthemum, famous for blooming in fall and winter, will actually bloom anytime the light around him becomes sufficiently diminished. And, as you're about to discover, each of chrysanthemum's energetic properties might be seen as having to do with shining light into darkness or shoring up one's strength when it may otherwise begin to wane. Coincidence? I think not.

Chrysanthemum's name (from the Greek *chrysos* for "gold") means "gold flower." This is another indication of his bolstering, brightening dynamic, as many magical teachings consider gold to be the symbol and actual physical manifestation of the spirit-sustaining, life-giving essence of the sun.

Magical Uses

Longevity

Chrysanthemum's most famous magical ability might be his penchant for bestowing longevity. He does this by infusing us with vigor, youthful energy, and a healthy hunger for fresh perspectives and new experiences. But be advised that he is not a general health tonic: he only works for people who have passed into what might be called the "autumn of life."

To promote longevity, take the essence or brew a cup of tea made with dried chrysanthemum blossoms (grow and dry them yourself or purchase them already dried at an Asian grocery store), and drink daily.

Mental Clarity

In his *Encyclopedia of Magical Herbs*, Scott Cunningham suggests drinking an infusion of chrysanthemums to "cure drunkenness." And while I can't guarantee chrysanthemums will help you pass a breathalyzer test, I will say that—whether or not you are drunk—chrysanthemums may help clear your mind and focus your thoughts.

Similarly, if you're looking to understand a situation better, if you'd like help making an important decision, or if you're just plain craving more mental clarity, I suggest spending time in quiet contemplation with a blossoming chrysanthemum. Relax, breathe, and focus your vision on the blossom. Allow your breath to naturally deepen and slow down, and allow your thoughts to settle. Then connect with the intelligence of the flower and silently let him know precisely what you'd like help with. You will receive the guidance that you seek. Remember to thank the flower for his help before you leave.

Optimism

If we didn't indulge in a little gloom and doom every now and then, we'd be a little out of balance, wouldn't we? But when gloom and doom become the natural way of things, our joy gets diminished, our energy gets depleted, and our motivation begins to dry up. As we've seen, when brightness begins to wane, there's no better time to work chrysanthemum into your magic and replenish your inner light.

SPIRIT SUNRISE BATH

Just before sunrise, add five fresh chrysanthemum blossoms (or twenty-five drops chrysanthemum essence if they're not in season) to your bath water, along with an orange cut into eight wedges, three to five drops of jasmine essential oil, and one-half cup baking soda. Light a yellow candle or two and, as the sun rises, soak for at least forty minutes. As you soak, feel your spirits rising like the sun.

Protection

When it comes to fears and dangers related to the mysterious, dark, or unknowable, chrysanthemum is your man. Carry a fresh blossom to guard against earthbound entities, psychic attack, and other invisible dangers. To protect a space from unsavory unseen guests, you might hang garlands or wreaths containing chrysanthemums at doors and windows. If you're afraid of the dark or to prevent nightmares, sleep with a fresh blossom under your pillow. And if you feel constantly beset by fears related to the invisible realm, take four drops chrysanthemum essence under the tongue every morning and night until you feel settled and safe.

Solving Mysteries

Chrysanthemum's ability to shine light into the darkness makes him a wonderful ally when it comes to solving mysteries. Try silently tuning in to a blossom. Explain what you are trying to discover and why it's important to you, then request help. Then, when you get the okay, gently pick the blossom and keep it with you until the mystery is solved. At that time, return the blossom to the earth near the plant from which you gathered it. Be sure to express gratitude, and as a gesture of thanks, pour out a bit of wine or ale or place a silver dollar or shiny dime near the plant.

Soothing Grief

Real grief isn't just a passing thing. It's a deep current of energy that flows through our lives as an important accompaniment to love and joy. The older we get, the more grief we feel as we reflect on old times and remember our loved ones who have transitioned. But there are times—such as after the recent loss of a loved one—when grief can be so acute that it can feel all but unbearable. These are the times when chrysanthemum can help by bolstering our fortitude and shining the light of hope into our hearts. In times like these, he also helps by shining light past the veil of time so that we can feel connected to our loved ones even though they are no longer in this physical world.

For this purpose, try surrounding yourself in chrysanthemums—planting them in your yard and bringing them into your space. And if you know someone experiencing profound grief, you might consider giving chrysanthemums to him or her as a gift.

Magical Correspondences

Element: Fire
Gender: Male
Planet: Sun

Cinquefoil

This delicate, five-petaled flower possesses a lovely synthesis of soft, other-worldly energy and potent lucky mojo. Certain species of cinquefoil have been traditionally employed by herbalists and magical practitioners for a large number of uses, from treating diarrhea to inducing prophetic dreams.

Indian strawberry (a.k.a. "mock strawberry"), a species of cinquefoil, is like strawberry's wild hillbilly cousin. Though strawberries and mock strawberries are actually completely different plants, they appear highly similar in almost every way—the two main exceptions being that the blossoms of the Indian strawberry are yellow rather than white, and the fruit they bear is smaller and said to be lacking in flavor. While this variety of cinquefoil is mainly known as an attractive blossoming groundcover, the plant's healing and detoxifying properties—which are believed by some herbalists to contribute to the prevention and healing of tumors—have been incorporated in both Eastern and Western herbal healing systems.

However, since there is so little information on this available to the layperson, and because the plant is sometimes described as "mildly toxic," I don't suggest employing anything other than the flower essence for healing purposes unless you have access to expert knowledge. I am only relating this information because a plant's physical healing properties provide windows into the dynamics of its metaphysical and vibrational healing properties.

Magical Uses

Creativity and Playfulness

Remember when you were a child and the mere picture or mention of a faery, unicorn, or monster could send you into another world via your imagination and sense of youthful awe? Although as adults we often seem to think that the words *my imagination* should be preceded by the words *just* or *only*, the truth is that no matter what our age, our imagination allows us to tap into something that is not only very real, but also vital to our happiness, creativity, and the future of the planet. Blossoms of cinquefoil—through activating our imagination and sense of playfulness—create an energetic window into this something.

This aspect of cinquefoil's magic can also provide wonderful support for naturally dreamy and sensitive children who may be feeling closed off or less playful due to any sort of emotional challenge.

For any of these purposes, try spending time with a flower or taking the essence. Or, if you'd like to stimulate your creative and playful mind, you might soak in the following bath.

IMAGINATION INCUBATION BATH

Draw a warm bath and dissolve one cup sea salt in it. Light a yellow candle and a stick of rosemary or vanilla incense. Add nine fresh Indian strawberry blossoms or nineteen drops cinquefoil essence to the water, along with an aquamarine crystal. Before getting into the water, place your left hand on your heart and your right hand on your belly. Take some deep breaths and consider your intentions. Perhaps you'd like to find your direction with your next creative project, find a creative solution to a challenging situation, or rediscover a sense of playfulness in your relationship or career. Feel the feelings you'd like to feel regarding your creative and playful intentions. When this feels complete, get in the water and soak for at least forty-five minutes. As you do so, consciously relax your mind and allow it to freely wander.

Freedom and Liberation

Sometimes we just need to break away and rise above. Cinquefoil's energy—like an old friend from our "wild days"—can help us to cut loose and free ourselves from things like:

- limiting beliefs
- low self-esteem
- long-standing unhelpful patterns
- relationships that don't serve us
- inner restrictions or restraints
- sexual or social inhibitions
- fears and worries

Try taking two to four drops of the essence in a glass of water or sparkling cider (or, if your inner guru gives you the green light, an alcoholic beverage of your choice). Drink with the intention to liberate yourself from whatever you need liberating from. As you imbibe the flower's vibration via the beverage, feel your attachment to the condition, thought, pattern, or issue unraveling and dissolving, leaving you free. Or you might try spending time with the blossom or performing the bath ritual from the previous section with the intention to liberate yourself.

Healing

A core tenet of holistic medicine is that our mind and body are connected. As such, by helping us to dissolve and liberate ourselves from mental and emotional patterns that are no longer serving us, cinquefoil can be a good complement to physical healing endeavors, especially when they involve long-standing issues. Just to clarify, for serious medical issues I don't suggest using cinquefoil essence exclusively but rather as a gentle complement to other modalities. For this purpose, I suggest taking the flower essence regularly as needed.

Luck

Cinquefoil has an all-around positive energy that can help us to get into our most natural and harmonious life flow—in other words, he can help increase our luck. You might like to add cinquefoil blossoms or essence to any magical endeavor performed for the purpose of increasing abundance, blessings, or luck.

Magic

The realm of magic and the realm of the imagination are one and the same. In fact, both words contain a similar root: *magos*. If you're working on honing your magical abilities and becoming awake to the realm of magic in every moment, you might consider working with cinquefoil's vibration. For this purpose, try any of the previous suggestions or create the following mist.

MIST SMUDGE

Before creative visualizations, rituals, or other magical endeavors, mist the space with spring water into which you've added ten drops cinquefoil essence and ten to twenty drops thyme essential oil.

Prophetic Dreams

Traditionally, cinquefoil leaves have been employed as a smudge before bed to induce prophetic dreams about one's true love. Similarly, you can create the following mist smudge to induce prophetic dreams about your true love or anything else.

DREAMTIME MIST SMUDGE

Add nine or twelve drops cinquefoil flower essence to a mister of rose water, along with four drops neroli and eight drops lavender essential oils. Shake gently and lightly mist your bedroom before bed. Then, as you drift off to sleep, silently repeat what you would like to receive prophetic dreams about for as long as you remain conscious and focused. Phrase your statement in a positive way, as if you already know the answer to your query. For example, if you're wondering what city to move to, you might repeat, "I live in the perfect city, where I thrive in every way." Or, if you'd like to know how to meet a wonderful romantic partner, you might repeat, "I am in love with the most wonderful person, and she (or he) is in love with me." Be sure to keep a notebook and pen or a voice recorder next to your bed so that, upon awakening, you can capture any impressions you receive.

Wild Joy

Feel like your domestication is putting a kink in your joy? Been a little too long since you ran with the wolves and howled at the moon? Take cinquefoil essence as desired to help rediscover your inner wild man or woman.

Incidentally, getting in touch with your wild joy in this way can also help align you with your most ideal life path. After all, how can you follow your bliss unless you get wild and crazy enough to let yourself find it in the first place?

Magical Correspondences

Elements: Water, Air

Gender: Male

Planets: Uranus, Jupiter

Citrus Blossom

*T*here seems to be no end to the magical benefits of neroli and all varieties of citrus blossom (orange, lemon, grapefruit, etc.). Neroli is the fancy name for bitter orange blossom essential oil, named after the illustrious Princess Marie Anne de La Trémoille of Nerola. Simply encountering a blossoming citrus tree and inhaling the fragrance of her creamy white blossoms can lift your personal vibration, balance your emotions, open you up to wealth and luxury, soothe your stress, and generally fill you with delight.

Magical Uses

Heavenly Assistance

Once you inhale the scent of a citrus blossom, you'll know what I mean when I say that she is aligned with the heavenly realm. She soothes your mind, calms your emotions, and opens you up to the divine, angelic assistance that is always available to all of us. As such, she can help open doors, clear passages, precipitate opportunities, and orchestrate details in a harmonious way. To receive these benefits, you might try taking the essence, spending time with the flower, or soaking in the following magical bath.

BATH FOR DIVINE ASSISTANCE AND HARMONIOUS ORCHESTRATION

Draw a warm bath. After dissolving one-half cup sea salt and one-fourth cup baking soda in the water, add nine to twelve fresh citrus blossoms and five to ten drops neroli essential oil. Light a white or off-white soy candle and soak for at least forty minutes.

Beauty

In his *Encyclopedia of Magical Herbs*, author Scott Cunningham says that "fresh or dried [orange] blossoms added to the bath make the bather more attractive." And in *Aromatherapy for Everyone*, authors P. J. Pierson and Mary Shipley suggest "to regenerate skin cells and improve skin elasticity for mature skin, mix a drop or two [of neroli essential oil] with an application of an unscented face cream, and apply as normal." Additionally, you might incorporate citrus blossoms or neroli oil into rituals for increasing and enhancing physical beauty. A flower essence made from any variety of citrus blossom would also be a lovely way to emphasize physical beauty or help support any healthy appearance-enhancing regimen such as a weight loss or exercise program.

Clarity

When your mind is so full of thoughts, worries, and obligations that you seem to have forgotten why you are doing any of the things you are doing—or why you should even care—the scent of neroli essential oil, fresh citrus blossoms, or the essence of citrus blossoms might be just the thing to help you regain the clarity you crave.

AROMATHERAPEUTIC BRAIN DRAIN

Sit quietly with a notebook or journal nearby, relax, and simply inhale the scent of neroli essential oil or fresh citrus blossoms. Then, after a little while of sitting quietly, do a "brain drain": list all the things that are running around in your head, whether they're commitments, worries, fears, or anything else. Then take some time with each one and consider what steps you can take to minimize the stress each item seems to be activating. Perhaps you can drop a few of the commitments or delegate some chores to other members of the household. Maybe you'll feel moved to deal with things you've been putting off, or maybe you'll realize it's time for a vacation, retreat, or even just a little nature walk.

Comfort and Luxury

Considering the seemingly miraculous ways Princess Marie Anne of Nerola seemed to remain a wealthy and provided-for central member of the Spanish royal court, flower magic enthusiasts must wonder whether or not this had anything to do with her choice of fragrance. Indeed, the scent seems to send you into a realm of soft cushions and gentle breezes, which can't help but keep your personal vibration aligned with all things luxurious.

As you might imagine, this makes neroli essential oil (and the scent of fresh citrus blossoms) an excellent choice for magical and aromatherapeutic endeavors related to raising your prosperity consciousness and attracting wealth and desirable conditions. It's an especially good choice when you want to begin receiving wealth and luxury in an especially cushy and receptive way, such as in the form of gifts, windfalls, or delightfully convenient financial opportunities.

Additionally, neroli essential oil and the fragrance of citrus blossoms can be excellent to help balance those of us who can sometimes err on the side of workaholism. The fragrance helps us relax, enjoy the fruits of our labor, and allow blessings to flow to us rather than feel like we have to constantly hunt them down.

Emotional Balance and Stress Relief

Neroli essential oil is used by aromatherapists to help soothe premenstrual and menopausal stress and irritability, as well as general tension and stress. As you can easily experience for yourself, the fragrance does seem to immediately lift you out of the illusion of discord and put you smack in the middle of an even keel.

Happy Children

When children feel safe, protected, loved, and provided for, they experience inner security and carefree attitudes that are the basis of a happy childhood. And all of these feelings can be enhanced by the fragrance of citrus blossoms. For this reason (provided the child likes the scent), it can be an excellent idea to diffuse neroli essential oil in your home after your child experiences any sort of personal trauma or family crisis, including (but not limited to):

- divorce or separation
- abuse
- change of residence
- change of schools
- nightmares
- general fear
- bullying
- loss of a loved one

Happy Home

Citrus blossoms and neroli oil are wonderful ingredients for any sort of magical endeavor related to happiness in the home. The fragrance and energy aligns the home with the soft, relaxing, regenerative qualities that make home *home*. Additionally, the tranquilizing effects of the scent and vibration can help soothe tension and heal relationships.

Marital Bliss

Orange blossoms have been traditionally included in bridal bouquets to relax the bride and bless the partnership. Neroli and orange blossoms are classic ingredients in magic related to marital harmony and bliss.

Positive Thinking

Thinking is habitual, and when we get in a negativity rut, we usually have to employ a bit of extra elbow grease to get out of it. But get out of it we must, because our thoughts create and define our reality. And neroli essential oil and the scent of fresh citrus blossoms can help soothe and encourage the transition from a sense of struggle, worry, anger, and strife to one of ease, contentment, security, gentleness, and harmony. For this purpose, try diffusing the essential oil in your home or gently inhaling the scent of a fresh citrus blossom while repeating affirmations related to your desired change of inner dialogue.

Sensuality

Perhaps a significant reason why orange blossoms and neroli are traditionally associated with marital bliss is that they get us out of our heads and into our bodies. They remind us of the sweetness of life and slow us down so that we can fully appreciate the pleasures of the flesh.

And since a sensually alive person is a sexy person, this may be another dimension to neroli and citrus blossom's ability to increase our physical attractiveness.

Trust

For many of us, learning *not* to trust was a very important survival mechanism at one point in our lives. However, once we become adults, this throws a wrench in our plans to fall in love and settle down. The good news is, we can learn to trust again. We can see that we are no longer children and that not everyone is like the person or people who betrayed our trust so long ago. We can look our old hurts square in the face and work through them until they no longer have the same sort of power over us that they once had. And, to help these things along, we can inhale the fragrance of neroli essential oil and fresh citrus blossoms. The fragrance (and accompanying magical energy of the blossom), when directed with intention and accompanied by other therapeutic activities such as counseling, energy healing, and yoga, helps soothe our fears and open our hearts. It connects to the child within us and helps repair the places where that child feels broken.

Magical Correspondences

Elements: Water, Earth
Gender: Female
Planet: Venus

Clover

*I*t seems clover's leaves are often more famous than his blossoms—but why? Clover blossoms are ever so magical and endlessly lovely in their radiant subtlety. Paradigms of gentleness and purity, they also engender vibrant health, enhanced physical beauty, innate prosperity consciousness, and calm inner strength.

Magical Uses

Abundance

Our sustenance is, in fact, based not the visible manifestation of money but on the divine energy that underlies and animates all things. And this energy is endless! Once we realize this truth and allow our consciousness of God/Goddess/All That Is to grow and expand, we begin to notice that we already have everything we need. As a result, our visible resources begin to mirror our invisible awareness of our infinite supply.

To start this ball rolling, try spending time with blossoming clover and let him gently remind you of the divinely designed supply that is already in your possession at this very moment. You might also take the essence every morning during the waxing moon.

Beauty

Red clover blossom is a natural beautifier. In addition to endowing you with the magical energy of wild, divine beauty, when used correctly it can cleanse your blood and add radiance, elasticity, and clarity to your skin.

BEAUTY POTION

Boil four cups of water, then add a small handful of dried burdock root. Cover, reduce heat, and simmer for ten minutes. Remove from heat and add a large handful of dried red clover blossoms. Cover and let steep for one to two hours. Strain. Put two tablespoons raw apple cider vinegar in a wine glass and fill the rest with the herbal infusion. (Store the rest of the infusion in a glass receptacle in the fridge for next time.) Hold the glass in both hands and visualize a sphere of very bright golden-white light filling and surrounding it. Say "I am divine love" nine times. Drink. Repeat daily until desired level of beauty is reached.

BEAUTY BATH

You might like to perform this ritual when preparing for an event or moment during which you'd like your beauty and radiance to particularly shine forth. Gently and lovingly gather forty fresh, wild (organic) red clover blossoms, placing them on a clean cotton cloth in a basket or bowl. Wash them if necessary and then place them back on the cloth. Draw a bath. Light a white or off-white candle and a stick of vanilla or rose incense. Hold the basket or bowl in both hands and say:

Thank you, Great Goddess, for yielding and sharing these
blossoms, which are emissaries of your divine beauty.

Then strew them across the top of the water. Hold your hands over the water and visualize the water being filled with very bright, golden-white light. Say "I am divine love" nine times. Soak for at least forty minutes.

Faery Communication

All clover blossoms are members of that precious and esteemed group of flowers that help us connect and communicate with the faeries. They are like little energetic doorways into the faery realm. The best way to do this is to spend time outdoors near blossoming clover and let your mind wander and drift into daydreams. Also, if you have a faery altar (or if you choose to construct one), you may like to place clover blossoms on it. Working with the flower essence can help blur the walls between our realm and the realm of the fey.

Gentle Strength

As a character trait, strength must be balanced with gentleness in order to wield it in the most harmonious and effective way. Gentle strength is the trait that allows us to speak our truth with love so that we do not alienate or gratuitously offend. It allows us to maintain positive boundaries without unnecessarily stepping on anyone's toes. In short, it's the graceful ability to get our needs met while honoring and respecting the needs of others.

Just to clarify: possessing gentle strength does not mean that we never raise our voice or get angry. It just means that we do so only when the circumstances call for it and when we are honoring our deepest inner truth.

For those of us who were raised to think that speaking our truth is rude or out of line, and for those of us who learned that we had to bulldoze our way through life in order to be treated fairly or to receive our fair share, finding the balance of gentle strength can be an important consideration. And clover blossom (white especially) can help with this.

For this purpose, try sleeping with fresh white clover blossoms under your pillow, spending time with the flowers, or taking the essence.

Health and Healing

Red clover blossom traditionally has been used as a blood purifier and to treat breast cancer, menopausal symptoms, and skin problems. White clover blossom has been used to detoxify the system and realign the body with its natural state of health.

Energetically speaking, either or both can be used to restore vibrant health to the body/mind/spirit and to remind us of our most ideal state of holistic well-being.

For temporary or long-standing health challenges, supplement your other healing endeavors by taking the flower essence or creating the following charm. You may also like to create this charm as a gift for someone else (provided they are open to the idea).

Healing Charm

Gently and lovingly gather twelve fresh red or white clover blossoms. Place them in a small muslin bag, along with a white quartz crystal point that has been cleansed in sunlight. Tie closed with a green ribbon and anoint with eucalyptus or juniper essential oils. Hang from the bedpost or above the head of the healing person.

Protection

While some magical ingredients may be more potent protectors, white clover possesses a subtle emanation that can be a wonderful enhancement to any protection charm. For example, garlic, pyrite, and white quartz—especially when charged for the purpose—can repel negativity like nobody's business. White clover blossoms, on the other hand, can realign us personally with our natural state of positivity and perfection so that we have nothing to which negativity can stick. In other words, like attracts like, so when we vibrate with purity and positivity, we attract more of the same.

When you weave protective magic, you might consider adding a pinch of white clover blossom or white clover blossom essence so that your magic works on a number of levels and from a number of angles. For example:

PROTECTION CHARM

Empower a garlic clove in sunlight. Place it in a red flannel bag as you chant:

Protected and bound, safe and sound
If you don't wish me well, you won't come around.

Empower four pinches of dried white clover blossom in sunlight and add those into the bag as you say:

Clear and bright, happy and light
I radiate peace all day and all night.

Tie closed with a vibrant blue or white ribbon and anoint with angelica essential oil. Wear it under your clothes and close to your heart for extra protection in both physical and spiritual realms.

Purification

Just because something is subtle doesn't mean that it can't also be potent. And when it comes to spiritual and physical purification, that's clover blossom's motto.

Here are some ways clover blossom can be used for purification:

- Place two drops clover essence in a mister of rose water and mist an interior space to purify the vibrations. You can also mist your body and aura for the same purpose.
- Drink two to three cups white clover blossom tea per day to support physical detoxification.
- Drink two to three cups red clover blossom tea per day to support emotional detoxification (after abuse, a challenging breakup, etc.).

- Take four drops white or red clover blossom essence under the tongue or in water twice per day to support physical and emotional purification.
- Place fresh clover blossoms in bath water, along with one cup sea salt, for a physical/emotional/spiritual purification bath.
- After space clearing, arrange fresh clover blossoms and soy candles together on a plate and place in a central location in a room. Repeat in each room and area of the home, and light the candles to help set the new vibration in place and to further purify and uplift the energy.

Simplicity

If you feel overwhelmed or overextended, it just might be time to go back to basics. In cases like this, it's always best to start with clearing clutter. If you feel like you don't know where to start, start small: maybe just clear out a single drawer or cupboard. And then continue!

Once your clutter is cleared, establish new patterns of clarity and simplicity with the help of clover blossom (either color will work, but white is best for this purpose). For ideas, see the bullet points above in the "purification" section.

Magical Correspondences

Element: Air
Gender: Male
Planet: Mercury

Crabapple

otanists believe that crabapple is the result of a cultivated apple tree running wild, and I don't doubt it. She can easily be compared to a pristine, beautiful princess gearing up to be queen who suddenly rebels against her fate, lets her hair down, skinny-dips under a waterfall, and runs freely and gloriously through a meadow on a sparkly spring morning.

Crabapple is also one of Edward Bach's famous thirty-eight flower essence remedies, and in this form she's well-respected in holistic healing circles for her ability to purify the skin and infuse our awareness with feelings of freshness, purity, and self-love.

Magical Uses
Healing from Abuse

When we're abused in any way—mentally, physically, emotionally, or sexually—we sometimes harbor a deep feeling of being unclean or tainted by the energy of our abuser. If not consciously recognized and healed, we can hold on to this feeling for many years, perhaps even getting so used to it that we no longer notice its effects. Crabapple is perhaps unsurpassed in her ability to help us release this feeling by reaching deeply into our psyches and drawing out the poison so that we can feel like ourselves again. If you have the good fortune of being near a tree while she's in bloom, visit her. Sit beneath her, relax, and let her pamper you in her miraculously healing aura. If you don't have this opportunity, however (or even if you do), take the essence regularly until you feel the shift.

Freshness and Purity

Some of us (Virgos and Libras, raise your hands) can experience moments of obsessive cleanliness that stem from a feeling that we—or our homes or the entire planet—are dirty, disorganized, unkempt, or fundamentally *wrong*. At these moments, crabapple can set us straight and infuse us with the opposite feeling: that we, our homes, and the entire planet are fresh, ordered, harmoniously aligned, and fundamentally *right*.

To experience these benefits, soak for at least forty minutes in a hot bath into which you have added one cup sea salt and forty drops crabapple essence. To heal a long-standing emotional imbalance related to feeling unclean, you might also take two drops of crabapple essence under the tongue twice a day for forty days. (As a Virgo, I find that it's good to keep a bottle of crabapple essence in the medicine cabinet right next to the aspirin and bandages.)

Self-Acceptance, Self-Love, and Self-Worth

Are you like I was when I was in my early and mid-twenties, constantly berating yourself for your imperfections and obsessively thinking negative thoughts about your skin, waistline, ideas, and the sound of your own voice? Exhausting, isn't it? And as if that weren't enough, it drains your effectiveness, happiness, and magical power.

The good news? Crabapple. Spend time with her, work her into rituals, and work with the flower essence.

Magical Correspondences

Element: Air
Gender: Female
Planet: Venus

Crepe Myrtle

With a blossom that appears fresh and delicate but heartily retains its strength and beauty for prolonged periods even in the hottest climates, crepe myrtle's sweet vibration helps confer things like strength, resilience, youthful beauty, and graceful change.

Magical Uses

Enduring Partnerships

You know those relationships that are in it for the long haul—those "rocking chair on the porch someday" relationships? These are the ones that crepe myrtle's tender-meets-hearty vibration is directly in alignment with. Of course, while she can't transform a partner into someone he or she is not, if a relationship has the potential to last and thrive, she can help enhance and solidify that potential, smoothing the journey in the process. This is why crepe myrtle can be an excellent ally when entering into or supporting any sort of partnership that you desire to hold on to, including business partnerships, marriages or love relationships, and friendships. For example, you might employ the blossoms when decorating for a wedding ceremony or creating a bridal bouquet. Or you might bless a new home that you're sharing with a partner by misting it with rose water into which you've added five to ten drops crepe myrtle essence and ten to twenty drops neroli essential oil (see "citrus blossom"). You might also consider ceremoniously planting two crepe myrtle trees on your property. If you decide to do the latter, place them so that they are close but not too close, as Kahlil Gibran describes in this passage from *The Prophet*:

> *And stand together yet not too near together:*
> *For the pillars of the temple stand apart,*
> *And the oak tree and the cypress grow not in each other's shadow.*

Graceful Change

As the Greek philosopher Heraclitus famously pointed out, "The only constant is change." As such, learning to gracefully flow with the changes of life is synonymous with experiencing profound inner peace. In fact, flowing gracefully with change is something that can help support and smooth any issue or challenge that we may face. This is why, if you have crepe myrtle flower essence on hand, you might add a drop or two to any other essence or take it simultaneously to enhance the other essence's effectiveness.

If you're moving to a new home or starting a new job, or if your home or business is experiencing a change of residents or staff, you might bring fresh crepe myrtle blossoms into your living space or workspace to help smooth the transition and enhance feelings of security and positivity.

Inspiration

Part of crepe myrtle's affinity for long-term situations is her ability to help us find inspiration and freshness within the day-to-day conditions of our most important commitments. In other words, she can help prevent the burnout that comes from the illusion of "same old, same old." The truth is, each moment is completely new; crepe myrtle can help us remember that truth and be inspired by it. (Of course, she won't help us to stay in a situation that we have outgrown—rather, she will help us find the necessary stamina to be loyal to the things that truly nurture our soul.)

For this purpose, try taking the essence, planting a crepe myrtle in your yard, or misting your space with spring water containing ten to twenty drops spearmint, juniper, or eucalyptus essential oil and five drops crepe myrtle essence.

Stillness

Beyond all changes there is an eternal stillness. This stillness is the realm of the sublime. When we become conscious of it and tune in to it, life becomes sweet. We feel like we can cozy up to life and feel content with living in a quieter, less restless, more internal way.

Of course, if you feel restless because your soul is craving positive change, that is one thing. But sometimes we feel restless because we don't feel comfortable with ourselves or with the process of life. We turn on the TV just so we don't have to think or spend time alone in our own mind, and this is the type of thing that crepe myrtle can help with. By the same token, she can also help with things like:

- meditation
- yoga
- focus
- study
- peaceful, connected communication
- self-knowledge

Youthfulness

Finally, crepe myrtle's stamina, equanimity, and fresh inspiration all lend themselves to infusing one's mind, body, and spirit with an ageless, enduring beauty. You might add crepe myrtle essence to your bath water or cosmetics for an energetic fountain of youth effect, or create the following mist potion for an aura of youthful beauty.

FOUNTAIN OF YOUTH MIST POTION

Add eight drops crepe myrtle essence to a mister of rose water, along with a small aquamarine crystal and five drops lavender essential oil. Hold the mister in both hands and visualize very bright aqua-colored light moving like a fountain through and around the bottle. Shake lightly and then mist your face and neck (and, optionally, your body). Repeat as desired.

Magical Correspondences

Element: Earth
Gender: Female
Planet: Saturn

Crocus

*S*ome say that this divine, otherworldly flower first blossomed forth after Zeus and Hera made love on the hillside in an especially passionate way. Considering the profound coolness and peace of crocus's vibration, this was perhaps a demonstration of divine alchemy, as Zeus and Hera—successfully and in one glorious moment—transmuted their famously discordant polarity into balance and sublime quiescence.

Magical Uses

Banishing Nightmares

Crocus's cool radiance, soothing energy, and happy disposition combine to create an excellent magical cure for nightmares. For this purpose, try taking the flower essence or adding ten drops crocus essence to a mister of rose water, along with twenty to thirty drops lavender essential oil. Shake the bottle and then lightly mist the sleep area before bed.

Cooling Violent Emotions

In the Victorian language of flowers, one of crocus's meanings is "do not abuse." Perhaps this is because crocus possesses an energetic dynamic that helps cool anger and other violent emotions. She can be employed magically for assistance with protecting or disentangling yourself or another from domestic violence (or any other sort of violence) and harsh emotional conditions.

For this purpose, try planting crocus in your yard, bringing her into your space, or adding six to ten drops crocus essence to a mister of spring water, along with ten drops each of peppermint and spearmint essential oils. Shake and mist the space to create an atmosphere conducive to nonviolence and peaceful coexistence. Or you might secretly add two to three drops crocus essence to the food or beverage of one whose anger or violent tendencies you would like to disperse. (Incidentally, if you also add it to your own food or beverage at this time, it will not hurt and may even be helpful to your cause.)

Happiness

In the Middle Ages, healers recommended consuming saffron to bring happiness and joy, and the crocus flower is traditionally associated with the dawn and the earliest hints of spring, heralding new beginnings and the end of the long, dark night.

Wealth

Saffron, the most expensive culinary herb, comes from the stigmas and styles of the saffron crocus. Indeed, saffron's beautiful color and luxurious taste can help align us with the vibration of wealth and abundance. For this purpose, try empowering saffron with your intention to draw wealth and adding it to a savory dish.

Magical Correspondences

Elements: Water, Air
Gender: Female
Planets: Sun, Moon

Dahlia

While at first glance dahlia seems to have a sturdy temperament and a sunny disposition, if you take a moment to tune in to her energy, you'll find that she's characterized by decidedly delicate, otherworldly, moonlit qualities. Like the heroine of an Isabel Allende novel, she not only reminds us of the dark and mysterious aspects of life, but she also reminds us that those aspects can be beautiful and inspiring in their own right.

Magical Uses

Dreams

While dreams might appear to be more ephemeral and fleeting than waking life, if we examine what we know about both—namely that all we can know for absolute certain is that both are simply patterns appearing and disappearing in our consciousness—waking life and dreams actually are not so different. And when we choose to view dreams as valid and valuable life experiences, we gain access to entirely new levels of self-awareness and magical power.

Taking the flower essence right before bed and right after awakening can help us with all aspects of dream magic: astral travel, lucid dreaming, remembering our dreams, receiving or divining messages from our dreams, and weaving our dreams into our waking consciousness in ways that empower and heal us.

A sachet of dried dahlia petals under your pillow or near the head of your bed can work in a similar way, especially when magically empowered for the purpose.

Mystique

Want to surround yourself in a veil of otherworldly mystique? Dahlia's watery, lunar qualities can help you do just that. Consider the following potion.

....

Veil of Mystique Potion

After dark, in a candlelit room or by moonlight, add nine drops dahlia essence, six drops ylang ylang essential oil, and five drops lotus essential oil to a mister of rose water. Close the lid and shake. Hold the bottle in both hands and say:

> *As the moon ensorcells with her cool glow*
> *As the ocean conceals her depths below*
> *As the west wind o'er the earth doth flow*
> *Mystique surrounds me where I go.*

Mist your entire body and aura before any event or situation during which you'd like to be shrouded in an invisible cloak of wildly magnetic mystery.

Occult Wisdom

If you're drawn to magical studies, chances are you were a magical person of some sort—a witch, village wise person, shaman, etc.—in at least one past life. It's also quite probable that magical or psychic abilities run in your family. Dahlia can help us remember and activate the occult wisdom and magical abilities stored in our memories and genes, and she can facilitate our magical studies by connecting us with the lunar realm. To receive these benefits, take the flower essence or incorporate dried dahlia blossoms into magical workings related to enhancing your magical studies and fortifying your magical path.

Similarly, dahlia can be useful for rituals involving initiation or dedication to one's chosen magical path. For example, during an initiation ceremony, an initiate might drink from a glass or chalice of red wine or well water containing nine drops dahlia essence. (This would also work well for self-dedication or initiation ceremonies.)

The Sweetness of Shadows

Despite all the spiritual talk about white light and sunshine, the fact remains that there is beauty in darkness and sweetness in shadows. This is something goth kids and horror film enthusiasts already know, but the truth is, we all know it! Why else would Halloween be synonymous not only with death and fright but also with candy and fun, and why else would vampires in movies always be so wildly attractive?

While many might find the idea of beauty in darkness to be disturbingly deviant, there are actually a lot of benefits to this perspective. Excitedly looking into the shadows and ascribing a delicious quality to our fears and even our eventual death allows us to be more psychologically complete. In other words, instead of always trying to coast along the sunshiny surface of things and desperately struggle to "stay happy," we get to bravely gaze into the darkness and go deep.

Dahlia knows all about this. It's perhaps no coincidence that she's the national flower of Mexico, where the *Dia de los Muertos* (Day of the Dead) holiday epitomizes the celebration of the sweetness of death, shadows, and the dark side.

If you're ready to stop running from the dark side and instead face it with joy and delight, dahlia flower essence can help. Interestingly (especially when coupled with exercise and counseling), this can help with depression and other types of mental illness by releasing and activating energy that has formerly been trapped and stagnant because of fear. Please note, however, that employing dahlia for this purpose can sometimes cause things temporarily to seem worse before they get better.

Transmutation of Emotions

What we call negative emotions really only pose a problem when we hold on to them and they start to enslave energy by getting stuck in our consciousness. On the other hand, when we consciously process them and move through them, they eventually become things like wisdom, joy, happiness, energy, vitality, and freedom. In fact, we might think of "negative emotions" as dead wood. Just sitting around in the backyard for years on end, that wood will get crusty and stinky and start to attract spiders and mold. But if we throw it in the fire instead of letting it sit there, it becomes brightness and beauty that warms our hearts, brightens our lives, and fuels our joy.

Dahlia helps with this, which is another reason she can help with depression and other types of mental illness. She's also helpful for easing grief and healing long-standing childhood issues. Interestingly, this may be coupled with an activation and enhancement of our creative expression. Creative blocks may be healed and art may flow forth in abundance as we channel our old pain and formerly stagnant emotions into the formation of beauty.

For any or all of these purposes, try taking the flower essence or creating a ritual involving dahlias.

Magical Correspondences

Element: Water

Gender: Female

Planet: Moon

Daisy

*M*agically speaking, daisy is very potent, as she is a living, visible manifestation of simplicity itself. In the same way that roses bridge the world of the seen and unseen as tangible representations of pure love and devotion, daisies remind of us of our inherent innocence and purity; as such, they renew our positivity, refresh our spirits, and restore our health. What's more, they revive our inner knowing that we are eminently lovable, that we deserve to receive all forms of blessings and support, and that anything is possible. See what I mean? Magically potent indeed.

While the "daisy family" can refer to the entire, extensive *Asteraceae* family (which includes sunflowers, dahlias, asters, and chamomile, to name but a few), the daisy we're talking about here includes the flowers we generally recognize as daisy, such as the gerber daisy and *Bellis perennis* (English daisy or lawn daisy)—although chamomile flowers (and other energetically and visually similar members of the *Asteraceae* family) also share the properties listed below.

For African daisies, which are a completely different plant, see "African daisy."

Magical Uses

Health

Well-being is our natural state. As such, by connecting with the purity and simplicity of the daisy, we can release feelings of stress and being overwhelmed and complexity, and restore our inherent immunity and our body's natural ability to heal itself. Additionally, because daisy's energy is so clear and potent, she can lend strength to our personal power and magnetic field, and generally help fortify our overall well-being.

For this purpose, bring fresh daisies into healing rooms, plant daisies in the yard, spend time in quiet contemplation with daisy blossoms, take the flower essence, or otherwise magically incorporate her.

Health and Healing Mist Potion

Add ten drops daisy essence to a mister of spring water, along with ten to twenty drops eucalyptus or juniper (or a combo) essential oils and five drops white quartz gem elixir or a small white quartz crystal. Shake. Hold in both hands and visualize very bright green light filling the bottle as you say a quick invocation, such as:

> *Hygeia, goddess of health and healing,*
> *please infuse this potion with vibrations*
> *of healing, purification, and renewal.*
> *Thank you, thank you, thank you!*
> *Blessed be. And so it is.*

Mist yourself, others, and the space to promote an atmosphere of healing.

Simplicity

At first glance, modern life appears to be complex beyond all comprehension. As if that weren't enough, somewhere along the way we seem to pick up this underlying feeling that we need to figure everything out. And—since figuring everything out in a linear, "logical" way is almost categorically impossible—this makes for a lot of depression, fatigue, stress, and general ennui. Once we let go of this externally imposed need to force logic and scientific understanding on everything, the universe—and life as we know it—reveals itself to be absurdly simple and endlessly sweet; this is the wisdom of the daisy. Simply by spending some time in quiet contemplation with her, you can pierce the illusion of complexity. As a result, your stress will dissipate and your depression will evaporate.

Other ways to benefit from this aspect of daisy's wisdom include any of the suggestions in the "orientation" section beginning on page 3. Even the symbol of the daisy can be a powerful way to connect with her energy—for example, you might bring a painting of daisies into your space or incorporate daisy imagery into your spellwork.

Purification

As you might expect, daisy is also an expert at purification and can be especially useful when stress, worry, clutter, or any form of complexity or energetic congestion is involved. For this purpose, work with any of the methods suggested above. As a magical ingredient, she is also an excellent accelerator and amplifier when added to any purifying spell, ritual, charm, or mixture.

Wealth

Just as daisy helps amplify our body's natural healing ability by stripping away what is no longer needed and bringing us back to our natural, vibrant state, she can also help us rediscover our natural state of wealth and prosperity. By aligning us with our inherent purity and deservedness, she strips away our limiting beliefs surrounding receiving money, resources, blessings, and all forms of support so that we can receive the divine sustenance that is our birthright. For this purpose, I suggest bringing a bouquet of daisies onto your altar on the full moon, taking the essence, spending time with the blossoms, burying a dollar bill near the base of a daisy plant on a Thursday during a waning moon, or incorporating the flower into other rituals or charms such as the following.

WEALTH CHARM

On the day of a full moon, lovingly gather a fresh daisy blossom, and, in full sunlight, place her on a small piece of green cotton fabric, along with a dollar coin, eight allspice cloves, and a small citrine quartz. Hold your hands over the magical ingredients and say:

I simply receive wealth, I simply receive blessings.
I am perfectly loved and perfectly supported by
the God/dess (or Universe or All That Is). I am so grateful!
Thank you, thank you, thank you! Blessed be. And so it is.

Tie the fabric closed with hemp twine. Keep the charm with you, place it on your altar, or sleep with it under your pillow for at least one moon cycle.

Magical Correspondences

Element: Air
Gender: Female
Planets: Sun, Moon

Dandelion

A flower famous for wishes, dandelion is also a symbol of cosmic harmony. In his different guises he encapsulates all four elements as well as the sun and moon: in his yellow phase he is aligned with the sun and Fire as well as the Earth element, and in his white phase he is aligned with the moon and Water as well as the Air element. This can be especially helpful for magical workings aimed at equilibrium and yin/yang balance.

His name is derived from the French and means "lion's tooth," and—as you'll learn—he's an obvious favorite of the author Ray Bradbury.

Magical Uses

Animal Protection

Any part of the dandelion can be helpful for magic involving animal protection.

ANIMAL PROTECTION CHARM

Sew a small charm bag out of muslin. Add a teaspoon or two of dried dandelion root, along with the seeds from one white dandelion and a small white quartz point. Tie it closed with hemp twine, hold it in both hands, and say an earnest prayer or invocation to St. Francis asking for strong and lasting protection for your beloved friend. Place it near a photo of the animal to magically ensure his or her safety. (Of course, take precautions in the physical world too—shots, tags, checkups, etc.!)

Divination

Would you like to know whether or not you are truly in love? Try this little ritual suggested by the free-spirited Clarisse in the novel *Fahrenheit 451* by Ray Bradbury. Rub a yellow dandelion gently under your chin. If your skin turns yellow, you're in love.

To enhance your intuition, wear or carry a pouch of dandelion root or daily drink a cup of tea made by simmering a small handful of dandelion root for ten minutes and straining.

Happiness

Sunshiny yellow dandelions embody the energy of pure happiness, joy, and summertime. As Ray Bradbury describes in *Dandelion Wine*, you might make dandelion wine in the summer and then drink it in the winter to experience a bit of "summer caught and stoppered." This would be especially useful for those with seasonal affective disorder (SAD) or anyone who gets a little down in the winter months.

Simply taking the flower essence is also great for lifting the spirits, especially for those craving warmth and the sun.

Healing

Dandelion root is an excellent blood and liver purifier, which in turn can also have a positive effect on the skin. (See "Clover" entry.)

Dandelion root tea can have a strengthening and grounding effect on your energy field, and—when drunk regularly for a few weeks to a month—can help fortify and invigorate your overall physical health.

Dandelion leaves are also a nourishing addition to salad.

When your magical aim is inner balance and equilibrium for the purpose of sound physical health—if you feel a little off or if your immune system could use a bit of a boost—you might incorporate both yellow and white versions of the dandelion into your magical workings.

Inner Equilibrium Bath

Draw a warm bath. Light one yellow and one white candle. Place three yellow dandelion blossoms, two white dandelion blossoms, a handful of fresh dandelion leaves, and a handful of dried dandelion root into the bath water. Say:

> *Sun, moon, day, and night*
> *Earth below and fire bright*
> *Water of the lunar tides*
> *Breathe across the fields wide*
> *Balance me and make me whole*
> *Nourish my body and my soul*
> *Thanks and blessed be to thee*
> *As I will, so mote it be.*

Soak in the water for at least forty minutes while feeling yourself energetically adjust into a state of balance and strength.

Wishes

Children and whimsically minded folk everywhere agree that blowing the seeds off a fuzzy white dandelion while thinking of a wish will greatly increase its chances of coming true. This, of course, is a magical spell that the flower faeries teach to generation after generation of kids. (Do you remember a particular adult ever teaching you this practice? I rest my case.) And, after all, making wishes come true is a small price to pay for the wonderful service of helping give birth to a new crop of healthy dandelion babies.

Magical Correspondences

Elements: Fire and Earth (yellow), Air (white)

Gender: Male

Planet: Sun (yellow), Moon (white)

Datura

I love it when I have the uncommon pleasure of encountering datura growing wild in the dry hills of California. Her energy is evocative of an exotic and inscrutable sorceress or a deliciously dangerous secret. She is a wild queen of the otherworld, and I am utterly ensnared by her charms.

As legend and history have it, I'm not the only one. Native American tribes were known to imbibe a potion made from her to induce visions, ecstatic dancing, prophecy, and spiritual union with the Divine. What's more, she is associated with witches and flying.

WARNING: I do not recommend consuming any part of the datura plant, as she is extremely toxic. But never fear: datura's vibration alone is highly potent and can be effectively employed for any of the following magical aims.

Magical Uses

Astral Travel

For help with astral travel, take four drops datura flower essence (purchased by a reputable company or very safely and expertly made) under the tongue. For astral travel in your sleep, you can do this before bed. Alternatively, sleep with a charm bag filled with dried or fresh datura leaves and blossoms under your pillow.

Concealment and Invisibility

If you'd like to conceal or obscure your thoughts, motives, or actions for any reason, or if you'd like to render yourself as close to invisible as possible, consider performing a datura ritual such as this one: charge a dried or fresh datura blossom with your intention; wrap it in clean, white cotton cloth along with an iron pyrite; tie it closed with black ribbon or string; and carry it with you for the duration of the situation.

Discernment

In a situation where you need to discern other people's true motives, place a datura leaf and blossom into a small charm bag, along with a hematite. Hold the bag in both hands and charge it with your intention. Keep it in your pocket or elsewhere on your person throughout the duration of the situation.

Divination

It's said that the Incas as well as the Delphic oracle in Greece incorporated datura into the ritual work surrounding their prophecies. Similarly, you might employ her to aid your divination work (e.g., tarot, I Ching, crystal gazing, etc.). For example, before you begin, you might place a very tiny pinch of dried datura leaves and blossoms into a bit of water in a potpourri burner and light it.

Or, to preserve the clarity of your readings and increase the potency of your deck, sew a drawstring bag. As you do so, sew a dried and pressed datura leaf into the lining. Use it to store your tarot cards.

Enchantment

Magic involving utterly enchanting another person or group of people can be greatly aided by the use of datura. This is especially true when you'd like the enchantment to be combined with a level of deep respect and awe. (For example, before a presentation or performance of some kind, a job interview, or a date.) One way to do this would be to visit a blossoming datura in the wild. Sit near the plant and have a conversation. Begin by relaxing and tuning in to the datura, and, when you feel ready, silently express the situation you'd like help with via images and feelings. Then respectfully ask the blossom if she'd share her powers of enchantment and intoxication with you. If she agrees, relax even more deeply and allow her to infuse you with her energy of bewitchment, charm, and cool confidence and calm. When this feels complete, thank her with a small libation of beer, wine, or ale, along with three clean silver coins (such as quarters or silver dollars).

Magical Power

Datura can also be helpful for rituals designed to help you claim the fullness of your magical power and for initiation and self-dedication rituals. For example, before or during the ritual, you might place four drops datura flower essence (purchased from a reputable company or very safely and expertly made) into a cup of water or wine. Hold the cup in both hands and visualize very bright white light filling it. Before you drink, say:

This beverage is now filled with the light of potent magical power.
As I drink it, my strengths are nourished and my gifts are revealed.

Magical Correspondences

Element: Water
Gender: Female
Planet: Moon

Echinacea

With such a hearty, sturdy vibe, it's interesting to note that echinacea's name is derived from the Greek word for hedgehog. Although he reportedly received this name because of the spiny appearance of the center of his blossom, his energetic dynamic may also be accurately described by the comparison.

Magical Uses
Health and Healing

Employed as a veritable cure-all in herbal medicine (echinacea has been used to treat infections, colds, allergies, asthma, skin conditions, coughs, earaches, flu, fungal infections, and urinary infections, and as an all-purpose tonic and immune-system strengthener), echinacea's magical properties are also conducive to health and healing. For example, you might take the essence regularly during periods when you'd like to activate your body's natural healing wisdom and natural state of radiant health. Or you might sit in quiet contemplation with blossoming echinacea plants to allow your energetic field to resonate with their healing wisdom and receive healing guidance and messages. Additionally, consider charms, rituals, or mist potions such as the following healing mist.

HEALING MIST

Mist a healing room or create an environment conducive to healing with a mister of spring water into which you've added ten drops eucalyptus essential oil and five drops echinacea essence. You might also lightly mist the area around yourself or another person. Remember to shake before each use.

Fortification and Heartiness

Like the hedgehog for which he is named, echinacea can help us protect our soft vulnerability with a naturally strong outer armor. Provided you clearly intend it and magically direct your energy toward it, he can also lend strength and potency to any magical intention. For example, according to Scott Cunningham, some Native Americans employed echinacea "as an offering to spirits to ensure and strengthen spells."

For added heartiness and fortification in any life situation, you might have a conversation with an echinacea blossom, letting him know what's going on and how you could use an extra dose of strength. Then, if he gives you the go-ahead, lovingly gather the blossom, wrap it in a cotton cloth, and place it on your altar or carry it with you throughout the situation. You might also employ him in an essence, charm, or ritual.

Simplification

Because echinacea is adept at emphasizing helpful energies and conditions, he can also make it easier to recognize the energies and items that are no longer serving us. So anytime you feel overwhelmed and want to pare things down and return to a simpler, more grounded sort of life, echinacea can be an excellent ally. Try planting him in your yard, taking two to three drops of the essence first thing every morning or last thing every night, or spending time in quiet contemplation with him.

Support for Healers and Health Care Professionals

For holistic healers and mainstream health care professionals alike, healing can be a rewarding yet highly challenging gig. If we aren't careful (or even if we are), we can sometimes pick up challenging energetic patterns from our patients and clients, or we can allow our own energy to be depleted as we heal. Echinacea can help with both these challenges by simultaneously strengthening our energetic protection and bolstering our natural state of well-being. For this purpose, I suggest taking the flower essence before and after engaging in healing work of any kind. Or you might prefer to take it in the morning and evening during vacations or weekends to recharge your healing batteries.

Success through Service and Joyful Work

Like a happily buzzing bee hard at work creating the golden sweetness we call honey, echinacea can help us dissolve joyfully and whole-heartedly into our work in a way that yields sweet success. So if you'd like to magically open doors to joyful work opportunities or fortify yourself for a productive and prosperous work period, employ echinacea. Plant him in your garden, bring his flowers into your workspace, take the essence regularly (until your goal is reached or you've sufficiently absorbed the desired energy), or mist your workspace with spring water containing ten to fifteen drops rosemary essential oil, five drops peppermint essential oil, and five drops echinacea essence. Or perform the following bath ritual to call in more work or a new job or to infuse your current job with more joyful productivity.

BATH RITUAL FOR JOYFUL PRODUCTIVITY

On a Thursday when the moon is between new and full, add three fresh echinacea blossoms or ten to twenty drops echinacea essence to your bath water, along with one-half cup organic clover blossom honey. Light a yellow candle near the bathtub and hold your hands over the water as you mentally direct golden-white light into the water. Say:

All doors are open for prosperous and joyful work.
I love what I do, and I irresistibly attract sweet success.

Relax as you soak for twenty to forty minutes.

Magical Correspondences

Element: Fire
Gender: Male
Planet: Jupiter

Forget-Me-Not

The name forget-me-not is said to come from the story of a knight who picked some of the flowers for a sweetheart while they were out walking. When he fell into a river and began to drown, he threw the flowers to the maiden and said (in German) *Vergiss mein nicht*, which means "forget me not"!

Magical Uses

Clarity and Focus

Simply gazing at this blossom's clean blue petals, along with the sunshiny burst of white or yellow at the center, infuses the mind with freshness and calm. Indeed, the flower's vibration is highly clarifying and can help with matters that require sustained attention and focus, such as studying, test-taking, performing, and so on. For this purpose, you might take the essence regularly as needed.

Health

Forget-me-not's organizing and clarifying wisdom can help bring the body, mind, and spirit into alignment while harmonizing the organs and generally enhancing holistic well-being. For this reason, forget-me-not can be a useful ingredient to essence mixtures and rituals designed to enhance physical or mental health.

Love

As you may expect, forget-me-not can be a useful ingredient in love magic when it's your intention to keep yourself fresh in the mind of another. Of course, as with most love magic, you must be careful with this, as you don't want to encroach on someone else's free will. So while you might want to incorporate forget-me-not into a ritual designed to strengthen the bonds in an already existing marriage, you might *not* want to incorporate forget-me-not into a ritual designed to enthrall the thoughts of a certain specific someone. If you must, you might add an addendum to your intention such as "only if it is pleasing to _____ and in completely accordance with his/her free will."

Memory

Forget-me-not essence or blossoms can be an excellent general memory enhancement or pick-me-up. This can be helpful for tests and also to help reverse the effects of memory loss. To benefit from this aspect of the flower's magic, you might plant forget-me-not in your yard or take the essence.

Organization and Efficiency

When organization and efficiency are crucial, forget-me-not can help. For example, taking the flower essence can be a wonderful companion when clearing clutter or streamlining your workday.

Perspective

Like a good friend and a voice of reason, forget-me-not can lift you out of a stressful mindset by helping you gain a truer perspective. After all, almost nothing is as important as we think it is, and this too shall pass. So when life feels overwhelming and you can't see the proverbial forest for the trees, you might try spending time in quiet contemplation with forget-me-not or taking the essence.

Success

Because of forget-me-not's clear, balanced, organized energy, this flower can support our magical intentions related to success. Forget-me-not does this by keeping us focused, streamlining and maximizing our efforts, and helping us maintain a healthy, sustainable perspective. For this purpose, you might take the flower essence in any of the ways directed above, spend time in quiet contemplation with a blossoming forget-me-not, or incorporate the blossoms into spells or rituals designed for the purpose.

Magical Correspondences

Element: Air

Gender: Balance of male and female

Planet: Venus

Foxglove

While foxglove can be fatally toxic (do not consume!), Western medicine has employed her heart-healing and strengthening properties since the physician William Withering experimentally applied a traditional herbal healer's remedy to a patient in the second half of the eighteenth century. Foxglove is now the main component in the family of life-saving heart medicines known as digitalin.

On a subtler and more mystical note, faeries love her, she's highly protective, and she can help us get in touch with our wildness, joy, and magical power.

Magical Uses

Courage

Through simultaneously bolstering our heart energy and protecting our heart chakra, foxglove can help infuse us with the courage to live our greatness, follow our dreams, speak up for ourselves, and generally thrive in the midst of any number of formerly fear-inducing (or shyness-inducing) conditions. This can be especially helpful for situations such as:

- auditions
- interviews
- social gatherings
- sports events

- necessary confrontations
- performances
- starting a new job
- stepping out of your comfort zone in any way

To receive foxglove's courage-enhancing benefits, try taking the essence (since she's toxic, only make your own if you are very comfortable with doing so safely; otherwise, purchase from a reputable dealer) or employing her in any way mentioned in the "orientation" section. You also might create the following mist potion.

LIQUID COURAGE MIST POTION

Add six drops foxglove essence to a mister of rose water, along with six drops geranium essential oil. Shake well. Mist your body and aura before any event during which you'd like an extra dose of courage and protection.

Faery Connection

One might think of faeries as nature devas or nature spirits—the sentience of things like plants, rocks, the earth, the air, the sunlight, and the water. It follows that people who are drawn to this book (like you) are already profoundly connected to the faery realm. Still, taking a moment to consciously connect with faeries can be a wonderful way to spiral more deeply into the magic of the natural world and to the fun, whimsical, magical aspects of our spirituality.

Faeries love foxglove. When we cultivate and spend time with foxglove, we can more easily perceive the faeries and curry their favor. For this purpose, plant foxglove plants in your yard, cultivate them from seedlings, or spend quality time with them while they are blossoming.

And if you'd like to bring out your wild, faerylike nature and dwell more consistently in the realm of faery, consume the essence regularly as desired. (On a side note, this will activate your wild beauty and bewitching charm, so don't be surprised if you find yourself drawing more admiring glances and romantic overtures.)

Heart Healing

From a holistic perspective, although they occupy the same space, you might think of us as having two hearts: a physical heart and an energetic one. Still, the physical and spiritual worlds are inextricably linked—they support, enhance, and mirror one another—so these two heart centers are actually like two sides of a single coin. And foxglove's magic can help heal, support, and strengthen both. For example, magically employing foxglove can help support any of the following conditions (though this would *not* take the place of appropriate medical or psychological attention):

- a broken heart
- depression
- grief
- gear
- high blood pressure
- any physical heart conditions or challenges

Protection

Negative energy doesn't want to mess with foxglove: she bites! In other words, like the heroine of an action movie, she might be a good guy, but you definitely don't want to be on her bad side. This is probably why—as author Scott Cunningham relates—housewives in Wales derived a black dye from foxglove, which they used to paint protective crosses on their floors in order to "keep evil from entering the house."

Foxglove's protective magic can be especially helpful for those who are overly sensitive or who feel especially emotionally vulnerable or open for whatever reason. She can help us create natural boundaries and get in alignment with our inherent protective intuition.

Here are some ideas for employing her protective magic:

- Mist yourself with the liquid courage potion to create a protective shield.

- Take the essence.

- Plant foxglove near your front door and perhaps (for added protection and as desired) any other door to the outside of the house.

- To protect your home from negative people, entities, or energies, and to help yourself feel safe in your home, on a Tuesday during the waxing moon, mix nine drops foxglove essence with a small amount of equal parts menstrual blood and olive oil. Using this mixture, very lightly anoint the outside of all door frames three times: once on each side and once in the middle of the top.

- Dry a foxglove blossom and tie it into a piece of red flannel, along with a hematite and a clove of garlic. Keep it on your person for extra protection while out in the world, place it near an entrance to keep negativity from entering, or hang it near the head of your bed to protect you while you sleep.

Magical Correspondences

Element: Water
Gender: Female
Planet: Mars

Freesia

*F*reesia is that dear friend whom you call whenever you need a pep talk, a confidence boost, or help making sense of it all. Her bright beauty, straightforward charm, potent energy, and buoyant joy can get your energy moving and cure what ails you, whether it has to do with your life conditions, emotional state, or both.

Magical Uses

Clarity

If you feel immersed in a mental fog or stuck in a conundrum, freesia can help clear things up for you in the most delightful way. Simply bring a bouquet into your home or workplace (the important thing is that you are near it for substantial chunks of time). Then mentally tune in to the flowers, silently thank them for sharing their energy and wisdom, and let them know what you'd like help with. Alternatively, you might take the essence once daily until the fog lifts.

Courage to Make Necessary Changes

You've heard this before, but since we can all use a reminder, I'll say it again: the only constant is change. And change can take the form of growth, movement, or decay. When things (or people) stop growing or moving, guess what? They begin to decay. Still, the fact that the word *crisis* is literally derived from the Latin for "turning point" just goes to show you how traumatized we humans can feel as we face looming (but necessary) life changes (leaving a job we're not crazy about, moving to a new city where we don't know anybody but where we've always wanted to live, leaving a relationship, beginning a relationship, etc.).

And this is exactly what freesia can help with. So you might like to employ freesia's magical benefits if you feel stuck due to a fear of moving forward in a necessary way, or even if you just feel stuck and you're not exactly sure what path to take (since freesia helps with clarity too).

For this purpose, I suggest adding nine fresh freesia blossoms (or twenty-seven drops freesia essence) to your bath water. Flick your fingers over the water nine times, saying *Solve et Coagula* ("dissolve and reform"—an alchemical mantra that encourages positive change) once with each flick, and then soaking for at least forty minutes. Any of the suggestions in the previous "clarity" section will also work great.

Healing Depression

Since depression is usually the result of a combination of a lack of the two magical intentions listed above (lack of clarity coupled with lack of courage to make necessary life changes—in other words, being unable to discover what's wrong and act on that discovery because of a cloud of fear), freesia can be employed as a magical antidote to depression. For help in this area, try the bath from the above section, or any of the other previous suggestions in any combination. For depression that has been going on for an extended period of time, I suggest taking two to three drops freesia essence under the tongue in both morning and evening consistently for at least three months. This will undermine and dissolve the causes of depression and help you create a new, more joyful momentum.

Self-Love

In the same way that honey may be thought of as the energies of sweetness and sunshine made manifest in the physical world, freesia may be thought of as the condensed wisdom and distilled energy of self-love come to life. So if you could use a self-love infusion (and who couldn't?), spend time with blossoming freesias, bring fresh freesias into your home or workplace, meditate while inhaling the fragrance of the fresh flowers, or take the essence before bed.

Removing Blocks

We say we're experiencing a block when we feel stuck in a particular life area such as romance or prosperity. Similar to the previous "courage to make necessary changes" and "healing depression" sections, removing blocks has to do with getting your energy moving in the most ideal way possible and flowing courageously with the constant change that characterizes the human life experience.

Transmutation

Some magical ingredients help us dissolve and banish old conditions; others help us construct and invoke new ones. And still others still help us transform the energies contained within old conditions into beautiful new ones. In magic this type of transformation is called transmutation, and freesia is an expert at it.

For example, say you often find yourself in the middle of a lot of bad vibes at work, and you really can't light a sage bundle or begin loudly chanting *om* without getting fired or everyone thinking you're crazy. But what you can do is bring in a bouquet of freesia. The cool thing about that is that you will be freeing the energy currently trapped in negative or challenging patterns, transforming it into positive, helpful energy patterns and putting it to work for you.

Or if you'd like to employ freesia's transmutation expertise on a more regular basis, you might make the following mist potion.

TRANSMUTATION MIST POTION

Place nine drops freesia essence in a mister of rose water, along with eighteen drops lavender essential oil and nine drops clary sage essential oil. Shake to blend, then hold the mister in both hands and say:

All that's dross shall turn to gold
All that's stuck shall clearly flow
Bringing brightest blessings clear and bold.

Womb Healing

In many ways, wombs are like hearts: they are emotional centers in the body that relate to the universal female mothering instinct, whether that's for our children, other people's children, other adults, animals, plants, the planet, or any other beings that we feel could use protection and support. Freesias hold the specific type of robust, feminine, compassionate energy that specifically can help heal sorts of challenges that might affect this energy center, such as miscarriage, abortion, sexual abuse, emotional issues related to conception or mothering, or any sort of gynecological conditions. To receive an infusion of this energy, surround yourself with freesias, inhale their fragrance, spend time in quiet contemplation with them, grow them, put four drops of the essence in your drinking water, add twenty to forty drops of freesia essence to your bath water, or construct rituals employing them for this purpose.

Magical Correspondences

Element: Water
Gender: Female
Planet: Venus

Geranium

*G*eranium absolutely sings with positivity and magical power. In addition to being beautiful and (as my dad once put it) "bulletproof" additions to any patio or yard, geranium wields a ton of magical properties, and she expresses all of them with reliability and potency. It's truly hard to think of a more useful or versatile magical ally.

Magical Uses

Exorcism

Geranium's bright and cheerful vibration is a powerful deterrent and repellent to negativity of all forms, including unsavory entities. To keep ghosts and other forms of negativity out of your home, place pots of geranium in your yard. (Red ones are best for this purpose.) You can also employ fresh red geranium flowers in exorcism rituals such as the following.

....

EXORCISM RITUAL

While the moon is waning, during the day (preferably when the sun is out), obtain one white jar candle for each room/area in your home. Place each one on a plate and surround the candle in a circle of sea salt. Place each candle and plate in a central location in each room/area and light. As you light each candle, center your mind and say:

With the lighting of this candle, I now request that any and all earthbound
entities and stagnant energy patterns go into the light or out the door.

Then stand in a central location. Visualize a sphere of golden-white light completely surrounding and encompassing your home. Place spring or well water in a glass bowl, hold the bowl in sunlight for thirty seconds to a minute (skip this step if the sun is not out), then go back inside. In any way that feels right to you, say a quick prayer asking for divine assistance to escort any earthbound entities or stagnant energy into the light or out the door. Also ask that your bowl of water be blessed and filled with divine light. Then, using a freshly cut red geranium blossom on a stem, fling a small amount of water throughout each room/area of the home while moving generally in a counterclockwise direction. When this feels complete, say a quick prayer of thanks. Pour any remaining water at the base of a tree, and place the geranium blossom there too. Allow the candles to continue to burn for at least an hour, then flush the sea salt down the toilet, dispose of the remains of the candles, and wash your hands.

Other ways to employ geranium for personal or residential exorcisms include adding geranium essence or essential oil to a mister of water or rose water and misting yourself, a loved one, or your home; diffusing geranium essential oil in your home; or anointing yourself or a loved one with geranium essential oil.

Goddess Energy and Feminine Healing

Considering geranium's powerful, goddesslike energy, it should come as no surprise that many aromatherapists think of geranium as *the* essential oil for feminine health challenges. For example, in *Aromatherapy for Everyone*, authors P. J. Pierson and Mary Shipley suggest the following:

For cellulite, premenstrual syndrome, and menopause, mix twenty
drops [geranium essential oil] in one ounce of carrier oil and
massage on body. For cellulite, massage on affected areas. For
premenstrual syndrome and menopause, massage on abdomen
and back, paying extra attention to the lower back region.

Additionally, geranium—in her blossom, oil, or essence form—can help with magical objectives relating to getting in touch with our goddess energy and the feminine aspect of the Divine (a.k.a. the Goddess). The common varieties of geranium relate to the strong, healing, and protective aspects of the Goddess (think Isis), while rose geraniums and some of the other hybrids possess a softer, more receptive, and more Venuslike vibration.

Happy Home

All of geranium's magical aspects lend themselves to a happy home: her vibration is at once grounding, nurturing, loving, strengthening, protective, morale boosting, and powerfully positive. Try placing potted geraniums in a few locations around the outside of your home to infuse your household with peace, love, health, harmony, and happiness. To strengthen the effect, you might take a moment to commune with each plant, requesting her assistance with this intention.

Health and Healing

Since geranium is brimming with life-force energy, she can help our bodies, minds, and spirits reacquaint themselves with their innate healing wisdom and their natural state of vibrant health. It should come as no surprise, then, that—as author Scott Cunningham writes in his *Encyclopedia of Magical Herbs*—

Curanderos (shamanic/folk healers) in contemporary Mexico cleanse and heal patients
by brushing them with red geraniums, together with fresh rue and pepper tree branches.

As rue and pepper tree branches are not always readily available, you might try this curandero-inspired healing ritual on yourself or a loved one:

Aura Brushing for Health and Healing

On the full moon or when the moon is waning, ideally outdoors in full sunlight (but it's okay if this isn't possible), using a small amount of red cotton yarn, tie a few fresh red geranium blossoms together with a few sprigs of fresh rosemary. Stand comfortably on the earth, consciously relaxing your body and mind. Take some deep breaths and then, starting at your head and moving downward, gently brush your aura with the bundle by holding it about six to twelve inches above your skin. Imagine you are sloughing off negativity and stagnation and refreshing yourself with beautiful bright light and life-force energy. If you are doing this for a loved one, follow the same directions but have them relax in a similar way, then brush their aura for them. When this feels complete, visualize yourself (or your loved one) in a sphere of golden-white light. In any way that feels right to you, say a quick prayer or invocation for vibrant health and overall well-being. Express gratitude to the Divine. Finish by releasing the bundle in a moving body of water or at the base of a tree.

Heart Healing

Whenever grief or heartbreak is an issue, geranium can be an invaluable ally. Try planting her in one or more pots or window boxes outside your home and lovingly caring for her. Choose a variety that speaks to your heart. Here is a general guide to the specific heart-healing properties of a few geranium varieties:

> *White:* purifying (for when we feel guilty or unclean)
> *Red:* strengthening, rallying
> *Pink:* a reminder that life is sweet; heart healing related to friendships

Purple / Lavender / Violet: creativity, healing to the spirit and inner child

Multi-Colored Petals: helps soothe grief after the loss of a loved one

Rose: heart-opening, receptive, romantic healing, strengthens self-love and self-esteem

Nutmeg: warming, healing to creativity and inner child

Mint: refreshing, renewing

Once you've planted your geraniums, it can be especially helpful to periodically sit in quiet contemplation with them and allow their strength to surround your heart and permeate your spirit. Additionally, you might like to take two to three drops geranium essence under the tongue or in water twice per day or to diffuse or wear geranium or rose geranium essential oil; be sure to dilute these with a carrier oil if you have sensitive skin.

Love

Through healing our spirit and grounding us in a feeling of safety and present-moment awareness, geranium can help us experience romantic love and sensual pleasure. Gabriel Mojay, author of *Aromatherapy for Healing the Spirit*, describes this energetic effect nicely when he writes:

> *[Geranium] oil's exotic, floral, and slightly spicy aroma is reflected in its well-known aphrodisiac effect—an effect that relates to its intrinsically sensual, liberating nature. Nourishing the feminine creativity of the Intellect…and the still, receptive aspect of the Will…geranium oil is ideal for the workaholic perfectionist—for the person who has forgotten imagination, intuition, and sensory experience.*

All these effects are important prerequisites to harmonious intimacy and romantic love. Additionally, rose geranium—with her soft, heart-opening, love goddess vibration—can help us summon and open ourselves more deeply to romantic love. Try taking the essence, diffusing or wearing the essential oil, placing pots of geranium in your yard, having a heart-to-heart with a geranium, or employing her in rituals related to romantic love.

Positive Energy

Looking at everything in the most positive light possible might be thought of as *the* strategy to a successful and rewarding life. After all, our thoughts and intentions are our most important magical tools, as they can serve as the pivot points of our energetic momentum. And sometimes, staying positive means taking to heart the phrase *Illegitimi non carborundum,* or "Don't let the bastards grind you down."

When not letting the bastards (or any aspect of your life experience) get you down seems to be a concern, geranium can certainly help. Her energy lends itself to rallying the troupes, improving morale, and reminding us of our intrinsic positivity and power. For general positivity, you might try anointing yourself with the essential oil, placing pots of geraniums in your yard, and otherwise magically employing her.

Protection

As noted in the "exorcism" section, geranium is a negativity repellent. Place pots of red geraniums near the outside of your front door or in window boxes and request their help with protecting your home from negativity. You might also employ geranium essential oil to anoint yourself, your children, your loved ones, or any item that you'd like to shield with protective energy.

Purification

To purify your energy field of negativity, entities, or psychic cords of attachment, you might try misting yourself with rose water into which you've added ten to twenty drops of geranium or rose geranium essential oil. You might also use this potion to mist your home or any area that you'd like to purify. (Incidentally, this is a great "magical first aid" to carry around in your purse for both protective and purification purposes.) Another way to employ geranium's purification powers would be to add a few drops of geranium essential oil to your bath water, along with a cup of sea salt, then soak for at least forty minutes. If you go this route, be sure to drink plenty of fresh drinking water as you soak. You might also employ geranium in any ritual performed for the purpose of purification.

Strength, Courage, and Resilience

As you might imagine, geranium's considerable positivity also lends itself to the qualities of strength, courage, and resilience. If you (or a loved one) have been going through a particularly challenging time, or if you seem to be beset by fear or worry, geranium can help. For this purpose, you can employ any of the usual remedies (essence, essential oil, fresh blossom, ritual), but I highly recommend spending time in quiet contemplation with a blossoming plant—ideally one that you care for personally. Relax, and tell her what you're going through. Feel all your feelings and offer them up to her, emptying out your mind and becoming as still as you possibly can. Then, from a feeling place (not a thinking one), simply allow yourself to receive her guidance and energetic support, which will arrive quickly and powerfully, literally infusing your mind, body, spirit, and energy field with the energies of strength, courage, and resilience. Added benefits to this technique include immune-system strengthening and a boost to your intuitive faculties, especially with regard to how to proceed with whatever situation may currently seem to be presenting a challenge.

If your entire family or household is going through an especially challenging time, you might place a white quartz crystal point in a pot of red geraniums, and empower both crystal and plant with the intention to help shore up everyone's resilience and morale. Place the pot outdoors somewhere where the geraniums will thrive (usually in bright sunlight), ideally in a place where each family or household member will see it or be in close proximity to it often.

Support for Children

Few flowers can boast that they can help with just about any challenge a child may be experiencing, but geranium can. These challenges may include (but are not limited to):

- health issues
- shyness
- friendships
- moving to a new town or school
- problems with bullies
- focusing in school
- feeling safe
- feeling nurtured
- going through a parental divorce
- the loss of a loved one

If your child or a child you know is going through one or more of these challenges, you might take her to a nursery and ask her to pick out any geranium that she likes (of course, don't force it if the idea doesn't appeal to her). Then help her to lovingly care for the plant. Here are some other ways to employ geranium's magic to support your beloved child:

- If she likes the scent, you might diffuse the essential oil in her room or in your home.

- You might put a single drop of geranium essence in her breakfast or breakfast beverage and another one in her dinner or dinner beverage.

- You might tie a few geranium blossoms and leaves into a piece of muslin, along with a lapis lazuli or rose quartz crystal, and empower it with your healing and supportive intention. Hang it over the head of her bed.

Truth

Because geranium is such a potent representation of life-force energy, which is totally aligned with Truth, she can help us discover and recognize what is true in any given situation. For example, say you are not sure if someone in your household is being truthful with you. To heal this situation, you might begin by releasing your worry and mental chatter as much as possible and consciously cultivating a patient and confident mindset, or a deep inner knowing that everything is perfectly unfolding for everyone's highest good. Then continually diffuse geranium essential oil in the space until you are naturally able to sniff out the truth. You might, for example, realize that it was actually a trust issue and that you never had any true reason to doubt your loved one's actions or claims. On the other hand, you may begin to clearly see the discrepancies as the inner workings of the situation are brought out into the open.

You might affect a similar dynamic by daily misting the space with rose water into which you've added four to five drops of geranium essence, or by putting geranium essence in everyone's dinner every day. If there is any situation that you would like to know the truth about, you might simply spend time with a blossoming geranium. Center yourself, relax your mind, and then let her know what you'd like help with. Again relax and receive any guidance she may offer. Even if you don't get a clear message right away, you will receive an infusion of energy that will allow you to see the truth more clearly in the future.

Magical Correspondences

Element: Earth

Gender: Female

Planets: Saturn, Venus (rose geranium)

*H*eather's overall energetic dynamic is one of nostalgia: she guides us toward reaping wisdom, comfort, and healing from memories and past conditions. Gently and with compassion, she helps us to make positive changes as we use the past as a springboard for our present evolution.

Magical Uses

Connecting with Ancestors and Ancestral Wisdom

Heather can be a great addition to an ancestral altar, which is an altar created to honor a deceased loved one. Or you might spend time with her in quiet contemplation, bring her into your garden or home, or take her in essence form to facilitate a deeper connection with your heritage, your ancestors, and with the wisdom encoded in the past.

Along similar lines, author Scott Cunningham notes that heather "has also long been used to conjure ghosts." However, please note that I recommend employing heather (or anything else!) for this purpose only if you are an expert in this area. Otherwise, you may find yourself with an unwanted guest (or several).

Healing Deep Issues

Because of heather's affinity for the past, she can be an excellent ally for any time you're delving deep to heal and release old issues. By connecting even more deeply with the issues, you become enabled to heal them even more deeply. For this purpose, try taking the essence or adding it to your bath water, incorporating the flower into a ritual or charm, or trying any of the previous suggestions.

Luck

Traditionally (particularly in Scotland), carrying white heather has been magically employed to enhance one's luck.

Memory

Heather's alignment with the past can also come in handy when your magical intention relates to strengthening your (or someone else's) memory. Try taking the essence or incorporating heather into a ritual or charm.

Physical Healing

Some herbalists recommend heather for kidney and bladder conditions, as well as for cystitis and rheumatism. To employ heather for this purpose, consult an herbalist or other holistic health professional.

Protection

In *The Meaning of Flowers*, Gretchen Scoble and Ann Field note that while red heather promises passion, white heather offers "protection from rash, passionate acts." Similarly, Scott Cunningham reveals that "heather is carried as a guard against rape and other violent crimes." Indeed, simply carrying her can be highly protective. For safe travel (or for safely traversing any situation), you might try creating the following charm.

CHARM FOR SAFE TRAVELS

Gently and lovingly gather a single flowering tip of a white heather plant. Place this blossom in a small muslin drawstring bag, along with an iron pyrite (being sure to cleanse the crystal first in bright sunlight, running water, or white sage smoke) and a pinch of mugwort. Hold the bag in both hands and say:

> *I call on angels to protect me, I call on the Goddess to protect me.*
> *The earth protects me, the sky protects me, the stars protect me,*
> *the planets protect me. I am safe now and in all directions of time.*
> *Thank you, thank you, thank you. Blessed be. And so it is.*

Safety-pin the charm to the inside of your clothes whenever an extra dose of protection is desired.

Transmutation

Heather is a master alchemist when it comes to transmuting violent, angry vibrations into soft, nurturing ones. She's also an expert at transmuting the pain of the past into valuable wisdom for the present and future. This can be valuable anytime we have a lot of seemingly negative energy floating around, because she can help us not just get rid of it, but channel it toward increasing our blessings and overall well-being. For this purpose, try bringing potted heather or a bouquet of heather into your space or misting yourself or your space with the following mist potion.

TRANSMUTATION MIST POTION

Add nine drops heather essence to a mister of rose water, along with ten drops ylang ylang essential oil, five drops tangerine essential oil, and a small lepidolite crystal that has been cleansed and empowered in sunlight.

Magical Correspondences

Element: Earth
Gender: Female
Planet: Pluto

Hibiscus

*M*agically speaking, hibiscus packs quite a punch! His potency is reliable no matter which of his many magical uses you're employing, and his diverse benefits weave together to create a richly complex energetic signature. What's more, as potion ingredients go, hibiscus blossoms are as delicious as they come.

With his relaxing, inspiring, passionate, sensual, and liberating aspects, hibiscus couldn't be a more perfect choice for the state flower of Hawaii.

Magical Uses

Freedom

While freedom is our birthright and a natural characteristic of every human being, we can sometimes appear to be unpleasantly stuck in some situation, condition, mindset, or relationship. No matter what the perceived cause of our seeming lack of freedom (fear, guilt, obligation, limiting beliefs, etc.), hibiscus can help us tune in to our inner freedom so that we can liberate ourselves and be the masters of our own glorious destiny.

To employ hibiscus's freeing benefits and liberate yourself from inner and outer constraints, try taking the essence, adding the essence or flower to your bath water, or drinking hibiscus tea.

Harmony and Relaxation

When we relax and connect with our senses, we begin to find the natural harmony and rhythm that is our natural state. If stressful thoughts or conditions are keeping us from experiencing this relaxation and harmony, hibiscus can help us rediscover it, even if we don't have time for a week-long mountain retreat or a sunny vacation in the Bahamas.

"Liquid Vacation" Potion

Using dried hibiscus blossoms or an herbal tea blend containing hibiscus blossoms (for example, any of Celestial Seasonings' Zinger series), brew a pitcher of tea and chill. Pour over ice in a tall glass and squeeze a small wedge of lime over it. Sit comfortably in front of the glass, consciously relax your body, and take some deep breaths. When you feel sufficiently relaxed, hold your hands over the glass and direct energy through your hands into the potion as you inhale deeply and then chant "Om." Inhale and chant two more times, then drink mindfully, consciously imbibing the subtleties of the flower's wisdom and taste.

Independence

None of us is 100 percent independent, nor would we want to be—we all rely on others in some way. Still, it's important we remember and know that at our core, we own our own power, make our own decisions, and are totally self-directed. This not only benefits us, but it benefits all our relationships and all the other people who are in those relationships with us.

So if you feel that you are not in your own driver's seat or that you fear the idea of being your own person and making your own way, hibiscus might be just the magical ingredient for you. You might magically employ this flower in any of the ways mentioned in the orientation, or try the following charm.

Independence Charm

At sunrise on the morning before a full moon, place a dried red or orange hibiscus blossom, an iron pyrite crystal, and a pinch of ground cinnamon in a small red cotton bag. Tie closed with hemp twine, and use the twine to attach a naturally shed feather to the outside of your charm. Hold it in both hands and say: "With the birth of this new day, I own my power and choose my way." Keep the charm close to you until the next moon cycle.

Passion

Is your life characterized by passion? Are you passionate about your work, your hobbies, your loved ones, your favorite social causes, and life in general? If not, put "infuse life with passion" on your magical to-do list ASAP—and find yourself some hibiscus!

Romance

Because hibiscus possesses the benefits of relaxation, passion, and sexual desire, he naturally lends himself to romantic magical intentions. And because of his free, independent nature, he's especially adept at helping us experience romance in ways that allow us to retain our autonomy, personal power, and sense of self, which is always ideal. Employ him in rituals and charms designed for the purpose of drawing or enhancing romance, such as the following.

Love-Drawing Cupcakes

Make your favorite cupcake recipe and add a pinch of dried hibiscus blossoms to the batter. Conjure up all the swirly, passionate, romantic, lovey-dovey feelings you can, and then stir in a clockwise direction as you direct this romantic energy into the batter. As they're baking, call on the goddess Venus. Ask her to bless your magic and help draw an ideal romantic partner into your life. (Just to qualify: I mean "ideal" from a divine perspective, not a human one. So instead of requesting that your partner be a specific person or have specific qualities, request that he or she be the best possible partner for you at this particular time in your life, whatever that may mean.) Then open the oven door and blow five kisses to the cupcakes. Add pure vanilla extract and a tiny bit of rose water to the frosting. As you eat, know that you are internalizing the magic and powerfully magnetizing your desire. (All you need to eat is one cupcake, so maybe do this with a group of friends or pass them along to friends who also want to manifest partners. Alternatively, you can eat one per day until they are gone.)

Sexual Desire

As we've discussed, hibiscus blossoms are sensualizing, relaxing, and heart-opening, so they naturally get us in touch with our sexual desire. For this purpose, I suggest drinking hibiscus blossom tea. Or, if you want to get fancy, you might make this love potion:

LOVE POTION PUNCH

Pour two glasses half full of pink champagne. Add a splash of chilled hibiscus blossom tea to each, along with a bit of rose water and some strawberry puree. Enjoy with a (sexual) partner.

Swift Assistance and Activation

Because of its potent energy and punch, powdered hibiscus blossom can help expedite any magical intention. So if it's a magical emergency or you're just in need of some especially swift assistance, you might like to add it to your rituals and charms. You might also use it all on its own as an activator; for example, you can sprinkle it in your wallet or over your bank statement to activate your finances, or sprinkle it over legal documents to get stuck legal situations moving in the right direction.

Magical Correspondences

Element: Fire

Gender: Male

Planets: Venus, Mars

Holly

A favorite magical ally to the Druids and a perennial Christmas decoration, the holly plant is perhaps not quite as famous for his delicate white flowers as he is for his bright red berries and glossy dark green leaves. Among flower essence enthusiasts, however, this is not the case. In fact, holly is one of Edward Bach's original thirty-eight flower essence remedies and is most commonly employed to help open the heart and align us with the energy of love.

Magical Uses

Divine Connection

The divine, heavenly realm—the world of the wondrous and the oneness of all things—is the truth behind the illusions of discord and separation that can seem to characterize our present life experience. And the holly blossom can help align us with this realm, which in turn can immediately lift our mood and benefit every aspect of our life. This magical benefit may be seen as a number of benefits, including (but not limited to):

- angelic support and protection
- alignment with the angelic realm
- divine support and protection
- opening or harmonizing the crown chakra (the spiritual center at the top of your head)

- alignment with the Divine
- gaining a truer and more helpful perspective on any given challenge or situation
- improving your personal vibration
- establishing harmony and peace among groups and households
- increasing your blessings by aligning you with divine harmony and flow

For any of these purposes, try working with the flower essence, spending time with the plant, or incorporating the blossom into charms or rituals.

Protection

The entire holly plant—including the blossom—is highly protective, but the blossom's protective powers are perhaps the most potent and concise. In fact, in the words of physician and premier flower essence pioneer Edward Bach, "Holly protects us from everything that is not universal love." Through aligning us with the divine realm and purifying the vibration in and around us, holly can help magically protect us from all number of seeming dangers, such as:

- fire
- accidents
- anger or discord
- any sort of bodily harm
- violence
- challenges and hassles
- wild animals
- toxins

- earthbound spirits (unhappy ghosts)
- negative or harsh energy
- hexes and curses
- jealousy or envy

As you feel guided, you might work with the flower essence, spend time with the plant, or incorporate the blossom into charms or rituals. To protect a home or other structure, you might add twenty drops holly essence to a bucket of warm water, along with ten to twenty drops lavender essential oil, and ritually wash the outside of the front door (and any other door to the outside) with the mixture.

Purification

Because he is so aligned with the divine realm (which is the utter clarity behind the illusion of all seeming energetic debris) and because his vibration is so full of love, holly blossom's energy is extremely purifying. To purify a space or a person, mist with rose water into which you've added ten to twenty drops of holly essence. Alternatively, you might use a sprig of blossoming holly to fling spring water around your space, your own aura, or the aura of someone else. Other ways to employ holly's purifying powers include any of the previous suggestions.

Sacred Space

All of holly's magical gifts (divine connection, protection, and purification) lend themselves to establishing sacred space. This means that he can be a great ally when blessing a home or business or creating the space for ritual, yoga, or meditation. For this purpose, bring fresh blossoms into the space, mist the space with rose water containing ten to twenty drops holly essence, or fling spring water around the space with a sprig of blossoming holly.

Magical Correspondences

Element: Air
Gender: Male
Planet: Mars

Hollyhock

No one knows how long hollyhock has been around, except perhaps hollyhock herself. We do know that a Neanderthal man was buried with hollyhocks some 50,000 years ago. It's said hollyhock hails from Asia and came to Europe during the Crusades, and that hollyhock was one of the first botanical immigrants to the New World.

From a magical perspective, hollyhock is a powerhouse of ancient power. It's as if this flower been absorbing and cataloging spiritual wisdom since the dawn of time—and if you're ready, hollyhock's happy to share.

On a practical note, be careful with hollyhock, especially if you have sensitive skin or allergies, as simply touching this plant can irritate the skin.

Magical Uses

Healing from the Past

Wherever the past is involved, hollyhock can help. So if you're tired of being mired in old stuff from your recent past, your distant past, your childhood, or even your past lives, you might want to pay hollyhock a visit, work with the essence, or otherwise employ hollyhock in your healing endeavors. Hollyhock can also be an excellent complement to therapies such as counseling, past-life regression, and energy healing.

Healing Land

Just like people, land remembers. As such, whole areas of land can seem to be oppressed or traumatized by past events and situations. If you feel that an area of land in your care isn't as nourishing and vibrant as it wants to be, or if you know that something negative may have occurred on it, it can be helpful to perform healing rituals to free it up to be its most beautiful, vivacious self. For example, you might draw a circle in the dirt large enough to stand inside and burn sage to the four directions, calling on faeries or devas of the land to help release and transmute negative energies into positive ones.

In addition to clearing rituals, planting hollyhock on the land can help release and transmute old energies and realign that particular corner of the earth with its original power and grace. That way, your home (or business) can thrive and your magic can be strengthened by the healthy earth energies swirling around you.

When planting hollyhocks for this purpose, relax your mind as you intuitively choose the places the seeds or plants naturally seem to want to be planted. Alternatively, you can tune in to the land and see where it seems to most crave hollyhock plants. To further fortify the healing effects, you might empower white quartz crystal points in sunlight and then bury them, with the points pointing straight up, about four to five inches from the top of the soil.

Reclaiming and Realigning with Heritage

Our heritage might be defined as our spiritual and emotional roots. Having a heritage to connect with can help us to feel grounded in the present while also supported and bolstered by the past. Whether the heritage we most connect with comes from our ancestors, our past lives, or both, hollyhock can help us reclaim it and realign with it in a healthy way. And if we fear we've lost, forgotten, or been seemingly disconnected from our spiritual or emotional roots, hollyhock can help us remember and rediscover them.

For either purpose, you might simply tune in to a blossoming hollyhock, take the essence, or perform a ritual like the heritage vision quest.

Heritage Vision Quest

Sit in a comfortable position in front of a blossoming hollyhock with your spine straight. Take some deep breaths and consciously relax your body as you gaze at the plant. Feel the weight of your body on the earth and come fully into the present moment. Memorize the feeling and appearance of the hollyhock as best you can, and then close your eyes while still envisioning the plant, as if you're seeing it through your eyelids. Take your time with this: open and close your eyes until you feel you have a clear and living picture in your mind's eye. Then silently, from your heart, communicate to the plant what you'd like help with. Explain why you'd like to reconnect with your heritage and how you feel this will help you. Then imagine that the hollyhock turns into a large, beautiful mirror. Gaze into that mirror and see what you see. It doesn't matter if it doesn't make any sense at first—just let your vision be what it is. When this feels complete, open your eyes. It might be a good idea to jot down anything you'd like to remember in a journal or notebook. Then be sure to silently and earnestly thank the plant.

You can repeat this up to seven times, as long as you do it no more than once per day. Each time you may go deeper, so if you didn't see anything the first time or if your vision was cloudy or distant, subsequent quests may yield more potent results. And, over time, the visions will be sown in your consciousness and remind you of or reconnect you with your heritage in the ways you most desire.

Reconnecting with Old Ways

The term "old ways" is often used to describe the traditions of people such as shamans, members of tribal cultures or folk religions, old wise women or men, and village healers. Of course, during way too many periods of history and even up to the present in some regions, people like this have been appallingly tortured and murdered because of the fear of witchcraft. Those of us with past-life memories of this type of abuse often crave reconnection with the old ways while simultaneously associating them with the horror we experienced. Even in this present life, many of us are raised with the false and hurtful idea that we will "burn in hell" if we practice anything remotely resembling the old ways. Needless to say, these fears can be an energy drain holding us back from being ourselves and accessing the fullness of our spiritual power.

One of hollyhock's missions is to heal us from anything holding us back from reconnecting with the old ways and to dose us with a potent infusion of magical wisdom and power so that we can go forth proudly and reclaim our magical heritage. (Interestingly, it seems this plant may have been hard at work with this mission even during the Burning Times, as the medieval botanist Albertus Magnus recommended rubbing hollyhocks on the hands to protect oneself during a trial by fire.)

Remembering Past Lives

Considering how fuzzy (or missing) so many childhood memories seem to be, is it any wonder past-life memories are usually so deeply buried? Still, even if you don't believe in past lives, consciously accessing past-life memories can be an extremely healing endeavor that can release old pain and untangle present challenges like nobody's business. (If you don't believe in them, you might think of them as stories emerging from your subconscious to help make sense of present challenges.)

If you decide you'd like to access past-life memories, try spending time with the flower or taking the essence—and be sure to pay attention to your dreams!

Strengthening Confidence and Spiritual Energy

The word *pride* can have positive or negative connotations, and hollyhock can give us a magical infusion of pride in its most positive sense. In other words, this flower can fill us with confidence and strengthen our spiritual energy field. Similarly (or perhaps identically), according to the author Judika Illes in *The Element Encyclopedia of 5000 Spells*, just as hollyhock's height allows it to dominate most gardens, it can be successfully employed in domination spells. What all this adds up to is if you want to boost your confidence and influence, hollyhock just may be the magical ingredient for you.

Try drinking a cold infusion of dried hollyhock blossoms (place a jar of water in the fridge overnight with a small bit of the blossoms inside, then strain) or eating a fresh blossom before any situation or event during which you'd like to shine with confidence and exude an increased amount of charisma. For this same purpose, you might also keep dried hollyhock blossoms about your person.

Strengthening Memory

Memory strengthening is just one more of hollyhock's specialties. Try taking the essence regularly for general memory strengthening. You might also plant hollyhock around your home to help fortify your memory in a long-term way.

Magical Correspondences

Element: Earth

Gender: Balance of male and female

Planet: Jupiter

Honeysuckle

*H*oneysuckle always makes me think of the time when I inhaled her delicious scent (allowing her delightful energy to lift my spirits and mood) before going to the grocery store. After shopping, I glanced in my rear-view mirror and noticed that I had a very noticeable coating of white pollen around my nostrils. After mentally replaying the conversation I had with the bagger (Bagger: "How are you?" Me: "Doing really great, thanks!" Bagger: "Really great, huh?" Me: "Yes, really, really great!"), I realized that his first guess about the identity of the powder around my nose would probably not have been honeysuckle pollen.

Magical Uses
Activating Intuition

Author Scott Cunningham recommends inhaling the scent of honeysuckle to allow your intuitive faculties to take over your everyday linear-thinking mind. This goes along with honeysuckle's overriding objectives, which are to get things moving, to help us release what may be holding us back, and to connect us with our healthiest and most divine flow, because tuning in to our intuition is simply tuning in to the eternal flow of the Divine Mind, with which we are already one. Honeysuckle also helps with this because she has such an earthy, sensual scent while also being connected to the Water and Air elements. This elemental makeup lends itself to helping us connect our day-to-day reality (Earth) with the invisible realm (Water, Air), which in turn connects us with our all-knowingness and endless supply of divine wisdom.

Awakening Sexuality and Releasing Sexual Blocks

Let's face it: in our culture, having a healthy relationship with our sexuality can often be a challenge. Between fear-based religious upbringings, Photoshopped magazine ideals, and over-the-top literary and cinematic love scenes, the imaginary burden of what we "should" or "shouldn't" be or do or look like can become contradictory, overwhelming, and altogether unmanageable. Not only that, but many of us have had past sexual experiences with which we associate shame or other types of pain.

The good news? Honeysuckle can help from a number of angles. First of all, her sweet and earthy scent can bring us into our bodies and connect us with our sensuality. Second, because she's an expert at helping us let go of everything that doesn't serve us, she naturally ushers those overwhelming fears, ideals, expectations, and old hurts right out the door of our consciousness. And third, her climbing, intertwining growing pattern lends itself to that natural intermingling of hearts, minds, and bodies that characterizes all sweet, passionate, and mutually trusting sexual encounters.

To release sexual blocks and help heal and awaken your sexuality, try taking the essence or spending time with the flowers. You might also perform a ritual involving inhaling the scent of fresh honeysuckle.

RITUAL TO RELEASE SEXUAL BLOCKS AND HEAL SEXUALITY

For this ritual, you will want to have one or more blossoming honeysuckle plants nearby. At the full moon, before bedtime, pour a small glass of blessed water around the roots of the plant and gently and lovingly pick two blossoms. Place the blossoms next to the place where you sleep, and get ready for bed. Turn off all the lights, then light an off-white, unscented soy candle next to your bed. Sit on or in your bed and hold the blossoms in both hands. Close your eyes and take some deep breaths while consciously relaxing your body. When you feel ready, inhale the scent of the blossoms. Fill your mind, body, and spirit with nothing but an awareness of the scent and the blossoms, then say: "I love myself just as I am." Continue to inhale for a few more breaths, then say: "I love my body just as it is." Continue to inhale and relax for a few more moments, and then say:

I forgive, I release, I renew. I come into the present.
I accept and flow with my desires. I am blessed, I am perfect,
I am beautiful. I am safe, and all is well.

Now gently crush and rub the blossoms on your inner wrists, belly, and heart. (If you have sensitive skin, just lightly brush yourself with the blossoms in these places.) Place the blossoms under your pillow. Extinguish the candle and go to sleep. Repeat every night until the next new moon.

Good Luck

It's said that honeysuckle growing near your home will bring good luck. Of course it must be true, because good luck is the natural state of things, and honeysuckle helps bring everything into its natural state by releasing fear-, ego-, and illusion-based blocks to this natural flow.

Letting Go/Endings and Beginnings

Although everything is changing, and change is the natural state of things, change can sometimes feel unsettling, scary, or sad. While changes such as breakups or losing one's job can naturally leave us feeling bereft, even moving to a home that we like a lot better than the old one can bring about a considerable amount of stress.

Honeysuckle can help us realize that even seemingly undesirable changes can actually be blessings in disguise or even portals into the endless flow of divine blessings that's constantly doing its best to get through to us. After all, helping us tap into this flow with courage and calm is honeysuckle's special gift.

For this reason, taking honeysuckle essence or having a plant close to the home can help us during times such as the following:

- moving or major residence-related shifts
- traveling (or just being out of the day-to-day environment)
- starting a new school or school year
- starting or ending a new job
- job changes
- starting or ending a relationship
- the death of a loved one
- clutter clearing or releasing old keepsakes and memorabilia

Also, according to physician and father of flower essence healing Edward Bach, honeysuckle can help support those who cling to an idealized version of the past in ways that hamper them from enjoying the present.

If, as author Judika Illes suggests in *The Element Encylopedia of 5000 Spells*, surrounding oneself in honeysuckle can increase longevity, perhaps we owe that to her ability to help us change with the times: inner flexibility and openness to change is a quality of youthfulness and resilience, just as a nimble branch can bend with the wind while a stiff and brittle one will often break.

Prosperity

If you've read the previous information about honeysuckle, you've no doubt figured out that honeysuckle has to do with divine and energetic flow. Like the word *fluid*, the word *affluence* is derived from the Latin word that means "to flow." It's no wonder, then, that one of honeysuckle's most traditional magical uses is to help activate prosperity and abundance and get those finances *flowing*!

And, as mentioned above, honeysuckle's elemental makeup also lends itself to prosperity—i.e., Earth (the material world) and Water and Air (the invisible divine flow that animates and nourishes everything). As you may have guessed, it can be especially helpful for those of us who feel there may be some sort of block to our natural flow of abundance. To experience these benefits, try working with honeysuckle in any of the ways mentioned in the above sections, or make and carry a charm such as the following.

ABUNDANCE CHARM

When the moon is full, place three fresh honeysuckle blossoms on a small piece of green or purple cotton. Add a shiny silver dollar, five shiny pennies, a citrine quartz crystal (all washed in salt water and saged), five allspice cloves, and a pinch of cinnamon. Tie closed with a piece of hemp twine. Keep it near you until your finances are flowing comfortably, then bury it near the base of a tree.

Weight Loss

Everything is connected: inner/outer, form/spirit, body/mind. As such, releasing old "stuff" from our minds and emotions can help us release extra weight on our bodies. As a matter of fact, the previous ritual to release sexual blocks will work just as well for weight loss. You can also try taking the essence regularly, especially during the waning moon cycle.

Magical Correspondences

Elements: Earth, Water, Air
Gender: Female
Planet: Jupiter

Hyacinth

One would be hard-pressed to argue that there are flowers more beautiful and fragrant as the hyacinth. Indeed, she steals the show in the early spring and is the reigning diva of any garden in which she appears.

Hyacinths are named after the beautiful Greek youth Hyacinth, who was deeply loved and adored by Apollo. It was said that Zephyr (the wind) was so jealous of their relationship that he killed Hyacinth. Where his blood spilled, a hyacinth flower appeared. (Although named after a male mythological character, hyacinth possesses a feminine essence and is therefore referred to in the text as such.)

Magical Uses

Abundance and Luxury

Sometimes we may unknowingly push abundance and luxury away because, on some level, we feel undeserving—when, in fact, just like a tree that receives nourishment from the earth and sun simply by virtue of being present and alive, abundance and luxury are our natural state. On an emotional and vibrational level, magically working with hyacinth reminds us that we are immanently deserving and helps us to receive prosperity and experience luxury as a matter of course.

Attracting Gifts

Admittedly, some magical objectives are more self-serving than others, but there is nothing unspiritual about receiving gifts, and being open to receive aligns us with our intuition and opens up the floodgates to our abundance. So if you're in the mood to work a little magic for the purpose of attracting wonderful favors and gifts, what can be the harm? That is, of course, as long as you don't interfere with anyone's free will by singling out specific individuals during such magical undertakings (in other words, do a general ritual without picturing any faces or naming any names). Hyacinth can help with this, because—just like twinkling eyes and a disarming smile—she elicits an exceptional level of generosity.

For this purpose, magically work with the essence or blossom as you feel guided or sit with her mindfully as you silently request her help with shifting your vibration to a more receptive, magnetic one.

Charm and Irresistibility

Most of us spend a good amount of time and money on things in the physical world that (we hope) make us a bit more charming and irresistible. On the magical side of things, hyacinth blossoms can help us do the same. This can be especially helpful for those particular evenings or events when you really want to attract positive attention and shine your irresistible light.

The potion below can help you in such occasions to do just that. Please employ it only once per moon cycle (otherwise its effectiveness will be compromised—and besides, you've got to leave *some* of the attention for those other folks).

....

Irresistibility Potion

While you're alone, add four drops hyacinth essence to a glass of pink champagne or sparkling juice. Make a toast to yourself in the mirror and drink as you gaze at your reflection and marvel at your natural charm and considerable attractiveness.

Glamour

Do you sometimes wish you were more glamorous? Putting two to three drops hyacinth essence under the tongue two to three times a day for an entire moon cycle (new to full to new again) can help you get in touch with your inner black-and-white movie star and exude the timeless glamour that you so crave.

Influence

In the French language of flowers during the Victorian era, hyacinth meant "I love you; you destroy me." While I'm not suggesting that you go about destroying anyone by employing the hyacinth's awesome influential power, I *am* suggesting that, like Obi-Wan Kenobi, you might occasionally want to use "the force" to let your words ring exceptionally and immediately true for the people who hear them. For example, this might be helpful during court cases, while you're trying to escape the clutches of Darth Vader and his evil empire, or any other time wielding a lot of influence might come in handy. Try incorporating hyacinth blossoms into spells or rituals designed for the purpose, or add three drops of the flower essence into a glass of chilled hibiscus tea. Before drinking it, empower it with your intention to dominate or persuade.

Magical Correspondences

Element: Water
Gender: Female
Planet: Venus

Hydrangea

While hydrangeas appear in a number of colors, the garden varieties often range from pink to violet to blue, and the acid content of the soil can cause them to change from one color to another. But no matter what color she is, hydrangea's sensitivity to slight changes and shifts, along with her very deep alignment with water and the watery realm of psychic awareness, combine to make her a special ally to those of us who might be called psychic, intuitive, or spiritually sensitive. This is especially true because, while it might seem contradictory, her sensitivity is coupled with a fierce energetic dynamic related to shielding and protection. Consequently, she can help us experience our psychic gifts while also honoring our boundaries and staying spiritually safe and sound.

Magical Uses

Boundaries

Those of us who are magically inclined can often have a particular challenge when it comes to maintaining healthy boundaries in relationships and in the invisible realm. This is because we can pick up on other people's emotions and on slight changes in the energetic environment, and the lines between us, others, and our environment can sometimes get blurred. What's more, our very bright light and potent power can cause others to—sometimes consciously but usually subconsciously—latch onto us and siphon off some of our personal energy.

Hydrangea's wisdom is about experiencing the fullness of your magical power while still standing in your strength and maintaining healthy emotional, spiritual, and physical boundaries.

For this purpose, I suggest any of the following:

- Plant hydrangeas around the perimeter of your yard or on either side of the front door or front gate, and ask them to help you maintain positive boundaries in your home and life.

- Take two to three drops hydrangea essence under the tongue or in water two to three times per day.

- Place a bouquet of hydrangeas on your altar and petition a god/dess of your choice to help you establish and maintain good boundaries.

- Incorporate hydrangeas into spells, charms, or rituals designed for the purpose.

Deconstructing Challenging Karmic Patterns

When you notice an ongoing or recurring unpleasant condition in your life, and you get the sense that you have it in common with older relatives and even ancestors (such as a specific kind of money or relationship issue), it's most likely a challenging karmic pattern that is interwoven into your family tree. Challenging karmic patterns can also be interwoven throughout your own past lifetimes and carry over into the present one.

When consciously charged with intention, hydrangea can help penetrate these types of patterns and work with us to deconstruct them so that they stop wreaking havoc in our lives and so that we don't have to continue to pass them down to wreak havoc in future generations or lifetimes either.

For this purpose, you might try sitting in quiet contemplation with a hydrangea, requesting help with your karmic challenge, and then relaxing your mind and allowing hydrangea to work her magic. Additionally (or instead if you don't have access to a flowering plant), at the full moon, you might take three drops hydrangea essence under the tongue first thing in the morning or last thing at night (whichever feels right). After you take it, place both hands on your heart and say:

> *With hydrangea's help, this old pattern now unravels, dissolves,*
> *and completely disappears. It is gone, gone, gone, never to return.*
> *Thank you, thank you, thank you, and so mote it be.*

Repeat each night of the waning moon.

Hex Breaking

According to author Judika Illes in *The Element Encyclopedia of Witchcraft*, "To be hexed is to be spellbound, cursed, or bewitched." From a certain perspective, the hex might be caused by an actual spell, curse, or bewitchment (i.e., a magical attack of some sort), or it might also be caused by something like a psychic attack (see page 191), a challenging karmic pattern (see above), or even a limiting belief or thought pattern that holds us under its insidious sway.

Whatever the source of the hex, hydrangea can help break it. Here are a few ideas for how to employ her for this purpose.

Cleansing Fire

Consciously tune in to a blossoming hydrangea plant or plants and respectfully request their help with the situation. If they give you the okay, gently and lovingly gather a bouquet. Leave a silver dollar and ten pennies as payment. Then dry the bouquet completely, perhaps by hanging it upside down from the ceiling. The first day after a full moon, build a fire in a fireplace or fire pit. Relax and take some deep breaths. Whether you know its source or not, intuitively get in touch with the energy of the hex, then hold the dried bouquet in your hands. Whisper to the bouquet:

Thank you for helping me cleanse and dissolve this hex!
Now is the time! Find it, break it, and snuff it out forever!

(Safely) throw the bouquet in the fire and watch it burn.

PURIFYING MIST

Place nine drops hydrangea flower essence and twenty drops sage essential oil in a mister of rose water. Shake to blend. The night after a full moon, mist each room and area of your home while walking in a counterclockwise direction and chanting:

Wash it out, clear it out, blessed be.
The hex is broken; I am free.

Finish by misting yourself. Repeat each night of the waning moon, making an extra batch of the potion when necessary.

UNCROSSING SACHETS

Sew or obtain one small red flannel bag for:

- your front door
- your back door and any other doors to the outside
- every inside door
- yourself
- any loved ones whom the hex may also involve (except animals—they don't need one to receive the benefits of the ritual)

The Flowers 189

For each sachet, also obtain:

- one garlic clove
- nine individual hydrangea blossoms (the small blossoms within the blossoms—not the entire flower head), gathered with intention and gentleness
- nine white sage leaves
- a small length of hemp twine

The day after a full moon, empower all ingredients by saying a simple blessing prayer over them and envisioning white light around them. Then take one clove of garlic and gently hit it with a hammer to release its essence as you say:

The hex is broken;
I (we) am (are) free.

Place the clove in the first bag, along with the nine blossoms and nine leaves. Tie closed with a length of twine. Repeat with each sachet. Attach one sachet to each door, keep one on your person, and distribute one to each additional person as necessary; you can also do this later if they are not currently in the vicinity. Then stand in a central location and say:

Broken, banished, and unwound, the hex is nowhere to be found.
Happy, healthy, glowing bright; our way is clear, and all's set right.

At the new moon, bury the blossoms near the base of a tree, then wash your hands.

Protection

Planting hydrangeas around your home can be an excellent magical protection measure, especially when you enlist hydrangea's help to keep all negativity out and only allow those with the truest and most positive intentions to pass. You can also dry and powder hydrangea, empower it in sunlight and with a simple blessing prayer or visualization, and sprinkle it around the perimeter of your lot.

Redirecting Curses and Psychic Attacks

You might think of a psychic attack as another's ill will sent in your direction that you have somehow—usually unconsciously—invited or allowed into your energetic field. As an alternative to simply breaking a hex, curse, or psychic attack, you can employ hydrangea to redirect it to its source, sort of like holding up a mirror to someone giving you a dirty look, shielding yourself from it, and forcing the looker to give the look right back to herself. If you choose to go this route, though, be aware that there may be a bit more karmic repercussions than if you were to simply break the hex and leave it at that. It's up to you!

One way to do this would be to perform the previous "cleansing fire" ritual, only replacing the magic words with:

> *Thank you for helping me reflect this hex (curse, attack) right back*
> *to its source! Now is the time! Find it, redirect it, and send it home!*

As the dried bouquet burns, hold up a small mirror (that has been empowered in sunlight) so that it is facing away from you as you make a complete 360-degree turn slowly, in a counterclockwise direction. Then, to keep the curse from coming back, affix the mirror to the outside of your front door. For extra strength, reinforce it by also performing one or two of the other hex-breaking rituals.

Restructuring Energy Field

One reason hydrangea is such an excellent magical ally when it comes to releasing negative energetic patterns is that she doesn't just get rid of the old, she also helps us restructure our energy fields and reconfigure our energetic dynamics in healthier, more positive ways. For example, if you're working on releasing old habits, such as an addiction or an unhealthy relationship pattern, taking the essence regularly would help with this. Or if you've recently moved or your living situation has recently changed and you're interested in establishing a happier home and more ideal residential dynamic, you might plant hydrangeas in the yard and respectfully ask for their help in that area.

Magical Correspondences

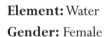

Element: Water

Gender: Female

Planets: Moon, Neptune

Impatiens

*O*ne of Edward Bach's famous original flower remedies and a component of the beloved Rescue Remedy, impatiens's wisdom has been employed by flower essence and holistic health enthusiasts for the good portion of a century. Although she's named for her seemingly impatient method of expelling her seeds from her pods quickly and at the slightest touch, she is actually an expert at slowing down, aligning with divine timing, and trusting the process of life. And when the moment warrants such behavior, she is also adept at helping us jump in and get things done. Considering both these aspects of her magic, she seems to be most concerned with helping us get into an ideal balance of enjoying the moment and getting things done. And this, of course, nourishes our happiness, reduces our stress, and supports our success in all life areas.

While only certain recognizable blossoms are usually found in gardens, impatiens's hardy and fertile blooms appear in an unfathomable variety of incarnations in the wild.

Magical Uses
Aligning with Divine Timing

While impatiens is best known for her ability to help us slow down and enjoy the moment, she is also an expert at helping us act swiftly when the time is right. In other words, she is all about lifting us out of the illusion of human timing and aligning us with divine timing. "Divine timing" may be considered an oxymoron, as time is an illusion, and the Divine is eternal, timeless, birthless, and deathless. However, divine timing might be defined as dwelling in the illusion of time while residing as close as possible to the truth of eternity. This type of perspective not only engenders happiness and peace but also helps bring about the ideal solutions and conclusions to all seeming problems and any situation in which we seem to find ourselves.

Practically speaking, impatiens can help when we feel:

- impatient
- worried
- disempowered
- overly attached to the outcome of any given situation
- overly detail-oriented
- lazy
- distracted or seemingly unable to focus
- overwhelmed by life
- hesitant to begin any project
- like we don't know where to start
- like we have to micromanage every little situation
- like we are not in the right place at the right time
- like time is not on our side
- like we are fighting against the tide rather than flowing with it
- like there is "not enough time in the day"
- rushed

For help with any of these conditions, bring impatiens into your yard, spend time in quiet contemplation with her, or take two to three drops impatiens essence two to three times per day under the tongue or in water. For general stress relief that includes any or all of the above challenges, you might try taking four drops Bach Rescue Remedy under the tongue first thing in the morning and as needed throughout the day.

Being Present

Like the title of Ram Dass's famous book, spiritual practitioners of every era and persuasion have endeavored to simply *be here now*. After all, what else is there to do but enjoy this mysterious life experience while we are having it? And, as you might expect after reading the "aligning with divine timing" section, impatiens can help us to do just that. When we enter the moment and let the past be the past and the future be the future—both conditions that exist only in our minds and are never actually here—we are happier and more peaceful, and everything seems to flow smoothly and work out in the most ideal possible way.

Naturally, this aspect of impatiens can help us to:

- connect with our loved ones

- enjoy the moment

- be awake to opportunities and blessings

- establish a meditation or yoga practice

- concentrate deeply

- let go of stress and worry

- excel at activities that require focus and relaxed attentiveness, including taking tests, sports, and listening to our significant others

Grounding

A positive side effect of aligning with divine timing and coming into the present moment is feeling grounded. This is because we are able to release everything that is extraneous and focus on what is here now: the present moment and the earth beneath our feet. For this purpose, try any of the recommendations above.

Magical Correspondences

Element: Water
Gender: Female
Planet: Mercury

agically and medicinally employed in many cultures (including Japan, America, Egypt, Arabia, China, France, and Greece), Iris, like the Greek goddess for whom she is named, is an iridescent bridge between the realm of humans and the realm of the Divine.

Magical Uses

Alignment with Inner Truth

Who are you *really*? While you'll never have a definitive answer in the scientific sense, each of us has a unique spiritual essence within us just waiting to be honored and expressed. And when we do express it, our divine gifts blossom forth, and we become clear, open channels of divine healing and love. But we can only express our inner truth once we get in touch with it and align with it, and helping us do so is one of iris's specialties.

To begin getting in touch with the deepest, truest essence of who you are, as you feel guided, try working magically with the blossom or essence.

Creativity

When we create, we are like prisms or crystals receiving and reflecting divine light and transmuting it into rainbows. The clearer and more receptive we are, the more we sparkle and the more beauty we spread out into the world. Just as the goddess Iris was a rainbow bridge of light between the human and the celestial realms, the flower iris can connect us to the ever-present divine download of creative light and energy so that we can express our creative visions in healing and beneficial ways. This allows us to transmute stagnant feelings and challenging emotions into beauty, and to experience countless benefits in every life area.

To open your creative channel with iris, try spending time with the flower, working with the essence, placing an iris in water near your creative workspace, or sleeping with an iris in water on your nightstand or otherwise near your head.

Energetic Balance and Calibration

Iris is a master energy healer. If you feel physically, emotionally, mentally, or spiritually out of balance, even if you're not exactly sure why, she can help make the necessary adjustments and get you back on track. Because, like a rainbow, she possesses all colors in equal measure, it's in her nature to add exactly what is needed and to absorb and release exactly what is not needed. You might think of her like a piano or guitar tuner for your chakra system. To fine-tune your energy in this way, take two to three drops iris essence under the tongue first thing in the morning, surround yourself with blossoming irises (indoors or in your garden), or try the following bath ritual.

Chakra Healing and Energy Calibration Bath

Draw a bath and dissolve one cup sea salt, one cup of Epsom salts, and one-half cup baking soda in the water. Light a white soy candle and place an ample supply of drinking water near the bath. Add forty drops iris essence. Remove your clothes. Stand above the water and hold your hands over it, palms down. Close your eyes and relax your mind. Say:

Iris, goddess of rainbows, divine bridge of color and light, I call on you!
Please infuse this water with your iridescent healing light.

Please balance and calibrate my aura, adding what is needed and removing what is not,
so that my body, mind, and spirit may sing and dance with the music of the spheres!
Thank you, thank you, thank you.
Blessed be. And so it is.

Feel iris's healing light moving in through the top of your head, down your arms, and out through your hands and into the water. Soak for about forty-five minutes, drinking water as needed. When you're finished, place the blossoms aside. Before the end of the day, be sure to return them to the earth by placing them at the base of a tree.

Intuition and Divine Messages

Not only is iris named after the divine messenger goddess herself, but her petals are most often indigo, purple, or white: the colors associated with the third eye and crown chakras, which govern intuition, inner knowing, and divine connection. Indeed, she is herself a doorway between our everyday human awareness and the all-knowing, all-seeing awareness of the Divine.

When consciously activating your intuition and psychic awareness, iris can be an excellent magical support. For example, you might create the following magical accessory inspired by the irises that were reverently placed on the brows of the sphinxes in Egypt.

FAERY CROWN FOR ACTIVATING INTUITION AND ENHANCING DIVINATION

Gently and lovingly gather an iris blossom or two and a length of ivy long enough to weave into a simple crown that will fit comfortably around your head. Using hemp twine, ribbon, or twist ties as necessary, tie or weave in the iris blossoms. Wear so that the blossom rests near the center of your forehead.

Love-Drawing

A Muslim friend of mine once taught me that in the Islamic religion, God is known by many descriptive titles, one of which is "The Subtle One." Those who desire to meet their partner call on this divine title when praying because there is so much subtlety involved with the alchemical correlation between the two souls who together make up what is known as "a perfect match."

Similarly, iris's subtle energetic precision can help us prepare for, and then draw, our perfect partner. Historically, powdered iris root (known as "orris root") has been employed in love-drawing spells, but the blossom works too. So if you're ready to embark on a lifelong romantic journey (pretty serious business, to be sure), you might perform the following spell.

LOVE-DRAWING SPELL

Within around ten minutes before or after sunrise on the morning of a new moon, approach a blossoming iris. Relax and tune in to her, and then let her know that you'd like to employ her in a ritual to draw your true love. Ask her if this is okay. If she says no, thank her anyway and retreat; you can try again at the next new moon (or in another year if she's no longer in bloom then). If she says yes, thank her by pouring a bottle of spring water and placing two lepidolite crystals near her base. Then gently and lovingly snip the blossom and wrap it in clean muslin or undyed cotton. At home, place the blossom in a small paper bag and leave it on your altar to dry. At the next new moon, by candlelight, at the same time (ten minutes before or after sunrise), remove the blossom from the bag and tie it into the muslin with hemp twine, along with two lepidolite crystals. Sleep with the charm under your pillow until your true love appears. Then return to the iris from which you snipped the blossom and bury the charm close by with an expression of heartfelt thanks.

Purification and Protection

Irises possess a very purifying and protective energy. For example, it's said that irises helped the Frankish King Clovis extricate himself from a river bank on which he was stranded by growing up through the water and revealing to him that the Rhine River was shallow enough to cross. This led to them being adopted as the symbol of French kings in the form of a fleur de lis.

In Japan, irises were placed on thatched roofs to purify the environment and protect from fire. And May 5 is known as "Iris Bathing Day," when iris leaf tea is added to bath water to protect the bather in the forthcoming year.

Additionally, irises are said to share the energy of the Virgin Mary, who has a very purifying and protective energy all her own.

Here are some ideas for employing irises for purification and protection:

- To energetically purify and protect your home, bring irises indoors and place them at or above thresholds.

- Create a protective charm by placing dried iris petals and dried yarrow in a charm bag and hanging it on or above the front door and any other doors that open to the outside.

- Employ iris petals in spells or rituals designed for purification and protection.

- Employ the fleur de lis symbol as a protective sigil in your magical work.

Walking Between the Worlds

As a goddess who walks between the worlds—the worlds of form and spirit, known and unknown, human and divine—Iris has been invoked in Greece to help successfully guide the spirits of women and girls to the afterlife. Traditionally, iris blossoms are employed to adorn caskets belonging to females.

All true magic is worked "between the worlds." In other words, perceiving and dwelling within the connection between the worlds is a prerequisite to successful magical workings. Consequently, if you feel stuck in one world or the other—or perceive things as only mundane or only magical but never both—iris can help you unite your vision and reclaim the fullness of your magical power.

Try working with the blossom or essence in any way mentioned above, or place five to six drops iris essence in a glass of red wine and drink it just before a spell, ritual, or divination work.

Magical Correspondences

Element: Water
Gender: Female
Planet: Venus

Jasmine

*P*assionate, luxurious, and prosperous, jasmine seems to magically encapsulate all that is wonderful and right in the world. Indeed, her appearance and scent evoke easy breezy days, sensual pleasures, and everything associated with the good life.

Fresh jasmine is known for being more fragrant after dark, which is why she's sometimes called the "Queen of the Night" in India.

Magical Uses

Abundance

As you may have already learned, jasmine essential oil is expensive! (Well, naturally.) Jasmine, like a breathtakingly beautiful woman, is a queen, and her elegance requires a certain monetary respect. This costliness is a natural side effect of her luxurious and sumptuous vibration.

Of course, the magical benefits of her abundant nature can be gleaned with just a few of her fresh blossoms as well (a much thriftier option).

....

ABUNDANCE CHARM

To help manifest a luxurious lifestyle and comfortable financial conditions, place a few fresh jasmine blossoms, a crisp dollar bill, and a white quartz crystal in a green satin charm bag. Tie it closed with purple velvet ribbon and keep it in your purse or near your checkbook.

Joy

We need joy like we need fresh air! If you come to the conclusion that joy has been conspicuously missing from your life, perform a spell or ritual incorporating jasmine, take jasmine essence, or surround yourself with the fragrance of jasmine. It will remind you of the best things in life and—by bringing you into your body and into the present moment—will help you to realize that you're already blessed beyond your fondest dreams. Here are a couple ideas:

....

Joy Potion (Nonalcoholic)

Brew a cup of tea using dried jasmine leaves and rose petals. Add four drops jasmine essence. Relax, take some deep breaths, and slowly drink.

....

Joy Potion (Alcoholic)

Place two drops jasmine essence in a glass of pink champagne and drink slowly. To make a full batch to share, place six drops in a bottle.

Sensuality and Attractiveness

Nothing enhances your sexuality and sexual attractiveness like getting out of your head and into your body. And just a whiff jasmine essential oil, jasmine absolute, or (better yet) fresh jasmine can immediately excite your awareness with the pleasures associated with being in a physical body.

Similarly, incorporating jasmine into rituals and spells aimed at enhancing your sensuality, the sensual connection between you and a loved one, or your sexual attractiveness will likely yield excellent results.

Bath Ritual for a Night of Irresistibility

Light one pink candle and one white or off-white candle and a stick of jasmine essence in the bathroom. By candlelight, draw a warm bath. Mix six drops jasmine essential oil or jasmine absolute into one cup sea salt and dissolve in the bath. Hold your hands over the bath water, close your eyes, and visualize very bright golden-white light coming up from the core of the earth, entering your feet, going up to your heart, down your arms, out through your palms, and into the bath water. Then envision the cool white light of the moon coming down from above, entering the crown of your head, going down to your heart, down your arms, out through your palms, and into the water. Say:

> *Great Goddess Isis, please infuse this water with divine magnetism and charm.*
> *Tonight may I dazzle, and may all who gaze upon me be smitten.*
> *Great Queen, I thank you!*

Soak in the tub for at least thirty minutes as you feel yourself becoming infused with the magic you've conjured.

Sexual Healing

Similarly, jasmine can help heal sexual inhibition and sexual issues. For especially long-standing issues, you might try nightly anointing yourself with the natural fragrance of jasmine (essential oil or absolute) and/or taking two to four drops jasmine essence daily for at least one month. And baths that incorporate fresh jasmine, jasmine fragrance, or jasmine essence can similarly soothe and heal emotional wounds related to sexuality.

Relaxation

Like a cocktail or a glass of wine after a hectic day (only easier on the liver), the scent of jasmine can take the edge off and ease you into a warmer, gentler, and more pleasant sort of mood.

Similarly, consistently surrounding yourself with the scent of jasmine can be an excellent remedy for long-standing stress, irritability, or worry. This, of course, is also part of her aphrodisiacal effect, and—since soothing stress is so conducive to physical healing—it's also perhaps why fresh jasmine has been traditionally kept in the bedrooms of bedridden patients in China.

Magical Correspondences

Element: Water

Gender: Female

Planets: Moon, Venus

Kalanchoe

*A*t first glance, kalanchoe might not seem too glamorous, but once you get to know him you're likely to love his friendly nature, understated wisdom, and "salt of the earth" personality.

Magical Uses

Grounding

Kalanchoe is very aligned with the earth, and he possesses sturdy, grounded energy. So if you're feeling flighty, ill at ease, or all over the place, you might want to bring a kalanchoe or two into your flower beds or outdoor pots. This can also help when you've recently moved to a new home and you want to establish roots and enhance feelings of ease, familiarity, and belonging.

Inner Fortification

Similarly, when you feel overly sensitive or have to traverse especially challenging emotional or energetic situations (jury duty, hospital visits, or Thanksgiving dinner with the extended family), kalanchoe can help fortify your defenses. For these types of situations, you might like to take two drops kalanchoe essence under the tongue just before bed the night before and again just before entering the situation. Things can roll off your back this way, and you will emerge relatively unscathed.

Harmony

When harmony (inner or outer) feels difficult to achieve because you feel uncomfortably buffeted by the ups and downs of your day or because you feel constantly harassed by life in general, try planting some kalanchoe near your front door in pots or flowerbeds. Then simply relax, tune in, and ask kalanchoe to share his wisdom and energy with you so that you can experience inner and outer harmony throughout your day. Every time you pass him, try to remember to thank him for doing so. You will feel an immediate sense of enhanced security and stability, and over the course of a few weeks you will begin to experience a steady increase in your overall level of harmony.

Protection

According to author Judika Illes in *The Encyclopedia of Spirits*, kalanchoe can help ward off the sinister creatures called *loups-garoux* (also known as werewolves) when planted in the yard. Similarly, you may employ kalanchoe in magic performed for the purpose of protecting yourself from negativity from seen or unseen realms.

Resilience

You can also employ kalanchoe's sturdy energy to help you do what you need to do during those times that seem to be especially rough. For example, perhaps you just went through a major breakup, and while you want to take at least a month off of work and just lie around crying and eating chocolate all day, you realize it's just not practical for a number of important reasons. Or perhaps you've just experienced the transition of a loved one, and now there are a ton of loose ends you've got to tie up, boxes you've got to pack, decisions you're expected to make, and so forth. During times like these, kalanchoe will happily come to your rescue like an old friend. He'll help you draw on inner reserves you didn't even know you had so that you can take care of what needs to be taken care of and emerge emotionally intact. For this purpose, I suggest taking the essence, spending time with the blossom, or creating a charm such as a kalanchoe blossom tied in a piece of muslin along with a white quartz crystal point.

These suggestions can also be helpful for children who are healing from abuse, whose parents have divorced or are divorcing, who are changing schools, etc. (Just to clarify: the magic of kalanchoe isn't about emotional healing per se, but more about getting through big changes and challenges with courage and grace.)

Magical Correspondences

 **Element:** Earth
Gender: Male
Planet: Saturn

Lantana (Shrub Verbena)

his feisty little guy is in the verbena family, but I can't for the life of me see the resemblance between him and his kinfolk (energetically speaking, that is). While they're both magical, beautiful, and helpful in a number of ways, lantana is strong, sunshiny, and sassy, while other verbena varieties tend to be etheric, otherworldly, and gentle.

Important notes:

- Lantana is not edible like many other verbena varieties, so do not consume any part of the plant.

- For information on the rest of the verbena family, please see the "Vervain (*Verbena*)" entry.

Magical Uses
Breaking Old Patterns

Lantana can be magically employed to act like a virus scan that can uncover and dismantle harmful patterns that may be stored in our consciousness, energy field, home, or workspace. Since we have all inherited issues stemming from childhood experiences and even further back into our ancestry and past lives, lantana can be a helpful ally in helping us end these patterns right now, during this lifetime, so that they never resurface in the lives of our descendants or future selves. For this purpose, I suggest taking the essence, spending time with the plant, or creating a charm.

Karma-Clearing Charm

Dry five blossoms in sunlight, and place them in a small cotton bag or tie them up in cotton fabric. Empower the charm with the intention to clear old karmic patterns, and hang it so that it's above your head while you sleep.

(Please note: magically speaking, though he is quick, lantana is not gentle. So this might be a little less than pleasant, like getting a tooth pulled.)

Exorcism

Lantana is so clear, dynamic, bright, and positive, it's hard for him to coexist with the stagnant, heavy, muddled, negative energy that characterizes unwanted ghosts and entities.

Here are some ways you can employ this aspect of his magic:

- Set a glass bowl outdoors in bright sunlight. Place a (cleansed) white quartz crystal in the bottom of the bowl and fill it with water. Float forty lantana blossoms (forty whole heads, not just forty tiny parts of the blossom) on top of the water. Hold your hands near the bowl and direct positive energy through your hands and into the water. After leaving the bowl in sunlight for one hour, fill a mister with water from the bowl. Add ten to twenty drops angelica essential oil to the mister. Close and shake well. Use the remaining water to feed plants around your yard or pour it out near the base of a tree. During a waning moon, shake the bottle and mist your home with the mixture to send entities packing. You may also employ this mist in other exorcism and space-clearing rituals.

- When exorcising entities or negative patterns from the energy field of a person, begin by calling on divine helper(s) of your choice. (Personally,

I'd call Archangel Michael and his angelic helpers.) Smudge the patient's entire aura with a smoking bundle of desert sage, feather sage, or sagebrush. Then set the sage aside (while leaving it safely burning) and sweep the patient's aura with a small bouquet of lantana blossoms. Finish by very lightly tapping the patient's third eye, heart, belly, and hands with the blossoms.

- Plant lantana around your home to keep negative entities (physical and nonphysical) from entering.

Getting Energy Moving

Sometimes our energy can get stagnant because there's something somewhere that we don't want to look at or something that we've learned we're supposed to repress. And once that happens, every aspect of our mental and physical health suffers. What's more, we find ourselves with a marked lack of motivation, direction, and clarity.

While it might not be entirely pleasant at first, lantana can help cure these challenges and get our energy moving in the right direction by taking us straight into whatever it is that we're so cunningly blocking from our own conscious awareness. And, since our bodies and minds are inextricably connected, this can also help get our organs moving and flowing in healthy and ideal ways. For this purpose, I suggest taking the flower essence regularly until your energy is moving in the way you desire.

Healing Depression

Depression is often the effect of blocked emotions and direction. As such, because of the energetic properties discussed in the "getting energy moving" section, lantana can help cure depression by getting you in touch with your feelings and ideal emotional flow. For this purpose, try taking the flower essence as recommended above or planting the flowers around your home and spending time in quiet contemplation with them. The smudging ritual from the "exorcism" section would also be a great option, so you might ask one of your especially magical friends to perform it on you.

Space Clearing

As mentioned, lantana can be a great space-clearing ally. Try smudging with a bundle of feather sage, sagebrush, or desert sage, then misting the space with the mist potion recipe in the "exorcism" section. Or add twelve drops of the flower essence and twenty drops clary sage essential oil to a mister of rose water to create a powerful, smokeless smudge spray.

Speaking Your Truth (and Coming Out of the Closet)

Lantana is sassy, saucy, and tells it like it is. Hence, if you're looking for a truth-speaking booster shot or inspiration to come out of the closet in any area of your life, look no further than lantana. First, he'll help you get clear on what your truth actually is. Then he'll help you clear your throat and speak up. For this purpose, try taking the essence or inhaling the fragrance while holding your specific truth-speaking intention.

Strengthening Boundaries

When our energy is strong and clear, and when we're in alignment with our feelings and inner dialogue, we naturally have good boundaries. In other words, we know who we are and who we aren't. We know what feels right to us and what doesn't. And we aren't afraid to let any of it be known.

This naturally strengthens and protects our personal energy field from dangers in both physical and nonphysical realms. For this purpose, I suggest inhaling the scent daily with the intention to strengthen your boundaries or taking two drops of the essence under the tongue or in water twice per day.

Strengthening Will

Since lantana helps us get clear on who we are and gives us a motivational jumpstart, it follows that he helps strengthen our will. This can be helpful when we're trying something new or moving through an especially challenging time. Lantana's will-strengthening action can also be helpful when we have issues with our third (or solar plexus) chakra, as he helps balance this chakra with the heart chakra so that our relationship with our personal power is balanced with (and healed by) love.

Magical Correspondences

Element: Fire
Gender: Male
Planets: Sun, Mars

Lavender

*T*he renowned medieval herbalist Hildegard von Bingen summarized lavender's essence succinctly when she said that lavender helps us with "maintaining a pure character." With profoundly purifying properties that span both physical and energetic planes, it is not surprising that her name comes from the Latin *lavare*, "to wash." She's a favorite of aromatherapists the world over, many of whom consider her essential oil to be among the most useful (if not *the* most useful) of all.

Magical Uses
Clarity
Lavender is aligned with the planet Mercury and, elementally speaking, is quite airy. These qualities lend themselves to the realm of thought and the conscious mind. Combined with the fact that her scent and energy are so highly purifying, lavender whisks away excess stress and mental chatter while magically imparting an exhilarating degree of lucidity. So, to transcend muddled thinking and gain clarity on a specific issue, you might want to simply inhale the scent of lavender. You could do this by:

- wafting a bottle of essential oil under your nose
- lightly crushing a fresh blossom between your fingers and inhaling
- diffusing the essential oil
- anointing your temples with the essential oil

For added power, you might say an invocation mentally or aloud just before you inhale, such as:

Lavender, thank you for clearing my mind and uplifting my spirit.
With your help, I am now in the moment and on my mark.

Cleansing

With antifungal and antibacterial properties, as well as an ability to purify the mind and spirit, lavender essential oil is highly cleansing on both physical and energetic planes. To cleanse and purify your body, mind, and spirit, you might add lavender essential oil to:

- bath water (alternatively, you might add dried lavender blossoms)

- body wash

- a mister of rose water (for a body mist)

- facial toner

- shampoo (as an added benefit, some aromatherapists claim that lavender oil can help with hair growth)

- your body (provided your skin isn't extremely sensitive, lavender is one of the few essential oils that we can apply "neat," or undiluted, to the body; for example, you might try anointing your heart and brow daily when spiritual or emotional cleansing is a concern)

To cleanse and purify your home (both physically and energetically), you might add lavender essential oil to:

- the washing machine (also consider adding a sachet or bundle of dried lavender blossoms to your stored clothes or linens, or put one in the dryer with your laundry to impart a fresh scent and feeling)

- a natural all-purpose cleaner

- an aromatherapy diffuser

- a mister of rose water or spring water (for a cleansing mist or smudge potion)

If you feel fundamentally unclean in a spiritual or emotional way, and to generally assist with physical or emotional detoxification efforts, you might like to employ lavender essence rather than (or in addition to) the essential oil or dried herb. Alternatively, you might add dried lavender to an herbal tea blend and drink at least a cup daily until you feel sufficiently cleansed.

Divine Alignment

Perhaps "divine alignment" is the best way to summarize all of lavender's endless magical uses. The scent and energy of lavender reminds us of our true divine self and clears the pathways within our life and energy field so that divine, healing, harmonizing, balancing energy can flow in the most ideal way. In addition to all the other magical uses listed in this chapter, the endless number of benefits of this dynamic may include:

- finding and flowing with one's most ideal career and life path

- expressing oneself in a healthy way

- self-esteem and self-love

- healthy sleep patterns

- recognizing one's own divinity

- feeling eternal

- going beyond the illusion of discord

- moving beyond fears and phobias

For this purpose, try employing lavender into rituals designed for the purpose, taking the essence under the tongue or in water, or inhaling the scent in any of the ways recommended in the "clarity" section. You may also add lavender to your bath water in the form of fresh or dried blossoms, essential oil, or flower essence. Growing lavender in your yard also can be an excellent way to align with divine energy.

Harmony and Balance

Mentally, emotionally, spiritually, and physically, lavender promotes harmony and balance. Not only can she can help us find sleep patterns that work for us, she can also help us to be balanced and harmonious with regard to just about anything, including but not limited to the following:

- love and relationships
- sexuality
- work
- family and household
- alcohol and sweets
- general health
- self-expression
- sleep patterns
- energy levels

For any of these purposes, or for balance in general, tune in to your intuition and choose a suggestion that you connect with from the above sections.

Healing

Aromatherapists employ lavender oil to support the healing process of numerous conditions, including (but not limited to):

- acne and other skin conditions (try adding to face wash or toner, adding to a steam facial, or applying neat)
- insect bites and stings (apply directly to skin or add to ointment)
- headaches (apply to temples, diffuse, or waft under nose)
- flu (diffuse)
- asthma (diffuse, anoint temples, anoint chest, or lightly anoint outside of nostrils)
- premenstrual and menstrual challenges (add to carrier oil and gently massage abdomen and lower back, add to bath water, diffuse, or waft under nose)
- constipation (add to carrier oil and gently massage abdomen and lower back, add to bath water, or diffuse)
- irritable bowel syndrome (add to carrier oil and gently massage abdomen and lower back, add to bath water, or diffuse)
- infections (depends on type of infection—apply to skin, diffuse, or drink tea made from dried blossoms)
- addictions (diffuse, anoint temples, or waft under nose)
- depression (diffuse, anoint temples, waft under nose, or add to bath water)

Joy

Lavender's vibration and scent both lend themselves to experiencing a balanced, sustainable, and highly potent level of joy. This can be helpful for treating depression and bipolar disorder, as well as general mood swings or other forms of mood-related challenges. It can also be helpful for any time we'd like to give ourselves an extra shot of joy or turn up the volume on our happiness. For this purpose, diffuse the essential oil, anoint yourself with the essential oil, keep a bottle of the oil with you and waft it under your nose every now and then, or take the flower essence.

Protection

Lavender is often employed in herbal insect repellents, and this physical property is mirrored on the energetic level by shielding our mood from little annoyances and helping us to rise above (or even avoid) the day-to-day hassles that might otherwise bring us down. And, since like attracts like, the scent of lavender can also protect us by keeping our energy clear and positive; that way, we will be likely to attract more of the same. This can be especially helpful for entering challenging work or social environments. For these purposes, try anointing yourself with the oil or even diffusing it in the space if you can. You might also create the following charm.

POSITIVITY CHARM

Cleanse a white quartz crystal by running it under cold water for two minutes, holding it in sunlight for thirty seconds, and burning white sage smoke around it. Then hold it in both hands and charge it with the intention to keep your energy clear and positive. Place it on a small piece of lavender cotton and tie it closed with a small piece of turquoise ribbon. Anoint it with lavender essential oil. Keep it in your pocket or pinned to the inside of your clothes when you traverse challenging situations, and refresh the essential oil periodically (perhaps whenever the scent begins to fade).

Relaxation and Stress Relief

Since stress can pose such a big challenge to every aspect of our happiness and physical health, it's no wonder that lavender is perhaps best known for its powerfully soothing and stress-relieving properties. In fact, according to aromatherapist and author Gabriel Mojay, experiencing the scent of lavender oil can be a helpful treatment for "nervous tension, insomnia, palpitations, and high blood pressure." It's even been said that the scent of lavender can help soothe and quiet wild animals.

For these purposes, try any of the aromatherapeutic suggestions recommended previously. You might also try anointing your pillow with the oil to help you sleep deeply and awake refreshed.

Relationship Healing

Author Scott Cunningham notes that "in North Africa, women used [lavender] to guard against maltreatment from their husbands." Indeed, in contemporary magic, lavender is commonly recommended as an ingredient that can help promote peace within marriages and marriagelike relationships while generally protecting against domestic unrest. (Of course, if the relationship is not for your truest good, magically employing lavender for this sort of intention will be more likely to help precipitate a split.)

Similarly, lavender can help us to shift our personal beliefs about romance so that we can attain the state of mind that is the most likely to attract a harmonious relationship.

Additionally, lavender can help with any sort of relationship healing, such as healing family relationships or relationships with colleagues.

To promote healing in a specific relationship, you might try the following ritual.

RELATIONSHIP HEALING RITUAL

Obtain or draw a small picture of yourself and a separate picture of the other person. (You should both be the only person in each picture.) Be sure that you both appear happy in the pictures, and if they are photographs, be sure that you are both, to the best of your knowledge, *actually* happy in the pictures. Also choose or draw pictures that "click" for you or intuitively feel right for the purpose. Place a fresh lavender blossom (that has been lovingly gathered) between the two pictures, facing them toward each other (sort of like a lavender sandwich). Then gently tie the "sandwich" together with pink satin ribbon and hold it between your hands. Visualize very bright white light coming down from above, entering the crown of your head, going down to your heart, down your arms, and out through your palms and into the bundle. Say:

> *Spirit of lavender, please heal our hearts, minds, and spirits.*
> *Align us with the Divine, align us with each other, align us with love.*

Then completely immerse the picture bundle in a glass or jar filled with dried lavender blossoms as you say:

> *Spirit of lavender, I now release this relationship completely into your wise and loving embrace.*
> *May it be healed and blessed in all directions of time. Thank you.*

Place the glass or jar on your altar or in a special place. You can keep it for as long as you like, but if you are ready to release it (perhaps when your relationship feels sufficiently healed), simply bury the contents near the base of a tree.

Releasing Guilt and Shame

Thanks to author Marina Medici, lavender (along with pine flower essence) has been my "go to" magical ingredient for guilt banishing since I first began practicing magic years ago. And—contrary to the belief of my Catholic grandmother, who famously asked, "Without guilt, how would anything ever get done?"—guilt banishing is an absolute must. While we all feel guilt at times, guilt is not a useful or a natural emotion. It is essentially self-flogging—a dysfunctional and abusive relationship with the self—rather than the much more effective and emotionally healthy pattern of (a) admitting one's mistake or lovingly recognizing one's pattern, (b) grieving over it and releasing it, and (c) constructively moving forward.

Similarly, the "emotion" we call shame is not something that benefits us in any way. It's essentially a response to an illusory perception—namely that we are not beautiful, lovable, exquisite expressions of the Divine.

And lavender can help with both. Try any of the aromatherapeutic or essence remedies suggested above or the following bath ritual.

....

Bath Ritual to Banish Guilt and Shame

During a waning moon, when the moon is in Cancer or Libra, draw a bath. Add one cup Epsom salts, one-half cup sea salt, and one-half cup baking soda. Light a white or off-white soy candle. Then add two handfuls dried lavender blossoms (lightly crushing them between your fingers as you do so) and/or twenty to forty drops lavender essential oil. Hold your hands over the bath water and take some deep breaths. Then visualize very bright white light coming down from above, entering the crown of your head, going down to your heart, down your arms, out through your hands, and into the water. See the water glow with a sphere of very bright white light. Say:

Spirit of lavender, thank you for cleansing me of all guilt and shame!
Thank you for aligning me with the truth of my being, which is divine love.
I now soak in acceptance, I now steep in forgiveness, I now radiate joy.
Thank you!

Keep plenty of fresh drinking water handy to drink as you soak for at least forty minutes and relax deeply.

Releasing Pain Associated with Unrequited Love

Lavender strengthens the physical and spiritual heart while balancing our mind/body/ spirit and aligning us with divine love, self-love, and love in general. In other words, she is a great ally to call on for healing a broken heart or for releasing pain associated with unrequited love. For this purpose, try any of the aromatherapeutic or essence remedies suggested above or employ lavender in a ritual designed for the purpose.

Magical Correspondences

Element: Air
Gender: Female
Planet: Mercury

Lilac

$\mathcal{V}$isiting the Descanso Garden's lilac garden when it's blooming in March and April is one of my most treasured and transcendent pastimes. But even breathing in the fragrance of cut lilac blossoms when they're for sale in front of my local market sends me into a dreamy, mystical, magic-drenched alternate plane of existence.

Indeed, the magic of lilacs is all about the otherworld, the doorway between the worlds, and the perception of things that may normally lurk just out of reach of our conscious awareness. She's also about high romance—not just passion and attraction, but classical-style romance: knight-in-shining-armor, sonnet-composing, sweep-you-off-your-feet romance.

Magical Uses

Chakra Balancing

To balance your energy field and the invisible wheels of light that are present along your spine, spend time in contemplation with blossoming lilac, inhaling the scent as you do so. You might also like to bring fresh lilacs into your space or healing room or employ the essence.

Magical Power

Fresh lilacs, lilac essential oil (rare, but it does exist), or lilac essence can help you slip into the space between the worlds where all magic is possible and enhance your abilities to perceive and work with subtle magical energies.

Passage Between the Worlds

Lilacs in bloom create a doorway of light between this world and the next. This can be useful in a number of ways, such as in the following rite.

DOORWAY OF LIGHT EXORCISM

If you feel that you are living with earthbound entities and you'd like to ask them to leave, place a vase of a few fresh-cut lilacs into each room and area of your home, and light a white candle near each vase (but not so close that it uncomfortably warms the blossoms). Stand in a central location, hold your hands in prayer pose, close your eyes, and envision a very bright doorway of light pervading your entire home. Being mindful of pet and fire safety, leave the house for five to ten minutes. When you return, leave the candles burning as you light a bundle of dried white sage (so that it's smoking, not burning—and be sure to carry a dish to catch any burning embers). Then move slowly but surely in a generally counterclockwise direction through each room and area of your home. Before extinguishing the sage, take a moment to sage your personal energy field. Extinguish the candles. Take all the lilac blossoms outside of the house and place them at the base of a tree, and be sure to take a shower or bath when you're finished.

Peace

Because of lilac's deep alignment with the subtle reality and the real truth of things (and perhaps because she's a member of the olive family), she can help establish peace where there has been long-standing grief, drama, heartache, or strife. If she can withstand the climate, you might plant her in the garden and request that she help establish harmony in the home. You might also place lilac essence in the water supply of any person or group of people who could use these benefits, or incorporate lilac blossoms, essence, or oil into any ritual performed for the purpose of establishing peace.

Psychic Abilities

Surrounding yourself with lilacs or lilac essential oil or taking the essence can enhance and reveal your psychic abilities, especially your abilities to perceive and communicate with the spirit world. You might also try conversing with a blooming lilac and requesting that she infuse you with her ability to see into the depths and into the true nature of things.

Romance

Delicious romantic adventures—at least a few of them—are an indispensable component of a magically and spiritually balanced life. If it's time for you to conjure up a bit of dreamy and dizzying romantic enchantment, incorporating lilacs into your magical workings is an excellent idea. For example, you might make a simple yet potent love potion by placing six drops lilac essential oil in a bottle of red wine and sharing it with a partner or love interest.

Sweet Spirit Summoning

To summon sweet and beneficent spirits into your space or to communicate with deceased loved ones, diffuse lilac essential oil or place fresh lilacs on your altar after dark and by candlelight. Relax, close your eyes, and inhale the fragrance by taking some deep breaths. Visualize the room filled with bright white light. Request an audience with your loved one or, alternately, request that sweet and beneficent spirits enter to protect you and your home and lend their wisdom and beautiful energetic essence. If you're requesting an audience with a loved one, continue to relax and allow your mind to be open to their presence.

Magical Correspondences

Element: Water

Gender: Female

Planet: Venus

*A*ligned with numerous goddesses, angels, and saints (including Quan Yin, Mother Mary, Venus, Archangel Gabriel, and Saint Anthony), and a traditional symbol of purity and protection, the lily just may be a visual manifestation of divine energy. With her strong and sweet fragrance, her perfect magical blend of delicate and bold, and her breathtaking appearance, she is a worthy representative of the heavenly realm.

Please be advised: as it says on a plaque at my vet's office, lilies kill cats! So if you live with one or more felines, you might want to find another ingredient or at least exercise extreme caution when working with lilies (or, to play it especially safe, employ the flower essence). Still, if you make it yourself, be extra careful and be sure you're in a cat-free zone.

Magical Uses

Angel Invocation

Lilies are especially aligned with the angelic realm: in fact, their energy might be thought of as one and the same. If you'd like to bring more angelic energy into your life, spend time with lilies, add lilies to an altar dedicated to the angels, or work with the flower essence.

Divine Assistance

In fact, lilies are not just aligned with angels but also with the entirety of the divine and heavenly realm—and especially divine energy that is both strong and feminine (see "goddess alignment" later in this entry.) And since, in truth, we are all fountains of the same divine radiance, the more we align with the divine realm, the truer, more authentic, and more harmonious our lives become. To receive these benefits, spend time with lilies, add lilies to an altar dedicated to the angels, or work with the flower essence.

Divine Love

If one were to attempt to describe divine energy, one word in the English language could be used more accurately for this purpose than any of the rest, and that word is *love*. Of course, the word love is also used in a lot of other ways, including "I love that restaurant" or "How's your love life?" But when we want to align more closely with the truest and most potent meaning of the word—i.e., divine love—every aspect of our life benefits, including all our relationships.

Divine Beauty

If it's your magical intention to radiate beauty that is so potent, pure, and goddesslike that you intimidate some people, lily is very likely the ingredient for you. To illustrate what I mean, imagine for a moment that Isis or Venus walked into a bar or nightclub: while she would doubtless be the most beautiful woman there, she wouldn't exactly inspire boldness in potential suitors. On the other hand, if someone were to approach her, there's a pretty good chance he'd be on the level. (And if not, she'd know it in a heartbeat.) But the point is, we don't always want to be beautiful just so that we can attract pick-up lines: perhaps we're preparing for our wedding or a special belly-dance performance or we're just ready to exude goddesslike beauty as a matter of course. In any case, to awaken your goddesslike beauty, work lily into your magic, take lily essence, surround yourself with lily blossoms, or create the lotion potion below.

"Beauty of the Goddess" Lotion Potion

Mix six drops stargazer, oriental, or Asiatic lily essence into a bottle of unscented lotion. Also add twenty drops ylang ylang essential oil and ten drops jasmine essential oil. Shake well. Hold in both hands, call on Isis or Venus, and ask her to bless the lotion with her blindingly beautiful divine essence. Apply after bathing or showering anytime you'd like to exude intense, mesmerizing, and, yes, intimidating beauty.

Entity Clearing and Protection

Because lilies are so aligned with the divine realm (like lilacs), they can create a doorway of light to help wayward spirits and earthbound entities cross over. For those stubborn spirits who want to stay in this realm, lilies can help move them out of the space and get them out of our hair. And lilies can also help protect spaces by preventing entities from entering in the first place. To experience these benefits, employ lilies in your own space-clearing rituals or try either of the practices below.

Stargazer Clearing Spray

If you live, work, or spend a lot of time in a place where you feel earthbound entities seem to gather and linger, you might want to add forty drops stargazer lily essence to a mister of rose water. Mist the space as necessary to evacuate the unwanted guests and lighten the energy.

Tiger Lily Protection

Author Judika Illes, in *The Element Encyclopedia of 5000 Spells*, suggests planting tiger lilies near windows and doors to prevent ghosts (a.k.a. earthbound entities) from entering the space.

Goddess Alignment

Anytime you'd like to invoke or align with the energy of the divine feminine, you might like to employ the magic of lilies. For example, you could place a bouquet on a goddess altar, add lily essence to your water, or create a "goddess garden" by planting lilies and other goddess-invoking plants (such as lavender and rosemary) near a statue of a particularly bold, beautiful goddess of your choice.

Harmony and Ease

Lily's very potent alignment with divine energy and assistance means that she can help smooth out life's little difficulties and infuse our lives with feelings of harmony and ease. So if you've been feeling harried, harassed, overwhelmed, or annoyed by life in general, try adding four or six drops lily essence to your drinking water in the morning immediately upon awakening. To help with clutter clearing (another way to bring in more harmony and ease), mist the space with rose water into which you've added six drops lily essence.

Legal Success

Provided you're in the right, lily's divine powers can help you realize swift and harmonious success in situations related to fairness and justice, such as court battles, neighbor or coworker disputes, and insurance claims. Work dried lily or lily essence into charms and rituals designed for the purpose, or perform the following ritual.

Lily Immersion Ritual and Charm for Legal Success

The night before the case, add forty drops lily essence to your bath water and soak for at least forty minutes. Before bed, add four drops lily essence to a cup of chamomile tea, sweeten to taste, and drink. In the morning, wake up before sunrise and drink a cup of coffee or tea containing four drops lily essence. As the sun is rising, place part of a fresh lily blossom in a small red flannel bag, along with a pyrite crystal and two cloves of star anise. Tie closed with hemp twine. Hold it in both hands and say:

I now invoke the swift and powerful assistance of the divine and
heavenly realms. Great Goddess Isis, queen of heaven, I call on you.
Thank you for staying with me and granting me success.

Safety-pin it to the inside of your clothes, ideally near your heart or belly. Bring a bottle of water with you to court containing four drops lily essence to sip.

Safe and Harmonious Travel

As you may imagine, lily's divine alignment and powers of swiftness and ease make her a wonderful ingredient for magic relating to travel. For example, if you'd like to conjure up a delightful trip to a certain locale, you might place a picture of that locale on your altar and put a bouquet of fresh lily blossoms next to it as you say a simple prayer invoking the assistance of Isis, angels, or simply the "realm of heaven." To help ensure a safe and harmonious voyage, add two drops lily essence to your coffee or tea the morning of the trip.

Magical Correspondences

Element: Water
Gender: Female
Planet: Venus

Lupine

With a vibration that is hearty yet whimsical and earthy yet other-worldly, and an essence that is aligned with both the sun and the water element, the divinely beautiful lupine is a bridge and a doorway between the realms.

Magical Uses

Dog Healing and Balancing

Lupine's name comes from the Latin word *lupinus*, which means "wolf." Indeed, the lupine's energy is aligned with the canine species, and the flower can be a lovely magical ally when it's your intention to support the emotional or physical healing of your furry best friend. Lupine also can be used to help your dog adjust to a big change, such as a new home or family member. For any of these purposes, you might plant lupine in your yard, add four to six drops lupine essence to a mister of spring water and mist the inside of your home, or try adding a single drop of the essence to your dog companion's water bowl each time you replace it.

Faeries

Especially when found in nature, lupine is a living portal into the world of faeries and plant spirits. To connect with these beings in a conscious way, you might try spending time in quiet contemplation with the plant or taking the essence.

Imagination

In the Victorian language of flowers, lupine represented "imagination," and it's no wonder: he's as whimsical as the day is long. For this reason, he can be a valuable ally when your magical intention involves creativity, healing your inner child, or helping your actual child (or children) feel emotionally relaxed and free. To receive these benefits, try magically working with him in any safe way you feel guided.

Otherworld Communication

According to author Diana Wells, "Those seeking to communicate with the dead at the Oracle of Epiros were fed a diet of lupine seeds, which induce a state of intoxication, perhaps making such communication more accessible." While I don't recommend intoxicating yourself with lupine seeds, I do recommend spending time in quiet contemplation with blossoming lupine while consciously opening your mind to the otherworld and the spirits therein. Similarly, you might drink a glass of water into which you've added four to six drops lupine essence before your mediumship efforts, or you might try the following.

....

LUPINE GAZING BOWL FOR OTHERWORLD COMMUNICATION

At midnight when the moon is dark, light a white or off-white soy candle in the pitch blackness (indoors or out, as weather permits and as you feel guided). Pour well water or spring water into a glass bowl and add three drops lupine essence. Also place three drops lupine essence under your tongue. Relax deeply as you close your eyes and take some deep breaths. When you feel centered and calm, visualize a sphere of very bright white light around yourself and say:

I now call on Archangel Michael and his band of mercy
(or whomever you usually call on for the purpose) to watch over me and protect me.

Then open your eyes, hold your hands over the water, and say:

Within this bowl with eyes of night
Beyond the day, beyond the light
I see into the other world.

Let your eyes go out of focus as you gaze at the water, and allow it to be a portal to the world of the spirits.

Magical Correspondences

 Element: Water
Gender: Male
Planet: Sun

Magnolia

*T*he wise and beautiful magnolia is so ancient that she actually predates bees. Indeed, gazing at a magnolia blossom awakens a primal connection to the earth and one's spiritual lineage.

Magical Uses

Awakening Ancient Wisdom

Deep within us, in our genetic memory and in our buried memories of old lifetimes, we hold ancient wisdom. Magnolia can help us remember this wisdom and allow it to be reborn into our present incarnation.

Pollinated by beetles, her symbolism of rebirth appears twice over: she is herself an ancient being alive and well in modern times, thanks to the continued attentions of the beetle, itself an ancient Egyptian representation of rebirth.

To help reactivate your ancient magical wisdom and power, you might visit a flowering magnolia and silently commune with her.

Fidelity

Traditionally, magnolia has been magically employed to help ensure one's partner's fidelity. In general, it's probably not a good sign if you're feeling so mistrustful of your partner that you feel it necessary to take magical measures to ensure his or her fidelity. Still, if we get a little insecure sometimes, who can blame us? The following ritual will help put your mind at ease.

"Shroud of Fidelity" Visualization

First, at any time in your life (not necessarily right before you perform the visualization), make friends with a blossoming magnolia tree. In other words, spend some quiet time with her and let her wisdom sink into your bones. Commune. Breathe. Become one. When this feels complete, thank her for her alliance and offer her a little gift such as a bottle of ale or a small white quartz crystal. Then, whenever you feel that little tug of jealousy, mistrust, or worry, no matter where you are, simply call your botanical ally to mind. Call your partner to mind as well and envision him or her completely encompassed in one of magnolia's blossoms. Deep in your heart, know that for the next twenty-four hours, they will not stray. (Or, if they do, you will be alerted to the truth.)

Goddess Energy

Femininity is not always gentle or demure. In fact, femininity also has a face that is strong and intense. Magnolia embodies this fiercer face of femininity and aligns us with the powerful goddess energy that already dwells within.

This can be especially helpful for women who are feeling uncomfortable about their age, as magnolia can show us the blinding radiance of our own true nature and help us claim our power and recognize our continuously flowering beauty.

To receive these benefits, visit a flowering magnolia. Relax and quiet your mind, focusing on the blossoms and the tree. Really get a feeling for her personality and her unique brand of potency and power. Notice how she is like a woman who is blindingly beautiful at any age because of the spirituality and sure-footed grace that shines through her. Then recognize this energy within yourself. See that it's already there, and allow its radiance to brighten until you can feel it shining out of you in equal measure.

Alternatively, work with the essence.

Independence and Personal Power

Because magnolia possesses the goddess energy described above, she can help us with issues related to independence and personal power. For example, you might create an "altar to independence" or "altar to personal power" in your home. Choose a small table or shelf and spread an attractive cloth over it. Place a small statue or picture of a powerful goddess, such as Isis or Hecate, in the center as a focal point. Then place a single magnolia blossom in water and add it to the altar, making sure to have picked it with reverence and gratitude. You might also add other items such as crystals, candles, incense, affirmations, or victorious-looking photos of yourself. (Just make sure the candles don't singe or uncomfortably heat up the flower.)

Wonderment and Awe

As children, something as simple as a butterfly can fill us with exhilaration and so much joy we can hardly contain ourselves. But as adults, this wonderment can sometimes seem to falter. Sometimes we can even get so jaded or numb that we plunge into depression and feel completely disconnected from our inspiration.

As a plant that's been around for millions of years and always finds it in her heart to burst forth in fragrant bloom once again every single spring, magnolia can help us refresh the sense of childlike awe that is our emotional, spiritual, and creative lifeblood.

To reap these benefits, try this:

WONDERMENT CHARM

Bring two glass bottles of chilled sparkling mineral water and a pair of scissors or shears to a blossoming magnolia tree. Place everything on the ground except one bottle of water. Hold it in both hands and mentally charge it with white light, then pour it around the base of the tree as you silently request that the tree help you remember your sense of childlike wonderment and awe. Hold the other bottle in both hands and mentally charge it with white light. Sit beneath the tree and slowly drink it as you relax, quiet your mind, and receive an infusion of energetic healing from the tree. (It doesn't matter if you can feel this or not—it is happening!) Then silently let the tree know you're about to gather one of her blossoms, and send her gratitude and love. Gently snip the first blossom that calls to you, and bring it home. Once you're home, tie it up with hemp twine in bright pink satin, along with a lepidolite crystal (that has been cleansed in sunlight, running water, and/or sage smoke) and a fresh sprig of mint. Place it or hang it so that it's a few feet above your head as you sleep. After one moon cycle, or when your joy returns, take the charm back to the tree, open it up, and leave its contents at the tree's base. Dispose of the satin and twine.

Magical Correspondences

Element: Earth
Gender: Female
Planet: Venus

Manuka (New Zealand Tea Tree)

*A*lthough it's a totally different plant, like the Australian tea tree (from which tea tree oil is obtained), it's said that New Zealand tea tree, or manuka, earned its moniker when Captain James Cook used its leaves to make a tealike drink for his crew. The two plants are also aligned when it comes to their antifungal and antibacterial properties. However, while the two are both used medicinally, manuka is more commonly used for decorative purposes as well.

Magical Uses

Body Chemistry

Manuka honey has been medicinally employed to help heal bacterial and fungal infections. Similarly, the vibration of manuka blossoms can help support healing related to yeast and bacterial infections, as well as skin conditions such as acne and dandruff. In addition to your other natural healing efforts (such as taking probiotics for yeast infections or applying Australian tea tree oil to acne or skin infections), try taking the essence or carrying a charm such as the following.

CHARM TO SUPPORT HEALTHY BODY CHEMISTRY

Dry five manuka blossoms in the sun. Then place them on a small square of natural-colored, natural-fiber cloth. Add an aquamarine crystal and a clove of garlic (be sure to empower both in sunlight first). Tie closed with hemp twine. Hold the charm in both hands and envision it glowing with very bright golden-white light. Say:

Perfect balance, perfect healing, perfect clarity.
I am safe, I am empowered, I am clean, and all is well.

Keep it close to your skin (perhaps safety-pinning it under your clothes) until the healing you desire has occurred.

Emerging from "Desert Periods"

A desert period might be defined as a time when we don't feel connected to our inspiration, our happiness, or our natural flow of good fortune and luck. Because desert periods are usually the result of an emotional block of some sort (created subconsciously as a method of shielding us from pain), manuka can help, as she's an expert at helping dissolve blocks of this sort, which helps reconnect us with our inner reserves of energy and joy. For this purpose, take five drops manuka essence under the tongue once per day, plant manuka in your yard, spend time around a blossoming manuka, or create a charm with manuka blossom crafted with this intention in mind.

Emotional Detoxification

Even painful emotions like sadness and grief are not toxic when they are pure. But feelings such as guilt, blame, self-punishment, self-loathing, and denial are tainted by the ego and therefore are *not* pure. In fact, they are not really feelings at all but externally imposed concepts that are not in alignment with our true identity, which is love. In other words, they seemingly disconnect us from the eternal flow of love that is our true nature. This seeming disconnection is unnatural and, just like harmful chemicals sprayed in the garden, feels harmful and toxic.

Of course, since the human experience is characterized by ego (or the illusion of separation), we all have these feelings at one time or another. The trick is not to fight them or give in to them but simply to recognize that they are based on illusion and have nothing to do with the truth of your being, which is love. This is what leads to emotional detoxification.

For help with this process, try spending time with the plant, taking the essence, or working fresh blossoms into a charm.

Holistic Balance

Whether it's your priorities, your schedule, your physical health, your state of mind, or all of the above, maybe you just plain old feel "out of whack." If this is the case, manuka can work on the vibrational level to help realign you in a way that feels nourishing, positive, and balanced in all ways. For example, you might try placing five fresh manuka blossoms in your bath water, along with ten drops Bach Rescue Remedy, one moss agate crystal, and one-half cup sea salt. Then soak for at least forty minutes.

Magical Correspondences

Element: Air
Gender: Female
Planet: Mercury

Marigold (*Calendula*)

The name *marigold* means "Mary's gold," and many believe that it was coined because the flower was used to adorn churches during the Middle Ages. Like early morning or late fall sunlight, you'll find that his energy can be at once soft and powerful or gentle and searing. Simply looking at his glowing, beneficent, sunshiny face is an immediate mood lifter and spiritual boost.

This entry refers to the marigold genus *Calendula*, or pot marigold. For information on *Tagetes*, or common marigold, please see the next entry.

Magical Uses

Cleansing and Detoxification

Both physically and metaphysically, calendula is an excellent cleanser and detoxifier. On the physical level, many herbalists recommend drinking calendula tea or tincture to help clear toxins, viruses, bacteria, and infections from the skin, liver, and gallbladder. The tea is also recommended to help clear fungus from the body and to help establish a healthy internal balance. Herbalist and author Jeanne Rose suggests using an infusion of calendula as a skin wash to treat eyes, irritated skin, and diaper rash.

On the metaphysical (magical) level, calendula can help clear energetic toxins stemming from our own thoughts and feelings, the thoughts and feelings of others, long-standing emotional or family issues, spending time in challenging environments, and so on. Like strong desert sunlight evaporating and purifying the lingering remains of a stagnant puddle, he does this in a straightforward and uncompromising manner. For this purpose, you might try drinking calendula tea or taking the essence.

Because everything is connected, calendula's physical and metaphysical detoxifying properties each have the potential to holistically bolster the other's considerable effects.

Detoxification Bath Ritual

If you're drawn to calendula and feel it's high time to clear toxins from your mind, body, spirit, emotions, and energy field, perform this bath ritual on a Sunday during the waning moon. Gather at least one full cup of fresh or dried calendula petals and/or blossoms, one tea bag or tea ball full of dried calendula blossoms, a good supply of drinking water, a white or neutral soy candle, and one cup sea salt. Place the tea ball or tea bag filled with dried blossoms in a mug and pour just-boiled water over it. Cover and let steep as you place the candle, salt, and drinking water near the bathtub and draw a warm bath. When the tea has steeped for at least ten minutes, remove the ball or bag and set the mug near the bathtub as well.

Close the bathroom door and light the candle. Add the sea salt to the bath and swish around until dissolved. Strew the cup of flowers or petals over the top of the water. Hold your hands over the water, take some deep breaths, and direct very bright light into the water as you say:

> *Great Goddess and Spirit of the Sun, please infuse this*
> *water with the powers of purification.*

Direct your palms toward your drinking water and repeat. Now direct your palms toward the mug of tea and say:

> *Great Goddess and Spirit of the Sun, please infuse this tea with the*
> *powers of purification. Thank you, thank you, thank you. Blessed be.*

Soak for at least forty minutes. As you soak, drink the entire cup of tea and a generous yet sensible portion of the drinking water. Once may be enough, but for more deep-seated or long-standing issues, you may like to repeat this ritual every Sunday of the waning moon (and following waning moons) until you feel sufficiently detoxified. (Optional: add gold essence or calendula flower essence to the bath water and drinking water.)

Happiness

If I had to choose one flower that utterly epitomized the essence of happiness, I might choose calendula. So if your magical objective includes happiness, you might want to consider working calendula into the mix. For example:

Happy Relationship Charm

Cleanse two small rose quartz hearts in a clear, moving body of water. Then, with two ribbons—one red and one pink—tie them into a piece of sunshiny yellow flannel with a generous pinch of dried calendula. Hold it in both hands and say:

Our hearts are joyful
We are bathed in love and light.

Visualize/imagine/feel your charm swirling with bright sunshine and pink light; then, in your mind's eye, see yourself and your partner embracing and being filled with and surrounded by this same light. When this feels complete, open your eyes and place the charm in your shared bedroom.

Health and Healing

Calendula's vibration generally supports health, healing, and overall well-being. For example, in addition to the healing properties listed in the previous "cleansing and detoxification" section, calendula tea or tincture can help soothe and heal the digestive system, reduce menstrual pain, and regulate menstrual bleeding.

Magically speaking, a pot of growing calendula flowers can help speed and support all forms of physical healing when placed in the patient's room. Planting calendula flowers in your yard or in pots can help bolster the overall healing energy of your home. Taking calendula essence, drinking calendula tea, or adding calendula essence to a mister of water and misting the space can also enhance the body's healing process. You might use calendula blossoms in magic worked for the purpose of healing as well.

If you're a magical practitioner of the poppet-making variety, you may already know that stuffing a healing poppet with dried calendula blossoms can be an excellent idea.

Healing Depression

Because depression usually harbors deep issues that demand recognition and sorting out, I don't suggest calendula as an initial magical depression remedy—for that I suggest something with more of a complex and radical dynamic such as freesia or lantana—but I do suggest calendula as a follow-up remedy to help clear residual clouds and establish new patterns of positivity and balance. For this purpose, spend time with the blossom or take the essence. You might also like to try the detoxification bath ritual on page 245.

Skin Healing

Calendula can work on both physical and vibrational levels to bring our bodies and minds into the type of balance that facilitates clear and healthy skin. In addition to the skin-healing properties and practices above, for the purpose of healing or clearing the skin, you might:

- take two to three drops calendula essence under the tongue two to three times a day
- drink calendula tea daily

- bathe your face in steam from hot water into which you've added dried calendula blossoms
- ask a calendula blossom what changes you can make to your diet or lifestyle to help support your skin-healing objectives
- create or find an ointment or skin treatment containing calendula
- otherwise work calendula blossoms into magic designed for the purpose

Magical Correspondences

Element: Fire

Gender: Male

Planet: Sun

Marigold (*Tagetes*)

agetes, or common marigold (a native to Central America and Mexico), while similar to its European counterpart *Calendula*, has a more pungent and complex vibrational profile.

It's said that the Aztecs used the marigold for spiritual and medicinal purposes, and even to this day he's featured prominently in *Dia de los Muertos* (Day of the Dead) celebrations. He's become similarly popular in India and Tibet.

This entry refers to the marigold genus *Tagetes*, or common marigold. For information on *Calendula*, or pot marigold, please see the previous entry.

Magical Uses

Death and Rebirth

In both India and South America, the marigold is associated with death and rebirth. During *Dia de los Muertos* celebrations in South America and throughout the world, marigold helps pay homage to the lingering aliveness of the spirits of the dead by appearing on countless skull-and-skeleton-adorned altars. When you consider the fact that his vibrational wisdom teaches about the enduring nature of our souls, the vibrant aliveness of our bodies, and life's inevitable continuity, this seems perfectly appropriate.

Indeed, for a number of reasons, marigold is a wonderful addition to an altar or ritual constructed for the purpose of honoring one or more deceased loved ones. These reasons include:

- He nourishes the spiritual journey of the deceased loved one(s) and lends movement, vitality, and flow to the cycle of death and rebirth.

- He helps soothe and comfort the living by reminding us of (and aligning us with) the endless cycle of death and rebirth.

- He opens the door between the worlds so that the nonphysical more powerfully translates to the physical and the physical more powerfully translates to the nonphysical. In other words, he facilitates a sense of connection between the living and the dead.

If you're going through a period of rebirth and transformation, if you'd like to more easily perceive the land beyond the living, or if you'd like to help support your grieving process, try working marigold into your magic.

Happiness

If it seems strange that a flower associated with death should also be associated with happiness, consider Halloween. This is the time of year when the veil between the worlds is said to be the thinnest, and it's no coincidence that it's also the time, from a cultural standpoint, that we seem to feel most comfortable with death. Our closeness to the other side allows us to glimpse the truth: that there is no end to life but only changes of costume and an endless game of hide and go "boo." We then (temporarily and figuratively) treat the entire process of life—but most notably death—as a game and as something associated with sweetness and fun.

Similarly, if we feel down and out, uncomfortable with the inevitability of our own death, or overwhelmed by the seeming seriousness of it all, marigold can help us to gain a truer perspective about the nature of life and death. He injects us with a boost of vitality, hope, and awareness of our eternal nature, which brings us back to our natural state of happiness.

Heart Healing

In his *Encyclopedia of Magical Herbs*, Scott Cunningham asserts that "marigolds, picked at noon when the sun is at its hottest and strongest, will strengthen and comfort the heart." In my opinion, this applies more to the *Tagetes*, or common marigold, than to the *Calendula*. (Although I'm sure either would be powerful if gathered with intention and with a strong, respectful connection to the energy of the blossom.) This is because the *Tagetes* marigold has a more potent, solid, dynamic vibration, which has the potential to lend support to the heart from a number of angles simultaneously. With Cunningham's suggestion in mind, if healing from grief or a broken heart is your magical intention, you might try the following charm.

HEART-HEALING CHARM

On a bright, sunny day without a cloud in the sky, when the moon is full (or up to few days before), a few minutes before noon, gently and lovingly tune in to a marigold blossom that is bathed in full sunlight. Take some deep breaths, relax, and have a heart-to-heart with the plant, letting him know exactly what you'd like help with. Allow yourself to receive any guidance he may offer at this time, and then, when you feel ready, ask if it's okay for you to gather one of his blossoms. When you get the okay, gently place a piece of red cotton flannel around the blossom and snip with scissors or shears. On your altar or another safe indoor space, spread the flannel out with the blossom on top, place a white quartz point (cleansed in running water and/or white sage smoke) next to the blossom. After one full moon cycle—when the moon again reaches full—tie the dried blossom and the quartz in the flannel using a piece of hemp twine or green ribbon. Using a safety pin, keep the charm on the inside of your clothes, next to your heart, until your heart feels sufficiently healed.

Protection

While marigolds facilitate a connection between the seen and unseen realms, they are excellent gatekeepers and powerfully dissuade unsavory entities and energetic conditions from coming through or hanging around. For this purpose, you might try planting marigolds in your front yard or hanging garlands on or above the doors. By the same token, the blossoms or petals (fresh or dried), when placed in the bedroom, help prevent bad dreams and keep you safe while you sleep.

If you're a medium or are studying mediumship, keeping a pot of marigolds in the room or taking two to three drops marigold essence in water can help you establish good boundaries while keeping your doors of perception open to the kinds of spirits you'd most like to chat with.

Success

Marigold's robust positivity, along with his alignment with positive spirits from the otherworld, can help stack the odds in your favor when it comes to things like court cases, job interviews, and other situations that might benefit from a dose of magical nepotism.

For this purpose, carry the fresh blossom in your pocket (after tuning in, asking for help, and lovingly gathering it), add the fresh blossoms or essence to your bath water, work with the essence, or otherwise magically employ *Tagetes* as you feel guided.

Vitality

Marigolds don't just symbolize rebirth as it pertains to those who have transitioned out of this world: they also symbolize and help manifest our own inner rebirth and a return of vitality after a period of feeling tired, drained, or otherwise weakened. For this purpose, plant marigolds in your yard or in pots, incorporate them into magic designed for the purpose, add them to your bath water, or take the essence. You might consider coupling marigold with pyrite (a mineral) for an especially vital magical punch.

Walking Between the Worlds

Marigold can help us permeate the veil between this realm and the spirit realm. He can also help establish positive boundaries so that we can traverse the otherworld with a sense of safety and attract positive spirits and experiences.

Magical Correspondences

Element: Fire

Gender: Male

Planets: Sun, Saturn

Morning Glory

This divine climbing plant has quite a magical résumé. In fact, it's said that Iroquois healers respected her power so much that even touching her was done with great care. Additionally, she's been employed by a number of Native American tribes—and, later, Spanish and European settlers—to receive visions and heal a variety of physical ills.

Still, due to her high level of toxicity, I don't recommend consuming any part of the plant other than her blossom's delicate vibration preserved in a very safely and expertly formulated essence. It's even said that her toxic elements can enter through your skin if you're doing a lot of barehanded pruning, so be sure to wear gloves!

Magical Uses
Awakening to the Magic of Life

Just as morning glory is quick to lift her face to greet each new day, she can help us open up to the magic of life like a blossom in the sun. Like a shaman, she also dwells between the worlds of form and spirit, and she can help us see behind the veil of time and the everyday world and gaze into the heart of the eternal.

To receive these benefits, visit a blossoming morning glory in the morning (while her blossoms are open). Sit or stand quietly, tune in to her energy, then silently request that she help you awaken to the magic of life. When you feel her assent to your request, gratefully blow her three kisses and offer her a bottle of fresh spring or well water by pouring it near her base. Tune in to her for a few moments more, thank her deeply, and then go on your magical way. Alternatively or additionally, starting on a new moon, take three drops morning glory essence under the tongue as the sun rises. After you do so, say "I am awake to the magic of life" three times. Repeat every day until the next new moon.

Clarity and Simplicity

When the hustle and bustle of everyday challenges crowd our consciousness, making us feel harried, overwhelmed, and like everything is a big old complicated mess, morning glory can help. She boils things down for us, reminding us that really, when it comes right down to it, how much money we have doesn't matter. Neither does keeping up with the Joneses or keeping the car spotlessly clean or making the perfect Thanksgiving dinner. She reminds us that all that matters is love, and that all that is real is this moment. In truth, there is no past, no future, no scoreboard, and no struggle. This simplifies everything and helps us to feel streamlined, joyful, and energized.

To align with this aspect of morning glory's wisdom, sit in front of a blossoming morning glory in the morning (while she is open). Since there will likely be dew on the ground, you might want to bring a towel or small camping chair. Sit with your spine straight, close your eyes, and relax as you consciously begin to merge with her beautiful, simple energy. When you feel aligned with her, with your eyes still closed, converse with her silently by saying something on your mind, such as:

> Morning glory, please help me to remember what is important and
> let go of what isn't. Please help me to come in to the present moment
> and to experience joyful simplicity in every area of my life. Thank you.

Another way to align with this wisdom (which you may do concurrently or individually) is to take three drops morning glory essence in a small glass of water as the sun rises, starting at a full moon and continuing until the following new moon.

Happiness and Harmony

Scott Cunningham states that "grown in the garden, blue morning glories bring peace and happiness." Indeed, if you consider all the other aspects of her wisdom stated in this chapter, happiness would be a natural side effect of having her around—particularly the blue ones, as their rich, velvety color is especially suited to awakening our personal divinity and bringing nourishment and balance to the soul.

Taking three drops morning glory essence under the tongue or in water as the sun is rising can also help confer happiness and harmony. (A blue variety would be exceptionally powerful for this purpose.) Repeat until you feel these energies have been sufficiently absorbed into your energy field, perhaps for one moon cycle.

Intuition and Divine Guidance

Blue morning glories resonate with the brow chakra, the seat of intuition, while the purple and white varieties resonate with the crown chakra, where our personal energy merges with the energy of the Divine. Magically employ them individually, according to your needs. An essence, essence potion, or charm incorporating one or more blossoms representing each of these two chakras (blue and purple/white) would be especially powerful for awakening intuition and aligning one with divine guidance.

Receptivity

Receptivity is an energy, or aspect, that is important to success in a number of life areas. For example, in order to experience harmonious relationships, we must be able to receive love and support. And in order to experience abundance, we must be able to receive opportunities and blessings. So if you feel that you have been blocking your natural flow of blessings by being all give and no receive, morning glory can help. For this purpose, on the evening of a full moon, you might try adding forty drops morning glory essence to your bath water, along with one cup sea salt and a moonstone. By candlelight, soak for at least forty minutes, drinking plenty of fresh water as you do so.

You may also (or instead) take three drops morning glory essence under the tongue before bed every night from the full moon to the new; as you close your eyes, envision a morning glory and consciously draw her energy into your personal energy field. Then think or say:

I am receptive to blessings. I am receptive to opportunities.
I am receptive to abundance. I am receptive to love.

Relaxation

When we simplify, harmonize, and align with the Divine, deep, natural relaxation is a natural result. Our stress is soothed, and we feel that we can relax into the moment and into the arms of the Divine. This is why morning glory can help with stress relief and sleep. For this purpose, try any of the aforementioned recommendations or simply drink a cup of chamomile, kava, or valerian tea (perhaps before bed or after work) into which you've added three drops morning glory essence.

Magical Correspondences

Element: Water
Gender: Female
Planet: Moon

Narcissus

*I*t's hard to think of a happier or more blissful flower than the narcissus, also commonly known as the daffodil. Like the gentle warmth of early spring sunshine, he awakens joy, enhances positive energy, and thaws out sorrow.

Magical Uses

Connection to the Otherworld

Narcissus, like lilac, opens the doorway of light between the physical realm and the otherworld. However, while lilac is more about the connection between us and our deceased loved ones, narcissus is more about life, springtime, rebirth, and the beneficent beings of light associated with these energies, such as angels and faeries.

Freedom from the Past

If we have negative or challenging emotions associated with the past, it's important that we acknowledge them and feel them fully. Still, at some point we must heal them and let them go so that they don't continue to taint our present and future moments. Narcissus can help us do this by bringing us into the present moment, aligning us with self-love and perfect emotional support, and enlisting the help of divine beings of sweetness and light to guide us and comfort us in exactly the ways that are most needed.

PAST-RELEASING RITUAL

If you're ready to heal your grief, anger, or other challenging emotions and let the past go so that you can embrace and enjoy the present as fully as possible, get a small glass bottle of blessed water, hold it in both hands, call on the God/dess to bless it, and imagine it filled with golden-white, divine light. Bring it to a blossoming narcissus on a sunny morning during the waning moon. Get comfortable (whether sitting or standing), consciously relax your muscles, take some deep breaths, and tune in. Feel your feelings as fully as you can, and then ask the blossoms to help you release and heal from the past so that you can move on. Feel yourself surrounded and blessed by the golden, sunshiny energy of the blossoms. Enter into this energy and let it permeate and shift your awareness. Then offer the blessed water to the plant by pouring it around the roots. Thank the plant and go on your merry way.

Present-Moment Awareness

Simply by inhaling narcissus's sweet scent and sitting with his powerful energy, we can begin to release excess thinking about the past and future and to realign with the present moment, which—in actuality—is the only moment there truly is. So if you're feeling harried, worried, scattered, or simply not present, take a time-out with a narcissus blossom or two and refresh your connection with the here and now.

Reclaiming Personal Power

If for any reason you've been feeling controlled, beaten down, or drained by others or life in general, narcissus can give you an infusion of self-love that will help you reclaim your personal power and free yourself from the seeming control other people and conditions have over you.

Taking two to three drops narcissus or daffodil flower essence under the tongue or in your water bottle daily can help with this. So can the following ritual.

"Reclaim Your Power" Ritual

On a sunny morning when the moon is between new and full, visit a blossoming narcissus plant or plants while holding two similarly sized white quartz crystal points. (Be sure to cleanse them first in cold running water or white sage smoke.) Bathe the crystals in sunlight for about one minute. Then hold them gently, one in each hand. Relax, take some deep breaths, and begin to observe and tune in to the blossoms. When you feel ready, conjure up the feelings of self-mastery and calm empowerment that you'd like to experience as best as you can. Feel this state of being as if it's already 100 percent true for you, and allow any associated pictures or situations to arise in your consciousness. Next, quiet your mind and allow yourself to receive wordless support and encouragement from the blossoms. When this feels complete, bury or place one of the crystal points next to the base of the blossoming plant(s). Keep the other one with you, and sleep with it near your head until the following new moon.

Self-Love

Self-love is perhaps narcissus's specialty. Simply spending time around narcissus blossoms imparts the wisdom of "Of course I love myself! What's not to love?" But if self-love is a deep and long-standing issue for you, or if you're encountering special challenges in this area in any way, plant narcissus in your garden or try taking the essence regularly for around a month or until the issue is resolved.

If this is coupled with being overly concerned about perfection or cleanliness, also consider concurrently taking crabapple essence.

Spiritual Refreshment

If your spirit could use a pick-me-up, connect with blossoming narcissus flowers to discover the refreshment you seek. If you simply relax and tune in after inhaling his fresh fragrance, you'll receive a wordless, organic sermon on the sweetness and magic of life. The floodgates to the miraculous will be lifted for you, and beings of light and love will whisper messages of hope and renewal from just beyond the veil. Even if you aren't consciously aware of it, it is happening.

Romantic Love

Self-love is the number one prerequisite to drawing and maintaining healthy, harmonious, and passionate romantic love. As such, narcissus naturally helps with romantic love as well.

Magical Correspondences

Element: Air
Gender: Male
Planets: Venus, Neptune

Nasturtium

With the magical energy and spiritual wisdom associated with creativity and nonconformity, it is no wonder nasturtium was a favorite of Benjamin Franklin and Claude Monet, both of whom had gardens full of them.

In the Victorian language of flowers, a nasturtium meant something like "just kidding." It was a way of showing the recipient that he or she was being teased. Similarly, in Latin the word *nasturtium* translates into "nose twister," although that is commonly believed to be because of his pungent and peppery smell.

Magical Uses

Banishing Prejudice and Supporting Tolerance

Because he helps us remember that there is plenty of room for all kinds of people and belief systems, and because of his ability to change our minds and help us see things in new ways, nasturtium can be a wonderful magical ingredient for humanitarian spells and rituals aimed at banishing prejudice and establishing pluralism and acceptance. For example, if you do social work or teach school in an area where racism seems to be an issue, you might like to put some nasturtium essence in rose water and mist the space before a meeting between usually opposing factions. Or if your heart is aching for the state of a certain country where prejudice often seems to prevail, you might place a representation of that country on your altar, along with a few nasturtiums in water. And if you suddenly discover that *you* harbor prejudice toward a certain group of people (it can happen!), you might take the essence regularly until you feel that condition shift.

Choosing to Create Your Own Reality

If you're reading this book, you most likely (at least partially) subscribe to the idea that—through our thoughts, feelings, and beliefs—we each create our own reality. And when we do so consciously (in other words, when we *choose* to), we are completely empowered to create the conditions we'd most like to experience.

Furthermore, if you've been putting this idea into action for any length of time, you know that during especially challenging times in our lives, or times when we know that it's high time to make some positive changes, we sometimes have to reassert our choice to create our own reality. In other words, we have to put our foot down, make a point of lifting our spirits and aiming our thoughts and feelings in the right direction, and establish a new energetic momentum.

And during times like these, nasturtium can help. From a vibrational standpoint, he attacks the situation from a number of angles. First, he opens new doors in our consciousness and loosens old ways of thinking and believing. Second, he packs an energetic punch: he fills us with courage and stamina, and gets our energy moving. And third, he dissolves our fear of change so that we can be open to the beautiful new reality we're choosing to create.

And so, if it's one of those times, you might like to engage in some kitchen witchery—did I mention nasturtium is edible?—to get that energy flowing. For example…

"New Momentum" Salad

Make a salad with nasturtium leaves and blossoms, lettuce, purple cabbage, pine nuts, tomatoes, avocados, and your favorite vinaigrette. Carve the words *new momentum* into an orange candle; place it on the table, and light. Hold your hands over your salad and say:

Toward my goals all things now flow.
Into my sails all winds now blow.
If I choose it, it is so.

Enjoy. (If you try this with a partner or group, substitute "our" and "we" in the incantation.)

Creativity

If increased creativity is one of your magical goals, take a hint from Franklin and Monet and grow a ton of nasturtiums in your yard. If you don't have a yard, consider growing them in pots. You might also add the essence to your drinking water. (And drink a lot of it!)

Freedom

Freedom and creativity go hand in hand. When we feel free, we feel creative, and when we feel creative, we feel free. Both have to do with allowing: allowing oneself to be oneself; allowing the Universe/God/Goddess/All That Is to animate us, guide us, and flow through us; and allowing the moment to be as it is (going *with* it, not *against* it). It's natural, then, that nasturtium helps with both.

So if you find that you just don't feel free in one or more life areas, a great way to employ nasturtium's liberating power is to add the essence to your drinking water regularly. Over time, this will help dissolve any possible energetic blocks and get you in the natural, divine flow of freedom.

Independence and Creating Your Own Archetype

Most (if not all) of us go through times when we rail against the ideas and ideals we were brought up with or absorbed from our culture. This usually happens when we realize that we feel limited or even trapped by these ideas and ideals. For example, many of us feel, on some level, oppressed by the idea that we're supposed to be a certain amount of "sexy" or "hot" (as defined by media) at all times, and that if we're not, we're not valuable or lovable. Others may feel oppressed by the idea that "responsible people" have "real jobs," and that if we try to do our art professionally or open our own business, we're being juvenile or unrealistic.

In cases like these, what nasturtium helps with is not banishing these ideas from the face of the earth, but rather banishing these ideas from having power over our individual lives and helping us to establish whole new archetypes that are empowering to us. So instead of just railing against them ("If only I hadn't been brought up with those ideas, I could do what I really wanted to do"), we just notice that they weren't our ideas to begin with. Then we say "thank you for sharing," let them go, and establish new ones.

To help yourself get out from under those old, externally imposed oppressors, you might plant lots of nasturtium in your yard and around your home, and take nasturtium essence in your water as well. Then you'll find yourself saying, "There's a *new* sheriff in town!"

Protection

In *Magical Aromatherapy*, Scott Cunningham suggests that inhaling the pungent scent of nasturtium as you engage in protective visualizations will strengthen the visualization's magical effects. Swedish botanist Carl Linnaeus noted that nasturtium's leaves look like shields, while his blossoms look like helmets.

Since the overriding flavor of nasturtium's magic has to do with being strongly grounded in oneself, it follows that nasturtium would naturally fortify our personal protective energetic boundaries.

So, before any situation that triggers the feeling that you need a little extra energetic protection, you might eat three leaves and one blossom, or just inhale nasturtium's scent.

Releasing Fear of New Situations

It's said that moving to a new home is just as psychologically taxing for most people as the death of a loved one. Indeed, we are creatures of habit, and while moving out of our comfort zone generally makes us more comfortable in the long run, the initial discomfort it brings can sometimes be a deterrent to making the changes our heart most desires. Helping us release this fear is another one of nasturtium's specialties.

And if we've already made the change and are in the middle of the ensuing discomfort (e.g., if we've just gone away to college or started a new job), nasturtium can help with that as well.

For either of these purposes, I suggest taking the essence daily or misting your space with rose water into which you've added two drops nasturtium essence and eight to ten drops rose geranium essence until the fear and discomfort subside.

Magical Correspondences

Element: Water
Gender: Male
Planet: Neptune

Oak

While oak trees are known by many as numinous storehouses of ancient magical knowledge, they aren't exactly famous for their flowers—unless, of course, you're a student of the language of flowers or a flower essence enthusiast, in which case you are likely to have an inkling of the considerable magical wisdom of the unassuming little oak blossom.

Magical Uses

Abundance

As opposed to "fast money" magic or "get rich quick" spells, oak blossoms are in it for the long haul. They can help us create the energy shifts necessary for earning and receiving money in a sustainable and fulfilling way. This is not to say that they can't also help us out in a pinch, but they will do it with the expectation that any temporary financial fixes are ultimately for the purpose of the long-term goal of sustained financial well-being.

If abundance has been an ongoing challenge for you in the past, and you're ready to turn that around, you might try the following charm.

"FINANCIAL WELL-BEING" CHARM

On a new moon, visit a blossoming oak tree with a shiny silver dollar in your pocket. Stand near the trunk, place your hands on it, and relax as you exchange energy with the tree. Gaze down and think about how rooted the tree is into the earth. Gaze up and consider how he easily and naturally receives all the sunlight and water he needs. Consider how long he has been in this exact location and how long he will continue to be here in the future. Say:

Just as everything you need is always provided to you, so is everything I need always provided for me. Just as your roots go deep and your branches reach high, so do my roots go deep and branches reach high. Thank you for reminding me of my infinite wealth.

Then lovingly gather a cluster of oak blossoms. Leave the silver dollar near the base of the tree as a token of your gratitude. Once home, wrap the blossom in a dollar bill (folding it toward yourself), and then wrap that in a small piece of green cloth. Tie it closed with hemp twine. Hold it in both hands and say:

Everything I need is always provided for me. My roots go deep and my branches reach high. Thank you, thank you, thank you. Blessed be. And so it is.

Place the charm near your financial documents or checkbook, in your purse, in the prosperity area of your home, or on your altar.

Creating Your Own Luck

According to ancient Chinese wisdom, there are a number of factors affecting the overall luck quotient of any given person. Some of them we can't change: for example, when or where we are born or who our parents happen to be. But there's a considerable portion of our luck that we *can* change, and that has to do with how we choose to perceive and interact with the world around us. Changing this kind of luck, and aligning us with our luckiest possible stars, is one of the oak blossom's specialties.

GREEN TEA LUCK POTION

To change your luck for the better, make a cup of green tea just before sunrise on the morning of the new moon. Doctor it up according to your tastes, and then add four drops oak flower essence. Hold it in both hands and visualize very bright, oak-blossom-colored light (think spring green) filling and surrounding the cup. Say: "Luck is my natural state. Luck is my birthright. I am lucky beyond my fondest dreams." Drink the tea as the sun rises. Repeat each morning until the next new moon, and remember to notice and celebrate all your lucky breaks—even the seemingly tiny ones—each day.

Employment

Oak blossoms can help you in magical workings related to procuring employment of all sorts—and perhaps especially employment that falls under the hospitality category, as oak blossoms symbolize hospitality in the Victorian language of flowers.

....

EMPLOYMENT CHARM

On a Thursday when the moon is between new and full, visit a blossoming oak tree. After relaxing and tuning in to the tree, lovingly gather a cluster of blossoms. Leave a silver dollar near the base of the tree as a token of gratitude. Once home, bundle the oak blossom in a small piece of royal blue fabric, along with a hematite and a silver dollar. Tie it closed with hemp twine. Hold it in both hands and say:

> *I am in perfect vibrational alignment with the divinely perfect job for me, and in the realm of truth, I have already found this job and acquired it. It is now mine, swiftly, easily, and perfectly. Thank you, thank you, thank you. Blessed be. And so it is.*

Keep the charm near you when searching for job listings and submitting résumés or applications, and take it with you to job interviews.

Focus and Long-Term Determination

When we're in alignment with our divine talents and truest desires, we are able to focus as a matter of course. Hard work seems to flow out of us naturally and abundantly, and our inner critic takes a back seat to our all-encompassing determination. Oak blossom can help set us on this course.

....

But be aware: oak blossom will only help you focus on things that are in alignment with your heart's true desires. In other words, if you're taking a chemistry class because your heart of hearts wants to be a doctor, oak blossom will help you focus on chemistry. If you're taking a chemistry class because your *dad* wants you to be a doctor (but you want to be an artist), oak blossom will *not* help you focus on chemistry.

To infuse yourself with the focus and determination to commit to your goals and live the life of your dreams, take the essence regularly until you feel the shift.

Success in School or Work

Because of the attributes mentioned elsewhere in this entry, oak blossom can help us experience success in school or work. Employ oak blossoms in your magical workings for this purpose or try taking the essence.

Tapping Your Divine Energy Source

If you have low energy and you suspect the causes might be that you seem to have misplaced the joy in your life and you're disconnected from your true desires, oak blossom can help you reconnect and get your energy moving in a healthy way.

To reap these benefits, visit a blossoming oak and silently tune in to the blossoms, allowing yourself to receive an energetic infusion and a potent dose of oak blossom wisdom. Additionally or instead, create a charm with the blossom or take the essence.

Magical Correspondences

Element: Earth
Gender: Male
Planet: Sun

Oleander

Considering I was terrified of the oleander plant in the backyard of my early childhood home—I actually had nightmares about it!—I am intrigued by author Scott Cunningham's statement that "Italian magical thought says that keeping any part of an oleander in the house brings sickness, disgrace, and misfortune of every kind to its inhabitants." Similarly, herbal expert Andrew Chevallier relates that grazing livestock instinctively steer clear of oleander, which is highly poisonous. I can't help but think that my magical child self was somehow onto all of that.

Still, despite her fearful reputation, when correctly employed, oleander possesses a good little selection of potent magical benefits. In fact—while I *emphatically* do not recommend trying this at home—oleander-derived medicines have been successfully employed in both ancient and modern medical systems to treat a whole gamut of health issues, including cancer, ringworm, asthma, psoriasis, and heart conditions.

Magical Uses
Emotional Healing

Whenever I go to the desert, I feel my emotional heaviness and pain come to the surface. Then, once I recognize and feel my feelings, their heaviness and toxicity begin to dry up and disappear. I feel cleansed and disinfected, like a thoroughly laundered blanket on a sunny clothesline. I share this because it's an excellent way to describe the manner in which oleander works her magic to help heal our lingering, festering emotional wounds: she can help lift and evaporate them like moisture in the desert sun.

For this purpose, try taking two drops of the flower essence in a small glass of water morning and night, starting at the full moon and continuing until the new moon. Continue throughout the entire following moon cycle until the next new moon if additional healing is needed. Please only make the flower essence yourself if you are very confident with the process—otherwise, purchase from a reputable company.

Additionally or alternatively, spend time in quiet contemplation with a blossoming oleander, requesting her assistance with healing and purifying your specific emotional challenges.

You may also like to employ oleander to support the healing of any type of physical condition that you believe may stem from a deep-seated emotional issue.

Strength

Nobody messed with my Italian grandmother Cecelia, and I mean *nobody*. She may have been small, but she was unquestionably and immediately the boss of every situation in which she found herself. If your personality could use an injection of boss lady (or man) mojo, you may want to employ oleander's unique magic in this regard.

By the same token, oleander can help infuse you with a shocking amount of resilience and courage. This can be especially helpful for those of us who may feel vulnerable because of our extreme sensitivity, or for anytime that you need to carry on when you seem to feel more like giving up. For this purpose, try either of the suggestions from the "emotional healing" section above.

Protection

As you know, when plants or animals are poisonous, it's generally because they evolved that way in order to protect themselves from other life forms. And oleander is generally considered to be one of the most (if not *the* most) poisonous ornamental plants. What's more, considering that all her other magical attributes (healing, strength, and transmutation) lend themselves to powerful energetic protection, she can help us establish magical boundaries through which negativity will be highly unlikely to penetrate. To employ oleander for this purpose, whether you want to protect yourself from physical, emotional, or spiritual harm of any kind, I suggest creating the following amulet.

PROTECTIVE AMULET

Tie a pink or red oleander blossom into a piece of red flannel, along with a clove of garlic, a pinch of rue, and nine safety pins. Anoint with frankincense oil. Hold in both hands and say:

To the left, I am safe.
To the right, I am safe.
Above me, I am safe.
Below me, I am safe.
To the north, south, east, and west, I am safe.
There is a circle of protection around me.
Oleander, garlic, and rue form a powerful boundary
Through which no negativity can penetrate.
Thank you, thank you, thank you.
Blessed be. And so it is.

Carry the amulet on your person whenever extra protection is needed. Or, to protect a loved one (if they are away and you can't give them the amulet in person), place a picture of the loved one on your altar and place the amulet so that it touches the picture in some way, and adjust the chant accordingly ("*you* are safe").

Transmutation

Oleander's magical dynamic can help dismantle and then transmute what is no longer needed (or was never needed in the first place) into beautiful, helpful, bright, fiery energy to fuel your happiness, luck, and success. Perhaps this is why author Judika Illes (in *The Element Encyclopedia of 5000 Spells*) recommends incorporating oleander into lucky mojo bags. Other ways you can incorporate the transmuting effects of oleander include:

- Tye an oleander blossom into a piece of red felt and hang it on or above your front door to transmute all negativity into positivity at the main entry point for energy in your home.

- Mist your workspace with spring water into which you've added two to four drops oleander essence and ten to twenty drops rosemary essential oil to transform negative workplace energy into good vibes and success.

- Spend time in quiet contemplation with a blossoming oleander plant and request her assistance with transmuting all your old emotional baggage into blessings, abundance, and luck. Once you make this request, relax and allow her to heal you in this way, like a reiki healer or shaman would.

Magical Correspondences

Element: Fire
Gender: Female
Planets: Saturn, Mars

Orchid

*A*s perhaps the most extensive of all flower species, when it comes to the magical properties of this elegant, queenlike bloom, there are many variations on the theme. But regardless of the variety, we can say that orchid's exotic beauty, otherworldly presence, and unique botanical characteristics put her in a class by herself. As a matter of fact, as I typed that last sentence, I heard her say in my mind, "Rose, *Shmose*." (She is not known for her humility.)

In this entry you will find some general guidelines, but to learn the properties of a specific variety, simply tune in to her energy and allow her to speak for herself.

Magical Uses

Beauty and Elegance

It is obvious that orchid's elegant, refined, pristine beauty is far from ordinary. And she can help us to possess extraordinary beauty as well. To receive this benefit, you might place a living orchid in your bedroom or dressing area. Or you might create a simple beauty potion by placing a few drops of the essence in bubbly water, champagne, or rose petal tea.

Expressing Uniqueness

One only needs to look at the lives of the world's great artists, inventors, and entrepreneurs to see that, if we channel them correctly and express them in constructive ways, precisely the things that may make us feel weird or odd are the things that have the potential to bring us the greatest success and respect. Not to mention, expressing one's uniqueness is one of the great joys of life. We only need to consciously step beyond our fear of failure and ridicule by expressing the gold that is at the heart of our uniqueness. And orchid can help us do just that.

For this purpose, bring living orchids (or paintings or photos of orchids) into your home or workspace, take two to three drops orchid essence under your tongue in the morning daily as needed, put ten to twenty drops orchid essence in your bath water, or mist your space or yourself with rose water into which you've added ten drops ylang ylang essential oil, five drops vanilla essential oil, and five drops orchid essence.

Goddess Energy and Queenliness

Orchid can help us possess the confidence and regal attitude that will allow us to claim our throne and reign supreme. This can be especially helpful for times when we're working on our self-esteem and decisiveness, or when we seem to feel as if anyone or anything holds authority over us. It can also help if we are getting our sea legs with a position of authority or if we are entering into any situation where personal authority and queenliness will give us an advantage. For this purpose, try any of the previous suggestions.

Ecstasy and Sexual Pleasure

As in the book *The Orchid Thief* and the film *Adaptation*, some kinds of orchids have been employed to reach ecstatic states (though I am not suggesting that you try this at home). Similarly, orchids in general are vibrationally and visually evocative of eroticism and ecstatic spiritual states. For example, I don't believe it's a coincidence that the paphiopedilum orchid is named after Paphos, where, according to author Diana Wells, "Aphrodite was worshipped and prostitutes were available."

To employ orchid's ecstatic and aphrodisiacal properties, try bringing live orchids into your bedroom or meditation area, taking two to three drops of the essence under the tongue or in wine or champagne, putting ten to twenty drops of the essence in your bath water, or misting yourself with a mist potion of rose water into which you've added ten drops ylang ylang essential oil, five drops vanilla essential oil, and five drops orchid essence.

Fertility

In addition to resembling the female genital, orchid's name is derived from the Greek word for testicle, and in China she is a symbol of abundant offspring. Additionally, as author Diana Wells puts it, "Orchids go to extremes to propagate themselves."

To magically assist with conception, take the essence once per day or bring live or cut orchids into your space.

Harmony

In *Feng Shui Symbols*, authors Christine Bradler and Joachim Sheiner suggest employing orchids to assist with marital harmony and to transmute harsh energy into harmony after an argument or discord of any kind. They also note the I Ching's statement that "two people living in harmony diminish harshness, because words spoken in harmony carry the fragrance of orchids." For this purpose, bring the potted orchids into your space, give a potted orchid or bouquet of orchids as a gift, or mist the space and people involved with the orchid mist potion suggested above.

Similarly, potted and cut orchids in the home can assist with a general feeling of household harmony and domestic bliss.

Romantic Love

Because orchids possess that otherworldly, transcendent vibration that is reminiscent of falling in love, orchids can help draw a new love or infuse an established relationship with feelings of excitement and newness. For this purpose, you might place two orchids side by side in a special place in your home, sit in quiet contemplation with an orchid to absorb her energy, incorporate orchid into rituals designed for the purpose, or create a love potion.

Love Potion

Add five drops orchid essence to a bottle of pink champagne, along with five drops vanilla extract and two petals from one homegrown or organic red rose. Share with a partner or date.

Spirituality and Intuition

Orchid has a very refined, spiritual vibration that can help one to pick up on subtleties and intuitive messages. To help enhance your spiritual and intuitive connection, take the essence or spend time with the blossoms.

Wealth and Luxury

While the lilies of the field may remind us of the many blessings that money can't buy, orchid's vibration reminds us that our supply comes from the Divine; that the Divine is infinite; and that, as such, there is absolutely nothing wrong with enjoying the blessings that money *can* buy. Furthermore, by replacing our limiting beliefs and attitudes about wealth and luxury, and by infusing us with her resplendent, affluent vibe, she can help align us with our most ideal and luxurious life flow.

Magical Correspondences

Elements: Water, Air
Gender: Female
Planets: Venus, Neptune

Pansy (also Viola and Violet)

A memorable component of Ophelia's dying bouquet, pansies—as well as violas and violets—are domesticated descendants of wild violas, and all have similar vibrational properties. Most pansies/violas/violets found in gardens are cultivated solely for aesthetic reasons, while wild violas (technically *Viola tricolor,* or heartsease) are medicinally employed by herbalists to heal a number of ailments.

These flowers have a clear magical mission, which is to multiply the amount of divine beauty in the world. When it comes to humans, they do this through example and by attuning our thoughts and ideas to the frequency of beauty.

The word *pansy* is from the French word *penser,* which means "to think," and violas purportedly got their name from the divinely beautiful Greek nymph Io.

For convenience's sake, henceforth the name pansy will be used, although this entry is inclusive of all members of the viola/violet family.

Magical Uses
Calming Stress Relief
Standing in the shade and gazing at a pansy will immediately envelop you in a sense of velvety coolness and calm. You can also benefit from this property of pansy by bringing fresh pansies into your space or taking four drops pansy essence under the tongue or in water as needed. A cool bath into which you've added thirty drops pansy essence or fresh pansy blossoms can help soothe anxiety and panic attacks.

Clarity

If your thinking has been muddled or you've been pondering an important decision, spend time in quiet contemplation with a pansy (ideally while you're both in the shade) or take the essence as needed. Or, on a piece of paper, clearly state what you'd like clarity on and why. Then fold it in half twice and set it under a bouquet of fresh pansies on your altar.

Gentleness

When we treat ourselves harshly or engage in anything excessive, pansy can help balance us out with a good dose of gentle serenity. For this purpose, take the essence regularly and place one or more fresh pansies on your nightstand (or otherwise near your head) while you sleep. And just a drop of pansy essence in water can help us heal the emotions of our children or animal companions when they've been acting angry or violent. Administer on a daily basis until no longer necessary.

Ideas

Pansies can help us receive the types of divinely inspired ideas that eventually germinate into beautiful things, such as businesses, nonprofit organizations, and works of art. They do this by clearing our mind and attuning us to a vibration that allows divine inspiration (in the form of beautiful thoughts and ideas) to flow through. This can be helpful for things like meetings, brainstorms, think tanks, and creative endeavors.

Love

As I mentioned above, pansies are characterized by the energy of divine beauty. As such, they also hold the energy of divine romantic love—not the passionate, sensual aspect of it but the intellectual and intuitive connection shared by the happiest and most intimate couples. They can help both draw and renew this type of love. For either purpose, you might construct an altar such as the following.

LOVE ALTAR

On a Friday when the waxing moon is in Pisces or Libra, assemble a simple love altar with a bouquet of nine fresh pansies, two rose quartz hearts, two violet candles, and a small piece of paper on which you have written exactly what you would like to manifest, as if it were already true. Light the candles, and conjure up the feelings aligned with the satisfaction of your desire. In the following days and weeks, allow the candles to burn at intervals until burned all the way down. When the pansies begin to wilt, place them at the base of a tree.

Love Divination

Another specialty of pansies is giving us insight into our partner's true thoughts. In fact, just spending time in quiet conversation with pansies and requesting their assistance in this area can help you gain the insight that you seek. Similarly, if you're doing a tarot or I Ching reading (or similar) for the purpose of learning more about a potential partner or a present romantic relationship, you might set a bouquet of fresh pansies on the table. Or you might try…

WATER GAZING

After dark, when the moon is in a Water sign, fill a clear glass or black ceramic bowl with spring or well water. Place it on a small table covered by a black table cloth. Place four soy votive candles at each corner of the small table. Turn off all electric lights and light the candles. Float two fresh pansy blossoms on the water. Sit comfortably in front of the table and relax deeply. When you feel ready, ask your love-related question. Then let your eyes go out of focus, gaze at the water, and—in your imagination, with your gut feelings, and with your physical sight—allow yourself to see what you see and know what you know.

Purity

Pansies help purify us on every level: mind, body, and spirit. Wild violas (*Viola tricolor*) are used as a purifying remedy for the skin, bladder, and lungs. Pansy flower essence can help purify our thoughts and feelings, and heal us from feelings of spiritual or emotional pollution. During Elizabethan times, pansies were associated with the pure and innocent aspects of romantic love.

Self-Exploration

The more we get to know ourselves, the more we love ourselves and the happier and better-adjusted we are. Indeed, negative self-talk and low self-esteem have everything to do with the illusion and misinformation that we are less than divine. Pansies support the sort of self-exploration that leads to an understanding of our own intrinsic beauty and worth.

- To put the brakes on negative self-talk and begin to replace it with gentle and loving self-exploration, put three drops pansy essence and two drops white chestnut essence (a Bach flower remedy) in water and drink first thing in the morning and first thing before bed until no longer necessary.

- To support the conscious unfolding of your own beautiful spirit and to help you find direction based on your heart's true desires and deepest joy, spend time in quiet contemplation with a pansy (ideally while sitting in the shade, which is aligned with pansy's cool, introspective vibration).

- While you're exploring your depths and getting to know yourself better, grow pansies in your garden or place a small bouquet of them on your altar.

Magical Correspondences

Element: Water

Gender: Female

Planet: Neptune

Peony

*P*eony is so beloved in Asia, he just may be the Asian equivalent of the rose. Throughout the Western world as well, this lush, sweet-smelling blossom has been revered for centuries for his healing and protective abilities.

Magical Uses

Cleansing

Energetically, peony is an excellent cleanser, bringing freshness and healing to the emotions and physical body by removing blocks, old patterns, and challenging attachments. For this purpose, try misting yourself or your space with rose water into which you've added six to ten drops peony essence, bringing peony blossoms into your space, using a peony blossom to flick blessed spring water around yourself or your home, or bathing in water into which you've added fresh peony blossoms or twenty to thirty drops peony essence.

Healing

Peony's name comes from the Greek Paeon, a student of Aesclepius, the god of medicine. As the story goes, Aesclepius became dangerously jealous of Paeon's healing abilities, and Zeus transformed him into a flower to rescue him from Aesclepius's wrath. Not surprisingly, in ancient Greek medicine the peony was employed to heal a number of different complaints. Paeon, of course, is also a word that has come to mean a song of praise and is traditionally associated with praise to the solar god Apollo, another deity associated with powerful healing.

To support physical healing, wear a necklace of fresh peonies, place a bouquet near the healing bed, or take the essence. You might also lovingly care for a peony plant in your yard, gently letting him know the health challenge you'd like help with (for yourself or another) and respectfully requesting that he lend his healing expertise.

Prosperity and Luxury

According to author Terese Bartholomew in *Hidden Meanings in Chinese Art*, "the peony is the flower of wealth and honor" in China. Similarly, authors Gretchen Scoble and Ann Field point out in *The Meaning of Flowers* that peonies "were flowers that only the rich could afford to grow in Japan. Therefore the peony symbolizes prosperity for the Japanese." Indeed, the peony—with his soft, abundant petals and sweet, heavenly fragrance—evokes feelings of luxury and comfort. And since what we focus on and feel expands, magically working with peony can help us attract and maintain luxurious conditions in our lives.

Protection and Exorcism

In Western folk magic, peonies have traditionally been employed for protection against imps, faeries, ghosts, "lunacy," and nightmares, and for help with exorcism rituals. For energetic protection, carry or wear a peony, or plant peony in your yard. You might also incorporate his blossom or essence into protective rituals and exorcism rituals. For protection against nightmares, sleep with a fresh peony blossom under your pillow, add two to three drops peony essence to a cup of chamomile tea and drink before bed, or bring a bouquet of peonies into the bedroom.

Success and Confidence

Although rarely used in holistic medicine today, peony roots and seeds have been traditionally employed as sedatives and antispasmodics. This relaxing aspect of the peony's vibration, along with his alignment with wealth and honor, make him an excellent ally for job interviews, presentations, performances, and any other situation in which a relaxed, calm, confident mind is of the essence.

Magical Correspondences

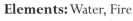

Elements: Water, Fire
Gender: Male
Planets: Sun, Moon

Petunia

*I*f your only encounters with petunias have been in pampered and manicured gardens, perhaps you didn't realize that these domesticated beauties are quite recent descendants of a hearty South American wildflower and very close relatives of the tobacco plant. Indeed, beneath her seemingly demure façade, wild beauty and adventurous freedom abound.

Magical Uses

Beauty

Physical beauty, environmental beauty, and beautification of people, objects, spaces, and situations are all included in petunia's magical repertoire. For this purpose, plant her in your yard, take the essence, add two to three drops of the flower essence to a bottle of face or body lotion, employ the essence or blossom as you feel guided, or create the following mist potion.

BEAUTIFICATION MIST POTION

Simply add six drops petunia essence to a mister of rose water, along with ten to fifteen drops rose geranium essential oil. Shake gently before use. Mist yourself or your space as desired.

Carefree Joy

Need a little more of that carefree joy associated with summertime, vacation, and childhood? Petunia might be the flower for you. For this purpose, take four drops of the flower essence once per day in a bottle of water (sipped over a period of time), add twenty to forty drops petunia essence to your bath water, plant the flower in your yard, or incorporate the flower or essence into rituals or mixtures designed for the purpose.

Domestic Bliss and a Happy Home

Just as petunia lends herself so gracefully to domestication while retaining the wild freedom at her energetic core, petunia can help us blissfully embrace the settled lifestyle without having to surrender our spontaneity and creative juice. This can be especially helpful for newly married couples or for anyone still making peace with the concept of living in one place or in one situation for an extended period of time. To benefit from this aspect of her magic, cultivate petunias in your yard, take the essence, or mist yourself or your space with the beautification mist potion.

Inspiration

Like inspiration itself, petunia's energetic dynamic is about channeling pure grace—starlight, freedom, and wild joy—into the physical realm. For this reason, petunia can help lift and rouse your spirits, activate your creativity, and generally infuse your life with inspiration. Try spending time in quite contemplation with petunia or employing any of the other suggestions presented in this entry.

Fresh Perspective

If you feel that a fresh perspective is just the thing you need to help get you out of a creative (or any other type of) rut, petunia might be an excellent flower to work with. Incorporate her into essence mixtures or rituals designed for the purpose, or try any of the previous suggestions.

Magical Correspondences

Element: Earth
Gender: Female
Planet: Venus

Pittosporum

*S*aid to originate in Japan, this divinely sweet-smelling little blossom has become a popular landscape addition to many gardens, and she now generously proffers her multilayered and multifaceted magical properties throughout a number of countries and regions.

While the essential oil is difficult to find, she has potent aromatherapeutic benefits when inhaled while still in flower form. To experience her magic and vibrational resonance any time of year, you might create a pittosporum flower essence or, if possible, purchase a bottle from a reputable dealer online.

Magical Uses

Abundance

Pittosporum whispers, "In this moment, all is well. You have everything you need. The universe is showering you with luxurious gifts, vibrant health, and an endless flow of abundance *right now*."

ABUNDANCE-INFUSION MEDITATION

On a Thursday during a waxing moon, after compassionately and gratefully removing a few pittosporum blossoms or blossom clusters from the plant, put them in water and place them near your meditation area or somewhere comfortable where you won't be disturbed. Near the blossoms, light a green candle. (You might also want to play some entrancing and soothing instrumental music.) Sit comfortably, with your spine straight, and relax the muscles in your body. Now, gaze at the blossoms as you clear and relax your mind. Bring them to your nose and inhale their scent. Breathe the scent all the way down to your belly, and visualize/imagine/feel the energy of the scent radiating throughout your entire body and aura. Set them back down and continue to relax. When you feel ready, pick them up and inhale again, repeating the visualization. On a feeling level (rather than a thinking one), allow yourself to know that all your needs are met and provided for, and that you dwell in an abundant universe. Feel your abundance flow freely: from you, to you, and around you. Decide to fully enter this flow.

Stay with this feeling and meditation for as long as feels right to you. Then extinguish the candle and leave the blossoms on your altar or nightstand. When it's time, return them to the earth by placing them at the base of a tree.

Balance

If your life feels off-kilter or you generally feel a little out-of-whack, put your nose up against a pittosporum blossom and inhale. Feel the scent working on emotional, mental, and spiritual levels to bring your mind, body, and spirit into balance and balance your polarities (masculine/feminine, giving/receiving, acting/holding still, thinking/feeling, etc.). You might also take the essence regularly until you feel your balance is restored.

Falling in Love

If you find or suspect that you're falling in love and you feel worried about the process (or just plain crazy), pittosporum can help. Because of her grounding, balancing, joyful, and sensual qualities, she's got all the bases covered when it comes to falling in love in the most harmonious way possible. You still might feel crazy, but at least it'll be a *good* crazy. Inhale the blossoms when possible and work with the flower essence.

Because she embodies the energy of falling in love in a harmonious way, and because like attracts like, when we're ready, she can also help us manifest the experience of falling in love.

"FALLING IN LOVE" CHARM

First, do not outline whom you will fall in love with or who will fall in love with you. This ritual must be done with no specific person in mind so that you can leave the outcome up the God/Goddess/Universe and consequently experience what is *actually* the best possible outcome, rather than what your ego thinks is the best possible outcome.

During a waxing moon, respectfully and gratefully obtain two flowering sprigs of pittosporum. Hold them in your hands and say:

> *I am falling in love with myself.*
> *I am falling in love with life.*
> *I am falling in love with someone wonderful,*
> *and s/he is falling in love with me.*
> *Thank you, thank you, thank you.*
> *Blessed be.*

Feel the sweet, dizzying, exciting feeling of falling in love. Place the sprigs in a jar and douse them in organic clover honey, filling it to the rim. Close the lid and tie the top with a pink ribbon. Store it in your refrigerator or your kitchen cupboard.

After a year has passed, you may rinse and recycle the jar. If possible, place the sprigs at the base of a tree or in a compost heap.

Sensuality

In a similar way to jasmine, pittosporum helps get us out of our heads and into our bodies. To experience this effect, inhale the scent from a fresh blossom. Feel the magical effects of the scent reaching all the way down to your belly and spreading out from there, relaxing your muscles and harmonizing your connection with your body and the earth.

Sexual Healing

For those who have been sexually abused or feel their sexuality has been harmed by unhealthy sexual relationships or harmful cultural messages, pittosporum is a God(dess)-send. She gets to the root of the issue very quickly and soothes it away with sweetness and self-love.

Weight Loss

When we overeat or hold on to excess weight, there's usually something we're trying to protect ourselves from or some emotional void we're trying to fill. Pittosporum heals these issues by soothing our fears and helping us feel nourished and supported by life on a deep level. As such, she is an amazing help when it comes to weight loss. Starting at a full moon, try inhaling the essence of the blossoms at least once per day until the next new moon. Additionally or instead, take two drops of the essence under the tongue twice per day.

Magical Correspondences

Element: Earth
Gender: Female
Planet: Jupiter

Plumeria

A divinely fragrant tropical flower and a frequent addition to Hawaiian leis, the endlessly blossoming plumeria is a veritable energetic fountain of youthfulness, and she imparts the carefree feeling of an endless summer vacation. In Asia, her heavenly nature is described in her name, which translates to "temple tree." Additionally, she is a famous addition to Indian incenses; fragrant smoke blends inspired by her or containing her scent usually include the word *champa*, as in nag champa, the beloved spiritual staple.

Magical Uses

Creativity

Writers, visual artists, and artistic folks of all varieties can benefit from plumeria's magic by simply inhaling the fragrance of a fresh plumeria or lighting a stick of nag champa incense. The scent playfully opens the top four chakras (heart, throat, third eye, and crown) to help divine energy and ideas and inspiration to generously and constructively flow.

Freedom

A favorite of hippies everywhere (in the form of nag champa incense) and residents of the Hawaiian isles (in the form of the blossom herself), plumeria is obviously no stranger to those to whom free thought and general "footloose and fancy free"-dom is paramount. To cut loose from old restrictions, try working with the essence, bringing plumeria into your yard, burning any incense with "champa" in the title, simply inhaling the fragrance of a fresh plumeria blossom, or incorporating plumeria (in incense, essence, or blossom form) into rituals or charms.

This liberating aspect of plumeria's magic may be the reason that she is associated with death and graveyards in a number of the tropical regions in which she thrives—perhaps she helps to free spirits from this earthly plane and send them into the light, or perhaps she helps free us from our fears and worries about death so that we can live life freely and to the fullest.

Healing Adolescents and Inner Adolescents

Being an adolescent wasn't all bad—in fact, if I remember correctly, some of it was unspeakably sweet. And the magic of plumeria is aligned with the sweetest and most lovely aspects of being an adolescent: for example, newly awakening sensuality, a wide-open future, and a sense that anything is possible. For this reason, plumeria can be an excellent magical ally for adolescents and for healing our inner adolescents. For example, if your teenage child is feeling awkward or wounded, you might give her a bottle of plumeria essence and have her take two drops under the tongue first thing in the morning and last thing before bed. If she likes the fragrance, you might find a perfume oil containing plumeria or frangipani (another name for plumeria). Similarly, if you experienced some sort of trauma when you were an adolescent that you haven't yet healed, you might try either of these cures yourself.

Long-Distance Relationships

In *The Meaning of Flowers*, authors Gretchen Scoble and Ann Field write that "plumeria stands for love in long absence, as for the sailor long at sea." From a magical perspective this makes sense, as plumeria blossoms year-round and exudes a harmonious combination of love, personal freedom, and eternal freshness. So if you're performing magic for the purpose of fortifying or enhancing a relationship that must endure extended periods of distance, plumeria might be an excellent ingredient to choose. For example, you might place two garnets side by side at the base of a potted plumeria and lovingly care for it, or you might burn nag champa incense at a love altar on which you have placed a photo of you and your partner.

Love

A heart that is falling in love is a youthful heart. And that joyful, eternally blooming falling-in-love energy is perfectly conjured by the scent and appearance (or even proximity) of plumeria. This makes plumeria a wise choice for magical endeavors related to magnetizing a new love or infusing an existing one with freshness and romance.

Youthfulness

It's no coincidence that witches are commonly portrayed as timelessly, suspiciously beautiful. Especially since there are ingredients like plumeria, who exudes an eternally blooming nature and whose smooth and creamy complexion seemingly never fades—even in extreme heat or after she's been picked. So, if youthfulness is your magical aim, you might add one to two drops of plumeria to your facial moisturizer or bath water, take the essence, or burn nag champa incense as you bathe or perform your beauty routine.

Magical Correspondences

Element: Water
Gender: Female
Planet: Venus

Poppy

oppy—with her ability to help us release our cares and relax into the arms of the Infinite—may be one of the most magically useful flowers. Interestingly, the opiates that are so famously, profitably, and often illegally derived from poppies are often valued for the same reason, although the vibrational and magical properties of poppy go about it in a much safer and gentler way.

Calm Energy

In addition to helping us sleep, poppies also help us release our stress, worry, and the fear-based motivations that drain us of our natural energy. If you find that you often feel simultaneously wired and drained (a condition unique to people who are motivated by stress), try taking three to four drops poppy essence regularly for at least two weeks to begin to restructure your motivation and align you with a gentle, sustainable supply of energy.

Please note: when employing poppy essence for this purpose, for the first week (and possibly into the second), your energy levels initially may feel worse before they get better. This is just because your old motivators will begin to fall away as your natural energy reserves begin to rebuild themselves.

Communion with the Infinite

Poppy specializes in reminding us of our true identity, as well as that of time and all of existence—which is, of course, infinity itself. As such, poppy can help lift our spirits, enhance our mood, and even heal depression. To experience these benefits, spend time with the flower or take the essence.

Invisibility

It's said that poppy seeds can help magically confer an ability to become invisible at will. This, you'll notice, is in alignment with poppy's vibrational pattern of allowing us to consciously merge with the Infinite. And if you ever come upon an occasion when an invisibility charm (or at least an inconspicuousness charm) might come in handy, including poppy seeds or poppy blossoms would be an excellent idea.

CHARM TO REMAIN INCONSPICUOUS

Run an iron pyrite and a moonstone under fresh running water for at least two minutes. Then place them somewhere safe and quiet on a white cloth in the light of the full moon for at least three hours. Next, place them on a small piece of black silk (ideally reclaimed or thrift-store purchased, then washed). Place one tablespoon poppy seeds and one fresh poppy blossom (any variety) on the silk as well. Hold your hands over the crystals and poppy ingredients and say:

No one notice
No one see
I am invisible
I am free.

Tie up the bundle with hemp twine by tying three knots, wrapping it around, tying three knots again, and then once more (nine knots altogether). Keep it with you when inconspicuousness is of the essence. Also, as your intuition dictates, be alert and take action or lie low—and wear quiet shoes!

Overcoming Addiction

It may be argued that addictions of all kinds stem from some form of fundamental disconnection between the addicted person and the Infinite. While heroin and other opiates (derivatives from the opium poppy) are some of the most addictive substances in existence, working with the vibrational wisdom of the poppy (whether we're addicted to recreational drugs, caffeine, alcohol, cigarettes, or any other substance) can help us remember and regain our conscious connection to the Infinite in a gentle, safe, and lasting way. For this purpose, take the flower essence daily as needed to help initiate, prepare for, and support your other substance-kicking activities.

Making Peace with Death

Traditionally and in *The Wizard of Oz* by L. Frank Baum, poppies symbolize eternal sleep. While "eternal sleep" might be interpreted as another way to say "death" (and poppies do indeed often appear as symbols as death), you'll notice that it describes death in a serene and restful way rather than in a way that inspires fear. And this makes perfect sense, because the energetic wisdom of poppies soothes the mind, helps us release our fears, and reminds us that we are, in truth, already one with the Infinite. In other words, it reminds us that death is nothing to fear and may even be deeply blissful and serene.

If you suffer from a debilitating or even just unsettling fear of death, if you or a loved one has been diagnosed with a life-threatening condition, or if you're supporting someone as they transition out of this life, you might want to work with the essence or surround yourself or the loved one with any variety of fresh poppies (planted in the yard or in bouquet form).

Perspective

Have you ever been running around, stressing out about all manner of things, and then, suddenly, something major happens—like, say, a loved one suddenly dies or becomes gravely ill—and it makes you realize how unimportant those things you were stressing out about actually were? If you have, do you remember how even though the occurrence was sad, the readjustment in your state of mind was a huge relief? And if you haven't, can you imagine how that would be true?

The wonderful thing about the spiritual wisdom of poppy is that it can help you gain that perspective without having to experience the crisis or upheaval. Once this happens, you'll find that your stress dissipates and your priorities feel more harmonious. To experience this, take the essence or spend time with a blossom.

Relaxation and Sleep

Like opiates, the energy of poppies can help us relax our bodies and minds, and sleep deeply and comfortably. Unlike opiates, working with the magical properties of poppies can bring out and help emphasize our own intrinsic predilection for deep relaxation rather than externally force it upon our internal systems.

If sleep or relaxation has been a challenge for you or a loved one, first be sure to cover or remove any large mirrors in the bedroom at night (which can be energizing and unsettling), and create as serene an environment as possible in the bedroom. Then you might like to try taking a few drops of poppy essence under the tongue before bed for sleep and in the morning and afternoon for relaxation and stress relief. You also might create the following sleep charm.

Sleep Charm

Simply pick a poppy and dry it. During the waning moon, place the dried poppy in a square of purple, white, or off-white flannel, along with one-half teaspoon dried chamomile, one-half teaspoon dried valerian root, one-half teaspoon poppy seeds, and a small amethyst crystal cluster. Tie it closed with hemp twine. Hold it in both hands and say:

Spirits of the nighttime deep
All night long please help me sleep
Replenish well as dreams unfurl
And float about your starry world.

Then place the charm under your pillow, hang it above your head, or set it on your nightstand.

Surrender and Release

If you're experiencing pain around the loss of something (which includes large changes of any sort), if you're facing the potential or pending loss of something, or if you're ready to let go of items or conditions that are no longer serving you, poppy can help you to let go of the past, embrace the present, and make room for the beautiful future. For this purpose, take the essence or work poppies or poppy essence into rituals designed to help you let go.

Magical Correspondences

Element: Air
Gender: Female
Planet: Neptune

Primrose

*D*uring challenging times, primrose is a compassionate spirit and a sympathetic ear. A veritable saint of the garden, he helps heal our emotional pain and transmute our suffering into joy.

Magical Uses
Admitting Feelings

If we don't acknowledge our feelings, we're paralyzed when it comes to healing them and moving on. Primrose can help us admit our feelings to ourselves so that we can move through them (rather than trying to go around them or above them) and eventually let them go. He does this by quietly setting the example of connecting with the earth, surrendering fully to the life experience, and holding the space for our feelings to emerge.

If you're not sure how you feel about something, or if you know you have pent-up grief, sadness, loneliness, or anger that you're ready to discover and deal with, visit some live blossoming primroses or bring some into your garden and spend some quality time with them. As you gaze at the blossoms, take some deep breaths, allow your thoughts to be soft and still, become aware of the area around your heart, and allow the primrose energy to do its thing. You may not consciously be aware of anything happening at first, but that's not the point. The point is that you simply let go and allow primrose to shift your inner landscape so that your feelings can more easily come to the surface. This may happen immediately, or you might feel the effects in the coming days and weeks.

Healing Grief and Heartache

By simply holding the space for our grief to be fully expressed, primrose helps us transmute our pain and suffering into wisdom and joy. That's why it's a good idea to spend time in quiet contemplation with primrose when you're experiencing grief or heartache. Working with the flower essence can also be helpful.

Hope Amidst Despair

Traditionally, it's said that primrose has the magical ability to protect from madness. I believe this ability comes from primrose's knack for shining the bright light of hope into the dreary cavern of despair. So if you're looking for the strength to carry on, try taking the essence or spending time with the blossom.

Relationship Healing

If you feel that your relationship could benefit from increased honesty, better communication, and a freer flow of emotions, primrose can help. Bring primrose into your garden, bring a bouquet of primrose flowers into your home, or put primrose essence in your and your partner's food. You might also surround a picture of you and your partner in primrose blossoms on the day or evening of a full moon and burn a red candle next to it.

Transforming Karma

If you feel that you're holding on to old, unwelcome karmic patterns of any kind, you might like to employ the transforming magic of primrose. Primrose can help you release and heal past-life traumas or childhood issues so that you can move forward victoriously and be free.

KARMA-TRANSFORMING BATH

Light a white or off-white soy candle and draw a warm or hot bath. Dissolve one cup sea salt, one cup Epsom salts, and one-half cup baking soda into the water, and add forty drops primrose essence. Remove your clothes and hold your hands over the water, palms down. Visualize very bright white light coming down from above, entering the crown of your head, going down to your heart, down your arms, out through your hands, and into the water. Visualize the water filling and overflowing with this light, radiating out in all directions like a smaller version of the sun. Then say:

> *Great Goddess, I call on you.*
> *Archangel Zadkiel, I call on you.*
> *Please fill this water with vibrations of healing and purification.*
> *Please release, remove, and transform old, unhelpful karma*
> *so that I may move forward and be free.*
> *Thank you, thank you, thank you.*
> *Blessed be! And so it is.*

Soak for at least forty minutes.

Magical Correspondences

Element: Earth
Gender: Male
Planets: Venus, Saturn

Rhododendron

*I*t is fitting that, in the Victorian language of flowers, azaleas possessed the seemingly contradictory meanings of temperance and passion, as the primary magical wisdom of this flower has to do with balancing our fiery, radiant, external personality with our watery, introspective depths.

Because of the magical similarity and often intertwining identities of rhododendrons and azaleas, all the sections in this entry refer to them interchangeably.

Magical Uses

Balance of Extroversion and Introversion

When we accept shyness as a natural part of life—for example, by allowing ourselves a natural warm-up period with a new acquaintance, letting ourselves off the hook or even laughing at ourselves when we're not Mr. or Ms. Smooth 100 percent of the time, or deciding not to go to a party simply because we're not in a social mood—everything gets a lot easier.

On the other hand, sometimes we also judge ourselves for our natural desire to be extroverted. For example, perhaps we learned as a child that we should never "be a show-off." Well, have you ever noticed that pretty much all of us, in one way or another, pay good money to watch other people "show off" their talents? What's more, our talents and performance urges often are ways that the divine energy (God/Goddess/All That Is) wants to shine through us in order to bring blessings to the world.

Rhododendron's wisdom has a lot to do with finding the balance between extroversion and introversion—i.e., how we relate to ourselves and how we interact with the world. She helps us learn how to shine our light in a natural way, while also taking time to go inward and honor our desire to be alone or lie low every now and then. This can be great for times such as:

- when you're starting a new business or venture that involves "putting yourself out there"

- when you feel socially awkward or shy to an uncomfortable degree

- when you want to perform or share your talents but some part of you is judgmental of this desire

- when you are exhausted by your social calendar and want to carve out more alone time

- when you want to temper your extroverted nature with a deep alignment with authenticity and a familiarity with your own emotional depths

- when you want to temper your introverted nature by connecting and sharing your talents with others

For any of these purposes, magically work with rhododendron in any (safe) way in which you feel inspired.

Balance of Gentleness and Greatness

In Japan, a country famous for both worldly greatness and respectful humility, azaleas have been considered sacred since ancient times. Indeed, an important aspect of this flower's wisdom is connecting with the deep stillness at our core so that we are anchored in serenity as we grandly shine our light out into the world.

Any of the suggestions in the previous section are ideal ways to employ rhododendron to help balance your gentleness (stillness/respect) with greatness (expansiveness/radiance) and vice versa.

Embracing Personal Power

In the language of flowers, another of rhododendron's meanings, according to author Adele Nozedar, is "Danger! Beware! I am dangerous!" To me, this mirrors the feelings that often come up when we start to connect with our unique talents and personal power. For example, we might feel like:

- other people won't like us if we are powerful
- being powerful equals being mean
- speaking our truth equals being rude
- being true to ourselves means alienating other people

But, in reality, we owe it not just to ourselves but to everyone else to be real and true to ourselves, even if we have to ruffle a few feathers every now and then. And rhododendron can help us discover our power, step into it, and radiate it out into the world without fear or apology. For this purpose, try any of the above suggestions, or perhaps whip up a batch of...

PERSONAL POWER POTION

During a new, waxing, or full moon, brew a pitcher or large jar of hibiscus tea (or a hibiscus blend, such as any of Celestial Seasoning's Zinger series), and chill. You might brew it as sun tea or in the traditional way. If desired, sweeten to taste with agave nectar. Add three drops rhododendron essence. Take it into the sunlight, hold it in both hands, and say:

Great Divinity, please infuse this potion with vibrations of power and strength. May it resonate within me, seeking out, intensifying, and amplifying my will, authority, and personal power. Thank you.

Finally, go inside (or stay outside if desired), and pour yourself a wineglass of the potion. Hold in both hands and say:

*I now step into my power. I now live my greatness.
I now fearlessly exert full dominion over my life and affairs.*

Then drink. Repeat this last step daily until potion is gone.

Mystique

In China, the azalea is a symbol of femininity and womanhood. And what is femininity and womanhood without mystique? And what is mystique if not a natural balance of what to conceal and what to reveal—an attractive equilibrium of introspection and extroversion?

Interestingly, this quality of rhododendron can also help female impersonators by giving them an infusion of finely honed feminine mystique.

But regardless of your gender or the gender you may be impersonating, rhododendron can help give you that attractive edge of inscrutable charisma and charm. Try taking the essence, adding it to your bath water, or misting yourself with rose water into which you've added ten to twenty drops.

Magical Correspondences

Element: Air
Gender: Female
Planet: Moon

Rose

Dubbed "Queen of the Flowers" by the poet Sappho, it's been said that the rose has the purest and most positive vibration of any living thing. Simply gazing at a rose blossom and inhaling her sweet, clean, and heart chakra–opening fragrance can lift your spirits, clear your mind, and align you with your truest and most divine self.

A highly cultivated flower, her origins go back to at least 3,000 years ago in Iran.

Magical Uses

Abundance

To fortify your wealth and draw even more of it, offer pink, red, and yellow roses or rose petals to the prosperity goddess Lakshmi as an expression of your gratitude and devotion. You might create an altar to her and light candles for her while expressing thanks for what you already have and respectfully requesting what you desire.

Beauty

Roses and beauty are all but synonymous. For a very simple beauty tonic to enhance your beauty and charm, lightly rub your face with a fresh pink or white rose petal. To maintain a youthful appearance, collect dew from a rose blossom at sunrise on your birthday and bathe your face in it. Remembering to do it every year it will enhance the effect.

Also, have you ever noticed that when someone deeply believes in and revels in her own beauty, you feel captivated by her charms? For this reason—and also because they will help open your heart—any of the suggestions in the "self-love" section below will also enhance your inner and outer beauty and overall attractiveness.

Clearing and Blessing

Simply misting yourself with rose water can immediately clear and uplift your aura/ energy field, make you more radiant and magnetic, and shift your vibration in a way that will align you with positive emotions and desirable conditions. Similarly, you can mist your home or any indoor space to clear and bless the energy.

Dreams

Sleep with the petals of a red rose under your pillow to dream of your true love and to help draw him or her into your life.

Sleep with the petals of a white rose under your pillow to prevent nightmares.

Emotional Healing

White, pink, or lavender-colored roses can be incorporated into magical workings that involve healing from any form of grief or heartbreak. Rose water, essential oil of rose, rose absolute, and rose flower essence can also be employed for this purpose.

Friendship

Pink roses are excellent gifts for friends, as they are expressions of the sweetness and openhearted energy that is at the core of all cherished and lasting friendships.

Pink roses are also very useful in rituals and spells to draw new friendships or deepen and fortify existing ones. For example, the following ritual would be great to perform when you've recently moved to a new town or any other time you feel ready to branch out a bit and make some new friends.

Friendship Ritual

Carve the word *friendship* into a pink candle, place it on a plate, and light. Spread the petals of two pink roses around the candle on the plate. Gaze at the flame as you say:

I am surrounded by the sweet light of friendship,
I am supported by the sweet light of friendship,
I radiate the sweet light of friendship.
I am blessed with an abundance of sweet and lovely friends, and for this I give thanks!

Allow the candle to continue to burn until it burns out, or extinguish and relight it at intervals. Then bury the petals and remains of the candle near the base of a blossoming tree.

Protection

Because of their pure and positive vibration, roses operate on the law of similars ("like attracts like") to preserve and protect their environs with pure intentions and positive energy. So consider employing rose water, rose incense, rose essence, rose absolute, or actual roses in protective blessings or rituals.

Similarly, the Romans scattered rose petals at banquets to protect against excess drunkenness and the negativity associated with it.

Purification

White roses purify and heal. Bless your house with a bouquet of white roses to bring a clear, fresh, positive vibration to a space and to support any sort of physical or emotional purification. For example, to purify the face of acne, perform this ritual during the waning moon.

ACNE PURIFICATION RITUAL

Boil a pot of water. Remove it from heat and float forty white rose petals on top. Cover your head with a towel, hold your face about a foot above the water, and bathe your clean face in the steam for eight minutes, coming up for fresh air when necessary. After the ritual, be sure to follow any inner guidance you may have about changes to your diet and skin regimen.

To clear the energy of your bed after a breakup or any other time you feel it's absorbed old energy that you'd like to be rid of, perform this ritual during the waning moon.

BED PURIFICATION RITUAL

Remove all the sheets and linens and wash them thoroughly. Mist the mattress lightly with rose water, and allow it to dry. Replace the clean linens, make the bed, and place the petals from forty white roses on top of the bed. Leave them overnight. (Sorry, but you can't sleep there for a night. Maybe camp out in the living room?) In the morning, remove them and place them at the base of a tree.

Romantic Love

Consider this: even the least magically minded person you've ever met knows that the gift of a bouquet of red roses or a single red rose is a very clear and potent expression of romantic regard. It's a knowing that spans seasons and generations and never seems to go out of style.

Needless to say, red roses are excellent for any form of love magic. For example:

ROMANCE MAGNETISM BATH

Light a red candle, draw a warm bath, and place the petals from one red rose in the water. Soak for at least forty minutes to surround and infuse yourself with the energy of romance and to help magnetize ideal romantic conditions.

Rose Petal Immersion

Completely immerse a picture of you and your partner in fresh red rose petals to increase passion and turn up the romance quotient in your relationship.

Pink roses also fall into the "romantic love" category, but they are less suggestive of sexuality and more evocative of the friendship side of romantic love. This is why you can use pink and red roses together in your magical endeavors (and with any of the suggestions in the previous "romantic love" section) for a well-rounded expression of romantic love. You might use just pink roses if you're in the earlier stages of a romance or if your relationship is in a stage when you'd like to concentrate more on sweetness and friendly connection and less on passion and physical attraction. Pink roses can also be helpful for increasing the harmony and warmth in a relationship.

Secrecy

In ceremonial magic circles, roses often symbolize secrecy, perhaps because they so elegantly and thoroughly hide what resides at their center. For example, the Rosicrucians have been known to hang a single red rose from the ceiling during their meetings to symbolize and seal the secrecy of all that goes on beneath it.

Self-Love

In truth, a human life is a flood of magical gifts from the Divine. And the key to the floodgates is self-love. In other words, the more we love ourselves, the more magic we experience in our lives. With that in mind, since roses can magically help us increase our self-love quotient, roses can magically help us with everything.

Simply surrounding yourself with any color of fresh roses—in your garden, in a vase, or in a bathtub filled with rose petals—can help you to forgive yourself, approve of yourself, cut yourself a little slack, let yourself off the proverbial hook, and generally love yourself more.

Misting yourself with rose water can have a similar effect, and it's a little more portable! You can carry a small mister in your purse or pocket for an emergency self-love boost.

The countless additional ways to receive the self-loving benefits of roses include:

- wearing essential oil of rose or rose absolute as a perfume
- taking a few drops of rose essence under the tongue or in water
- putting a bit of rose water in your drinking water to taste
- drinking tea made from dried rose petals

Spirituality

Because their vibration is so pure and positive, roses are wonderful altar additions and offerings to divine beings. Simply being near a rose or bouquet of roses can enhance one's meditation or yoga practice, since it clears the mind and aligns us so closely with the energy of the Divine. Rose water, essential oil of rose, rose absolute, and rose flower essence can all have similar effects. Additionally, the rose may be unsurpassed when it comes to enhancing your garden with a spiritual vibe.

In Sufism, roses represent the desire for what transcends this plane of reality—in other words, the part of us that craves connection with the realm of pure spirituality.

Magical Correspondences

Element: Water
Gender: Female
Planet: Venus

Sage Blossom

The cleansing and vibration-raising properties of sage's leaves have been known and loved by shamans and magical practitioners for centuries. Similarly, sage's blossoms are experts at clearing the way for clarity, serenity, and general positivity.

Magical Uses

Clarity

If you're feeling overwhelmed with thoughts or worries, simply spending a few moments with a sage blossom can help you press your inner reset button and find the clarity you seek. You might also try taking the essence or incorporating the blossom into your magical workings.

For example, the following potion can help calm what my mom called "busy brain" (the condition characterized by thoughts whirling around your mind and preventing you from sleeping). Additionally, it can help streamline our mental process while we sleep so that we can awake refreshed and clear.

DOUBLE-DUTY POTION FOR CLARITY AND SLEEP

Brew a cup of chamomile tea (or a chamomile blend). Sweeten with organic, responsibly harvested sage blossom honey. Add soy milk if desired. Before drinking, get into your pajamas and get ready for bed. Then hold it in both hands and say:

Divine Holy Mystery, please infuse this potion with vibrations of clarity and serenity.

Then relax and drink. When you're finished, say:

I now release all thoughts and worries to the Divine and my unconscious
mind for healing, resolution, and transmutation. I know that it is safe
to trust completely and release completely, and I happily do so now.
Thank you, thank you, thank you. Blessed be. And so it is.

Connecting with Inner Silence and Space Consciousness

In *Stillness Speaks*, spiritual teacher and author Eckhart Tolle writes, "A great silent space holds all of nature in its embrace. It also holds you."

If we just take a moment to tune in, sage blossom can guide us into an awareness of that great silent space very quickly. And from that space we can receive all the wisdom, guidance, perspective, and clarity that we could possibly desire.

In addition to sitting in quiet contemplation with a blossom for this purpose (which I highly recommend), you might take the essence, plant sage around the outside of your home, or soak in a warm bath into which you've dissolved a cup of sea salt and placed a few fresh blossoms or drops of the flower essence.

Deep Cleansing

You may or may not already know that there is an invisible aspect of your personal energy field that some call your akashic records. You might think of these records as something like the computer program that is your life, or your spiritual DNA. In other words, they hold information from this incarnation, past lives, and other dimensions of your being, and this information has an effect on your present life experience. As healers and magicians, we can consciously access these records to release ourselves from and rewrite negative or challenging programs (such as limiting beliefs, unhealed hurts, paralyzing fears, etc.), and this can positively affect the conditions we are currently experiencing.

One way to access these records would be to simply sit in quiet communion with a sage blossom and respectfully ask for help in this area. Then relax deeply and allow his essence and spiritual wisdom to go through your akashic field and perform a deep cleanse. Like a powerful energetic virus scan, this will streamline and purify your personal programming, making everything in your life easier, more successful, and more fun.

Emotional Detoxification

You know those times when you feel emotionally toxic, perhaps from a newly ended or currently problematic relationship, or because you recently traversed a particularly challenging or frightening time, place, or situation? Maybe it's not so much that you're wounded or broken-hearted but rather that you're emotionally out of whack in other ways, such as feeling drained, spooked, unbalanced, shell-shocked, or generally not right? Sage blossom can help with this, too, not just by removing the negative energy and programming but also by helping to ground us and to reestablish new, healthier, and more positive patterns and conditions. Along the same lines, sage blossom essence can help balance and detoxify the emotional landscape during emotionally challenging moments related to the feminine moon cycle (PMS, menstruation, or menopause).

Similarly, red or scarlet sage blossoms can help us heal the patterns associated with emotional wounds and broken hearts.

Emotional Disentanglement and Energetic Cord-Cutting

Sometimes we encounter a person who seems to leave us drained emotionally, spiritually, or physically. We might be very close to this person, we might interact with them in a limited capacity, or we might have encountered him or her for only the briefest of moments. Regardless, what is happening in the energetic realm might be described as being connected to this person with an invisible cord that is siphoning off our energy (this is sometimes called being "corded"). On some level (though most likely not consciously) this person intended to attach to our energy field, and on some level (again most likely not consciously) we allowed this to happen. This is a subtle demonstration of the old belief that "a vampire can only go where he's invited."

The good news is that by putting our foot down, disentangling from any situations that may keep us tied to this person, and defining our boundaries, we can also *unin*vite him or her. You can generally tell when unhealthy cords are cut because you experience an immediate rush of clarity, energy, and inspiration.

Sage blossom can provide excellent magical assistance with both the discovery of these unhealthy cords, the process of removing them, and protection from being re-corded in the future.

For these purposes, I suggest tuning in to a fresh, live sage blossom and requesting assistance, then closing your eyes, relaxing, releasing the situation to the Divine, and allowing the wisdom of the sage to do its thing. Additionally (or instead if you don't have access to a blossoming sage), I suggest taking the essence regularly until you feel the cord is sufficiently cut and new habits and patterns are sufficiently established.

Exorcism

You might think of sage blossom's energy as a spiritual compass pointing us toward health, wisdom, and clarity and pointing us away from negativity, unhealthy patterns, and people or entities with intentions that are not in alignment with our truest good. Because of this dynamic, sage blossom can help us exorcise earthbound entities (ghosts) and other undesirable energetic patterns from our home and personal energy field.

For these purposes, try any of the following ideas:

- Dissolve one cup of sea salt in bath water and add nine fresh sage blossoms, then soak for at least forty minutes. After you get out of the bath, visualize a sphere of very bright white light completely encompassing your body and energetic field.
- Mist your home with rose water into which you've added nine drops sage blossom essence and nine drops sage essential oil.
- Mist yourself or a loved one with the potion described above.
- Incorporate sage blossoms into spells or rituals designed for the purpose.

Meditation

Because sage blossom emanates serenity and stillness, he helps us establish the meditation habit and find meditative awareness in everything we do. For these purposes, try spending time in quiet contemplation with a blossoming sage or taking the essence.

Reclaiming Personal Space and Boundaries

Sometimes we need to reclaim our personal space and boundaries—for example, after a breakup, after a roommate moves out, after leaving a job, or even after hosting a visitor or visitors from out of town. Sage blossom—particularly the flower essence—can help with this. You might try misting your space and aura with rose water into which you've added nine drops sage blossom essence (and, optionally, nine drops sage essential oil).

Removing Blocks

As you might expect, sage blossom's clearing dynamic can also help us remove energetic blocks that we may be experiencing in any life areas. For support with dissolving and moving through any seemingly stubborn challenges, try one of the prevoius suggestions or incorporate sage blossom into a ritual or charm designed for the purpose.

Self-Respect

In the Victorian language of flowers, one of sage blossom's meanings was "deep or profound respect." And, magically speaking, this is very appropriate, as sage blossom can help us discover and foster respect for ourselves. In concert with sage blossom's other magical uses, this can be especially helpful for reestablishing positive patterns after moving on from a particularly unhealthy relationship or situation. To experience these benefits, try any of the previous suggestions or the following ritual.

DAILY RITUAL FOR ESTABLISHING SELF-RESPECT

Every morning upon awakening or every night before going to bed (whichever feels right), somewhere quiet where you won't be disturbed (perhaps in your meditation area or near your altar), sit comfortably, with your spine straight, and take some deep breaths. Place three drops sage blossom essence in a glass of water. Hold the water in both hands and say:

Divine Sage, Wise One, Great Holy Mystery,
Please infuse this water with vibrations of personal power, self-respect, and self-love.

Drink, then place both hands on your heart. Close your eyes. Relax your belly and breathe into your heart. When you feel ready, say:

I respect myself. I love myself. I honor myself. I treasure myself.
I have good boundaries. I trust my hunches. My every action is in alignment
with the Divine and my truest self. All is well in my world.

Finish by visualizing a sphere of very bright golden-white light surrounding your entire body and aura.

Magical Correspondences

Element: Air

Gender: Male

Planet: Jupiter

Snapdragon

*N*ot surprisingly, this sassy little specimen possesses a vibration both snappy and dragonlike: snapdragon is protective, fiery, and generally brimming with life-force energy.

Magical Uses

Hex Reversal

Author and witchcraft pioneer Scott Cunningham suggests placing fresh snapdragons on one's altar along with a small mirror in order to direct a curse or a hex back to its sender, and I must say that I love this idea. Snapdragon's bright, positive, don't-mess-with-me-or-else energy—especially when coupled with the ultimate symbol of deflection, a mirror—likely will not fail to send negative energy back to its source, provided you clearly set the intention, drum up a good amount of positivity and confidence, and visualize perfect success. Similarly, if you hang a mirror outside your front door to protect your home feng-shui style or employ protective mirrors for any other reason, you might anoint the top and sides of the mirror with the fiery protection oil on the next page. To neutralize and transmute any negativity that you fear may have been directed at you by another, you might take six drops snapdragon essence in a small amount of water twice per day.

Owning Your Power

You are powerful. Not only that, but you have opinions and preferences that matter. If, however, you have picked up somewhere along the way that when you express your power (even by simply sharing your opinions or preferences) you are being a "bitch" or a "jerk"—or that when you say what you think, you are stepping on other people's toes or that no one will like you—incorporating snapdragon into your magic can help. Will you win every popularity contest? Maybe not, but it's more important that you let you be you—and that you speak your truth with love, honor your own opinions, and own your own power.

Protection

Snapdragon's fiery energy protects against negativity from both seen and unseen worlds. For example, snapdragon is an excellent ingredient in charms created to protect one from ill wishes, ghosts, hexes, curses, stagnant energy, or emotions with challenging vibrations (such as jealousy or spite). For example, for this purpose, you might wear a fresh blossom somewhere on your person or tied into a cloth and safety-pinned to the inside of your clothes, take four drops of the essence under the tongue as needed, or create the following oil.

FIERY PROTECTION OIL

On a Sunday during the waxing moon and in full sunlight, place a small citrine quartz crystal and a whole clove of garlic in a medium glass bottle or small glass jar. Add nine drops snapdragon essence and eight drops geranium essential oil. Fill the bottle with sunflower oil, close the lid, and gently shake. Set the bottle in the sunlight, then direct your palms toward it (making sure no shadows fall on it as you do so) while you say:

Protected and safe.
A golden circle of fire surrounds.
Within and around, all is well.
Like shadows in sunlight, no negativity may remain.
Thank you, thank you, thank you.
Blessed be! And so it is.

To use, anoint your third eye (brow) and sternum (heart) before traversing challenging situations, lightly anoint the outside of every window and door bordering the outside of your home, anoint candles in protective rituals, or anoint vehicles or other objects as desired.

Truth

Snapdragon is associated with speaking one's truth as well as discerning the truth in any situation. For example, if it's your magical intention to see through any potential untruths in order to get to the heart of any given matter, you might keep a fresh snapdragon blossom somewhere on your person. By the same token, snapdragons are an excellent addition to the landscape of a courthouse or your home if you want to promote honesty and openness within it. For specific situations, you might visit a blossoming snapdragon and have a heart to heart about what you are dealing with, being sure to humbly request the flower's guidance in the matter, and finish by leaving a gift of a shiny coin or a bit of beer or ale.

Magical Correspondences

Element: Fire
Gender: Balance of male and female
Planet: Mars

Sunflower

What could be more descriptive of sunflower's solar correspondence than the absurdly simple name "sunflower" or even his botanical name *Helianthus*, derived from the name of the Greek sun god Helios? Not only is his magical signature specific and strong, it also appears to be instantly, universally recognized. Undoubtedly, this is due not only to the sunflower's sunlike appearance but also to the way his countenance worshipfully tracks the sun across the sky.

What's more, this American native has been so influential that many believe—as the University of Florida anthropologist Mary Pohl does—when the Spanish arrived in Central America and discovered that the sunflower was a potent symbol of the native solar deity, "the Spanish priests probably felt that the sunflower represented pagan worship and native political power and tried to wipe out its use" (Beckman 2008). Indeed, authors Gretchen Scoble and Ann Field point out that "in the Inca cultures of the Andes…the flower's image was hammered into gold and placed in the temple."

Magical Uses

Happiness

Sunflower's alignment with the sun and solar energy can help activate feelings of happiness, expansion, energy, vitality, and joy. As a result, he can be an excellent ally for alleviating depression or seasonal affective disorder (also known as SAD), or for simply increasing happiness in general. For this purpose, cultivate sunflowers, eat sunflower seeds, add sunflower petals to a bath, or add sunflower essence to your drinking water or bath water. You can also incorporate sunflower blossoms, petals, or essence into rituals or spells designed for the purpose, or create the following solar mist.

Solar Mist for Happiness and Joy

On a Sunday during the waxing moon (and ideally when the moon is in Leo), place a clear glass bowl of water in bright sunlight. Surround it with four clear quartz crystal points, all pointing in toward the center of the bowl at the four compass points. Float one sunflower blossom (that has been lovingly gathered) on top of the water. Let it sit, undisturbed and with no shadows passing over it, for one hour. Then fill a mister with the water. Pour the remaining water around the base of a tree, or use it to water the sunflower plant from which you gathered the blossom. Add five drops tangerine essential oil and four drops neroli essential oil to the mister. Close and shake. Mist your space to activate positive energy and happiness. (Please be careful not to get the mist on yourself, especially if you have sensitive skin, as the tangerine can be irritating.)

Health and Vitality

The light of the sun is invigorating, nourishing, and sustaining. Similarly, sunflower's vibration can help strengthen our energy field and boost our overall well-being; perhaps this why the sunflower is a symbol of longevity in China. To receive these benefits, incorporate sunflower essence, petals, blossoms, oil, or seeds into magical workings performed for the purpose of health and vitality. You might also like to cultivate sunflowers in your garden to absorb his vibrant, vitalizing energy through simple proximity.

Potency

Sunflower's energy is nothing if not potent, and perhaps this is why women have traditionally consumed sunflower seeds to help with conception. In fact, sunflower essence, blossoms, petals, or oil, or simply the plant itself (in your garden or yard), can assist with this magical intention for both males and females. By the same token, if you want to conceive of something other than a human, such as a business or an art project, sunflower also can help with this.

Personal potency (whether it involves conception or not)—i.e., strength, focus, determination, and personal power—can be increased by working with the energy of sunflower.

Power

It's said that Roman emperors wore crowns containing sunflower blossoms to invoke the power of the sun to magically ensure that their power would endure. This aspect of sunflower's magic can be helpful when we would like to:

- make a harmonious and sustainable transition into a role of increased authority
- exert authority (at work, at home, or in another group setting) in a peaceful and effective way
- step into our power so that we can more consistently effect positive change in our lives and in all our endeavors
- be assertive and stand up for ourselves
- positively shift the balance of power in any group or situation

For this purpose, take five drops sunflower essence under the tongue first thing in the morning for at least one moon cycle or as desired. You might also incorporate sunflower essence, blossom, petals, seeds, or oil into any form of magic performed for the purpose.

Radiance

Radiance is more than just beauty. It's also shining our light out into the world for others to see and enjoy. And it's being known and seen in the world in the ways we would most like to be known and seen. In other words, it's all the best connotations of the words *fame* and *popularity*.

Even though shining our light in this way and fully embodying our radiance is a natural, beautiful, healthy thing, we can tend to have baggage attached to it, which can sometimes take the form of being afraid of "showing off" or of simply being shy, denying or suppressing our talents, or being worried about what others think. Since sunflower is radiance made manifest in the physical world, it can be a wonderful magical ingredient to help us shine our light in the most nourishing, satisfying, life-affirming way.

Sustenance

Although they are quite lovely to behold, sunflowers are more often grown for their nutritional value than they are for their beauty. Indeed, the abundant sunflower seeds found at the center of the flower's large blossom are high in protein and possess wonderful health benefits. On the energetic side, this is mirrored by sunflower's prosperous, nourishing vibration. Incorporate sunflower essence, seeds, oil, petals, or blossoms into rituals or charms designed for the purpose of prosperity, nourishment, stamina, inspiration, or any other form of physical or spiritual sustenance—or simply plant him in your yard or display him in a vase on your altar or elsewhere in your home.

Strength

Not to be redundant—after all, I've already discussed the benefits of health and vitality, power, and potency—but sunflower is a natural choice for any sort of strength-related magical intention, whether the desired strength is mental, physical, or spiritual.

Truth

In *The Encyclopedia of 5000 Spells*, author Judika Illes recommends sleeping with three sunflowers under your pillow to reveal the identity of a thief, and a traditional ritual involves sleeping with a sunflower under the bed to reveal the truth in any situation. Perhaps this is because, just as the sun chases away shadows, sunflowers can help bring closeted or secreted things out of the unknown and into the revealing light of day. Similarly, you might like to incorporate sunflower into magic performed for the purpose of revealing the truth in any situation.

"The Truth Shall Prevail" Sunflower Charm

On a bright, sunny, cloudless day, when the sun is high in the sky and the moon is waxing, visit a sunflower. Relax and get in touch with the wisdom and energy of the blossom. Let the sunflower know exactly what you would like help with and why. Tell him the truth of the situation and request (from a feeling place, not a thinking one) that he shed light on the truth and bring a swift and successful resolution that is for the ultimate good of everyone concerned. When you feel that this is complete, ask if he will help with this situation and if it is okay to gather his blossom. When you get the okay, lovingly remove the blossom from the plant and gather it in a small green cotton cloth. Then, with a grateful heart, take a moment to pour a twelve-ounce bottle of beer or ale around the base of the plant as an offering of thanks.

Bring the blossom and fabric to an outdoor area where you will not be disturbed (such as a yard or secluded natural setting). Spread the fabric out and rest the blossom on top, allowing it to be in full sunlight. Gaze at the blossom, holding your palms near it so that you can direct energy into it without allowing shade to pass over it as you say:

The truth is heard. The truth is seen.

The truth is spoken. The truth cannot be denied.

The truth surrounds, the truth abounds,

the truth abides. In all ways, the truth is known.

Every shadow disappears into the light.

Every knot is unwound, every secret is unbound,

and all is now resolved.

In perfect harmony, and for the truest good of all concerned,

the truth prevails. Thank you, thank you, thank you.

Blessed be. And so it is.

Tie the blossom into the fabric with hemp twine, and keep it with you until the issue is resolved.

Magical Correspondences

Element: Fire

Gender: Male

Planet: Sun

Sweet Pea

With their delicately delicious scent, petulantly adorable blossoms, and luxuriously scrawling tendrils, sweet peas inspire instant devotion. Natives to the Mediterranean, they were beloved by the Victorians and are treasured additions to gardens (and roadsides!) to this day.

While they are members of the pea family, they are *not edible* and are, in fact, quite poisonous. Their scent, however, is safe to inhale, and sweet pea flower essence (since it is a vibration and not the flower itself) is safe to ingest when made correctly or purchased from a reputable company.

Magical Uses

Comfort with Luxury

Wealthy people and people who attract wealth are comfortable with luxury. They're in their element when they're indulging in the treats that strike their fancy. It feels natural to them. Whether or not their bank accounts are currently reflecting their inner state, they think things like, "Of *course* I'm hanging out in this cushy day spa! Of *course* I'm eating at this expensive restaurant! Of *course* I'm receiving those perfect sparkly sandals as a birthday gift!" They feel luxurious and they expect luxury, and so there is no way that luxury will not naturally envelop them to greater and greater degrees.

If we were raised with luxury, this is not so tricky. If we were not, or if we were raised with fears or limiting beliefs about the subject, we might need a little help cultivating this mindset so that we can attract wealth and luxury as a matter of course. And this is where sweet pea comes in. Like an elegant woman delicately sipping her beverage at a cocktail party or a picturesque winery, sweet pea luxuriates in the moment, enjoying blessings even as she attracts more of them. And she can teach us how to do this too.

To learn this wisdom from sweet pea, you might:

- Plant her in your garden and develop a relationship with her. Relax into her energy and let it permeate your consciousness and aura.

- Bring small bouquets into your home.

- Take two to three drops of the flower essence in a stemmed glass with water, wine, sparkling juice, or champagne daily.

Irresistibility

If you want to magically enhance your irresistibility and you're looking for an ingredient that will cast your charm in a decidedly coy and feminine light, sweet pea just might be your girl. For this purpose, you might:

- Be in close proximity to sweet pea on a regular basis by planting her in your yard or bringing bouquets into the house.

- Set the intention to absorb and radiate irresistible charm as you gently inhale her fragrance.

- Put two drops sweet pea essence in your perfume or body spray.

- Bathe in water into which you've added nine drops sweet pea essence.

Feminine Friendships

Cattiness and girly one-upmanship have got to go. They hide our beauty and diminish our power. In other words, no two females can possibly be cute or sexy in the exact same way, and the more we can love and admire each other's beauty, the more beautiful and powerful we will be individually and as a group.

A big part of what sweet pea has to teach us is how to embody our sexiness and feminine power to the nth degree while also appreciating the sexiness and feminine power of others fearlessly, generously, and without reservation.

Needless to say, this can help facilitate positive feminine friendships and peace among the feminine ranks. So, for any situation during which an elimination of cattiness might be helpful (say, for example, a belly-dance competition, a junior high-school sleepover, or a multi-performer drag show), sweet pea would be an excellent magical ally. Try:

- misting the space with rose water into which you've added nine drops sweet pea essence
- placing bouquets of sweet peas around the space
- wrapping a sweet pea blossom in cotton fabric and pinning it to the inside of your clothes (to protect yourself from cattiness)

Femininity and Feminine Power

Feminine power comes in lots of flavors: virgin queen, warrior goddess, and wise old crone, to name a few. Sweet pea's feminine power flavor is none of these. The feminine power associated with sweet pea is high-heeled, perfumed, lipsticked, and demure yet sassy—the perfect balance of understated and over-the-top, sexy, girly, love goddess flavor.

Not all of us girls are attracted to this flavor, but some of us are. And some of us *would* be attracted to it, but we've somehow forgotten about it or been shamed out of it or convinced ourselves that it wasn't really valid or valuable. For those women, realigning with the girliest of the girly can be a surprisingly empowering endeavor. But whatever the reason you'd like to realign with this particular brand of goddess energy, here are some ideas:

- Add forty drops sweet pea essence to your bath water, along with red and pink rose petals, and light a pink or white candle. Soak.

- Spend time in quiet contemplation with sweet pea blossoms.

- Set your intention, then inhale the scent of a fresh blossom.

- Create a love goddess altar and add a bouquet of sweet peas.

Magical Correspondences

Element: Water
Gender: Female
Planet: Venus

Tuberose

*E*qually lovely to gaze at and smell, tuberose's earthy, sweet, exotic fragrance is a treasured ingredient in perfumery, and she's revered in Asia and Mexico.

Magical Uses

Intuition

Tuberose is aligned with the moon, which astrologically governs both intuition and the psychic realm. Both her scent and her vibration help open and align the crown and brow chakras, where we receive divine guidance and psychic information. What's more, the scent of tuberose immediately takes us out of our heads and into our bodies: this deepens our intuitive abilities and allows us to integrate them into our everyday consciousness and express them in a useful way. Needless to say, tuberose can be an excellent ally when it's your magical intention to deepen, enhance, or hone your psychic abilities.

To receive these benefits, you might try placing a bouquet of tuberose or a single fresh tuberose flower on the table or desk where you are sitting while you perform intuitive counseling sessions of any sort (tarot, I Ching, psychic readings, etc.). Inhale her scent before your reading, as you relax your mind and come into a centered place. Repeat throughout the reading as desired. To generally increase your alignment with your intuition over time, anoint yourself with a natural perfume containing tuberose daily or take the essence.

Funerals

The Aztec word for tuberose is *omixochitl*, which translates to "bone flower." Some say this is because of her white, perhaps bonelike appearance, but I tend to believe that it's because of her traditional association with funerals. In fact, abundant vases and bouquets of tuberose sometimes surrounded the deceased at Aztec funeral rites in order to help open the threshold between the worlds and smooth the spirit's transition into the afterlife. In this regard, tuberose joins the ranks of sweet-smelling magical ingredients used in similar ways, such as sweetgrass, carnations, lilacs, and copal, not to mention the *Dia de los Muertos* (Day of the Dead) and Halloween associations between sugar and death—all of which suggest an inherent magical connection between sweetness and the afterlife. Tuberose, however, takes this a step further, as her scent becomes headier as the night deepens: a reflection, perhaps, of how we may find more sweetness the further we delve into the depths of the realm beyond.

Peace

Tuberose is very much aligned with love, and her scent and appearance are soothing to the spirit. Naturally, her presence, scent, and vibration can help increase one's inner peace or the peace within a couple, family, or group.

Protection and Purification

Since she is aligned with sweet spirits and the sweetness of the great beyond, tuberose helps establish the type of energy that negativity and negative entities don't like to hang around. For this purpose, try bringing her into your space, diffusing or wearing the scent, burning tuberose incense, or misting your space with rose water into which you've added some tuberose absolute and a few drops of tuberose essence.

Sensuality

Tuberose's scent is deeply sensual and can be employed as a potent aphrodisiac, especially at night, when her scent famously becomes more potent. (In India, she is called *rajani gandha*, which translates to "night fragrance-giver.") To get into the sensual mood (or help get someone else into it), simply anoint yourself with a perfume blend containing tuberose, bring fresh tuberose blossoms into your space, or inhale the scent in any form.

Wealth

Tuberose's luxurious nature can also lend itself nicely to wealth-drawing rituals. You might incorporate the fresh blossoms into rituals designed for the purpose or simply place them on your altar while setting the intention to draw more wealth into your life.

Magical Correspondences

Elements: Water, Earth
Gender: Female
Planets: Venus, Moon

Tulip

ew flowers can boast that their beauty inspired an entire country to go mad with a desire that eventually plunged it into financial ruin—but tulips can. The country was Holland, and the time was the 1600s. The tulips were so prized that their bulbs, like units of gold, underscored the entire economy for a time. It's said that when the number of tulip bulbs was found to be lacking, a depression commenced.

Many still marvel that a "mere" flower could have wielded so much power. But, of course, you and I know better.

Magical Uses

Beauty

The beauty of life, artistic beauty, physical beauty, emotional beauty, and, indeed, the pure, unadulterated essence and energy of beauty itself characterizes each and every blossoming tulip. Employ it in rituals for increasing physical beauty and tuning in to the beauty of life itself. You might also put ten to twenty drops tulip essence in your bath water to enhance physical beauty, or make a simple beauty and youthfulness potion by placing six drops tulip essence in a large bottle of spring water and drinking throughout the day.

Desire

Of course, when working magic, we never want to interfere with anyone else's free will. But is simply emphasizing our own innate desirability with the magic of tulips interfering with anyone else's free will? Certainly not. So try:

- putting a single drop of tulip essence on your lips along with your lipstick or lip gloss to incite others to kiss you
- adding tulip essence to your perfume or body spray to increase your magnetism and sensuality
- sweeping your aura (the area around your body, not your body itself) with a fresh tulip blossom or bouquet of tulips to surround yourself in a magical veil of desirability

Gratitude

Tulip's alignment with the heart can help us notice and feel grateful for all our many blessings. And because like attracts like, the more grateful we feel, the more we have to be grateful for. With that in mind, tulips can help us develop our prosperity consciousness and attract abundance and blessings of all forms. (But simply feeling grateful is a profound blessing in itself!)

To enhance your gratitude, you might take tulip essence or employ tulip blossoms in rituals designed for the purpose. You might also employ tulip blossoms or essence in rituals related to wealth and prosperity, especially if you realize that you could use a bit of help in the gratitude department.

Grounding

One might describe the feeling of being ungrounded in a number of ways. Some might describe it as feeling perpetually frightened and filled with anxiety or unease. Others might describe it as feeling overly exited or excitable and filled with enthusiasm and uncontrollable energy spikes. Still others might describe it as being absent-minded, spacey, or like having your head in the clouds. But whatever the symptoms, the energetic condition is the same: when we aren't grounded, our feeling of being connected to the energy of the earth is temporarily missing. This throws off our rhythm, our feelings of safety, and our inner equilibrium. As such, we may find ourselves with too much nervous energy and not enough nourishing energy.

But never fear: tulip can help. To receive an infusion of calm strength and to sync up your personal rhythm with the rhythm of Mother Earth, simply sit or squat on the ground and gaze at a blossoming tulip. Breathe in, breathe out, and repeat. Don't force yourself to breathe in any special way, but just notice your breath as it goes in and out, and notice how it naturally begins to deepen. Now consciously merge with the tulip. Feel how the air and light caress you, and then, as you gaze at the base of the tulip, feel yourself going deep into the earth. Stay with this for as long as it feels right, then thank the tulip. As you walk away, be conscious of the weight of your feet on the earth.

Heart Strengthening

The simple strength and loving beauty of the tulip resonates deeply with the energy of the heart. Spend time with tulips to help heal from grief or a broken heart, heal yourself from or fortify yourself against oversensitivity, and to support your physical heart. Tulip essence under the tongue can also help, as can the following brew.

HEART-STRENGTHENING BREW

In a tea pot or tea ball (or however you like to brew loose-leaf tea), place equal parts dried pink rose petals, dried red rose petals, dried hibiscus blossoms, and dried red clover blossoms. Boil water, pour into pot or cup, cover, and steep for ten to fifteen minutes.

Add two drops tulip essence and drink. Repeat daily for one moon cycle or until your heart grows strong.

In the case of physical heart challenges, obviously tulip essence is a complementary therapy rather than a primary one, so be sure to obtain appropriate medical counseling.

Love Goddess Alignment

Hathor, Venus, Radha, and Aphrodite, like many other love and beauty goddesses, possess the energies of both the sensual planet Earth and the passionate planet Venus. And guess what? So does the tulip. Imbibe her essence or incorporate her into rituals (like the one below) designed to bring out your sensuality, your passion, your divine beauty, and your inner love goddess.

....

"Be a Love Goddess" Charm

To make this charm, you will need to locate or plant a blossoming tulip somewhere outdoors that is sufficiently isolated or private. On or up to three days before the full moon, on a relatively sunny day, put on a flowy dress or skirt, pack a garnet and a garnet pendant on a chain, and visit the tulip. Take off your shoes so that you're barefoot and stand on the earth as you gaze at the blossom, consciously relax, and breathe deeply. When your mind feels clear and centered, hold the garnet in your hand and let it bathe in the light of the sun. Look at the tulip and say:

Tulip, I thank you for your divine beauty and your sensual strength.
I acknowledge and honor the love goddess in you.
I have come to ask you a favor, but first, I offer you this gift.

Place the garnet near the base of the tulip. Now hold up the pendant and let it bathe in the sun. Look at the tulip and say:

Tulip, like the love goddesses of countless cultures,
your divine beauty and sensual strength are infinite.
I humbly request that you share this divine beauty and sensual strength with me,
and that you assist with the awakening of the love goddess within me.

Dangle the garnet charm so that it's just above the tulip blossom. Say:

Please infuse this pendant with your love goddess energy.
When I wear it, may I remember my own divine beauty and sensual strength.
May I remember the love goddess that I am.
May I glow, may I radiate, and may I luxuriate in my own beauty
and in the beauty that is life itself.
Thank you, thank you, thank you.
Blessed be. And so it is.

Love

A Persian legend says that the first tulips were born from the blood of a grieving lover who rode to his death. This is a beautiful illustration of how love alone is real, regardless of what appears to transpire, and how love alone remains regardless of what appears to perish. Tulip's pure-hearted, loving energy make her an appropriate symbol for this legend.

In magical workings, employ red tulips to draw or support true, lasting romantic love and pink tulips to draw beautiful lasting friendships. White tulips can help with magic designed to cut through old baggage and get to the pure, open-hearted place where relationships can begin to thrive. If you live with your romantic partner, planting tulips (of any color) in the yard can help support your relationship. Tulips given as a gift are very fortifying to relationships, especially when mentally empowered with that intention.

Relationship Healing

Even though breaking up is hard to do, sometimes it's the right thing to do. Still, there are times when relationships can and should be salvaged. And when working magic for this purpose, you can't get much better than the tulip. Keep one or more potted tulips around or plant them in your yard. Have a heart-to-heart talk with them and ask them to swirl their pure, loving, and fortifying energies around your relationship to heal it in all the most necessary ways. You might choose red to bring in more passion, white to cool tempers and heal old hurts, peach or orange for a return to innocence and playfulness, and pink for heart-opening and disposition-sweetening.

Simplicity

If you're overwhelmed with all the details and complexity of modern life and you're ready for an infusion of simplicity, first clear your clutter. If you don't love it, don't use it, or don't need it, let it go. Then, to clear the energy, smudge your house with a bundle of dried white sage (light it so that it's smoking, and carry a dish underneath to catch any burning embers) or spritz your house with spring water into which you've added some sage essential oil, then bring in some tulips. You might also work with the essence.

Magical Correspondences

Element: Earth
Gender: Female
Planet: Venus

Valerian

Of course every flower is magical. But, like a wise old woman who lives alone in a cottage out past the edge of town, spending all her time brewing potions in a huge black cauldron, I think of valerian as being somehow synonymous with magic. Though she's best known for her relaxing and sleep-inducing qualities, her wisdom is vast and her powers are multifaceted. If there is a "must-have" magical plant, it is quite possibly valerian.

Magical Uses

Dream Magic

Valerian root has been traditionally employed to induce healing, inspiring, prophetic dreams. Valerian blossom can be used for the same purpose, albeit in a subtler sense. For example, taking valerian essence or misting your sleep area with the dream magic mist potion (see next page) just before bed can help with any of the following dream magic endeavors, particularly when coupled with a clearly set intention:

- inducing prophetic and problem-solving dreams
- inducing healing dreams
- inducing inspiring and wisdom-deepening dreams
- supporting astral travel

Dream Magic Mist Potion

Add four drops valerian flower essence, eight drops lavender essential oil, and four drops ylang ylang essential oil to a mister of rose water. (Optional: add a small apophyllite crystal or four drops apophyllite gem elixir—you might consider this when astral travel is your intention.) Shake and lightly mist your sleep area before bed.

Healing Depression

While it might seem counterintuitive to employ a relaxing magical ingredient to combat depression, a condition often characterized by lethargy and lack of enthusiasm, valerian can help, in fact, since depression stems from a lack of alignment with one's natural rhythm and most joyful life path. Have you ever been embarrassed to dance, then taken a shot or two of alcohol, only to find you're suddenly ripping up the dance floor? Same concept: valerian can help you relax, get into a natural groove, and merge with the divine music of life.

For this purpose, try cultivating or caring for valerian plants in your garden or taking two to three drops of the flower essence every morning and evening until your spirits improve and remain relatively balanced for at least one month.

Heart-Opening

Sometimes our hearts close and we stifle our feelings because we are reluctant to allow ourselves to experience our full range of emotions. For example, compassion can sometimes sting when we consider the pain or heartbreak experienced by someone we love. Similarly, joy is often accompanied by grief when we consider that every moment eventually passes away into the nothingness from which it came.

Because valerian helps us feel comfortable with our full range of emotions, she can help smooth our transition from a closed heart to an open one. This can support us in

346   *The Flowers*

attracting and maintaining harmonious relationships, as well as in rediscovering our inspiration and joy. For example:

HEART-OPENING ANOINTING OIL

Fill a tiny brown or blue glass bottle with a dropper three-fourths of the way full with sweet almond oil. Add five drops rose essential oil or rose absolute and three drops valerian flower essence. Before bed and first thing in the morning, shake gently and lightly anoint your sternum and heart area.

Influence

Traditionally, valerian root has been associated with the pied piper's all-encompassing influence over rats, and she's been employed magically to induce a similarly hypnotic effect over potential romantic interests. Naturally, you have to be very careful with any kind of magic that might encroach upon someone else's free will. With this in mind, you might employ the essence in rituals designed for helping you exert your influence over others in a gentle and harmonious way, whether your intention relates to romance, career, politics, or anything else. For example, you might try drinking the following potion to turn on the charm or increase the chances of getting your way in any given situation.

CHARISMA POTION

Fill a wine glass with sparkling apple cider. Gently crush two leaves of fresh mint between the fingers of both hands as you say, "My charisma is awakened." Add the leaves to the glass by opening your fingers with a flourishing flick. Lean down to the liquid and whisper, "My influence is vast." Then add four drops valerian flower essence as you say: "I am irresistible." Drink the entire glass before any situation during which you'd like to exert an exceptional degree of influence or exude an exceptional amount of charm. (Consuming the mint leaves is optional.)

Peace and Harmony

Valerian is adept at establishing peace within individuals, partnerships, and groups. You may like to employ the essence or blossom into rituals, charms, or potions designed for that purpose. For example, the following potion is great to have on hand to soothe discord and facilitate harmony.

PEACE POTION

Add four drops valerian essence to a mister of rose water, along with ten drops peppermint essential oil and ten drops lavender essential oil. Shake gently and mist the space to stop or dissuade arguments and help find peaceful resolutions.

Relaxation and Stress Relief

Magically speaking, valerian (both flower and herb) is perhaps best known for her ability to soothe stress and promote relaxation. If either of these are your intention, you really can't go wrong with valerian essence or blossom.

For this purpose, you might create the peace potion (above) and mist yourself and your space on a regular basis, employ the essence or blossom into rituals designed for the purpose, or take valerian essence regularly or as needed. For an extra relaxing and stress-relieving kick, you might add two drops valerian flower essence to a bottle of Bach Rescue Remedy and (similarly) take two to three times per day or as needed. Cultivating or spending time near valerian blossoms might also be a good idea.

Incidentally, an added benefit of employing valerian for this purpose is heightened sensuality and a gentle opening to intimacy. This is why it can be especially helpful and harmonizing for stressed-out couples.

Sleep

Valerian's healing abilities very heartily lend themselves to helping us get enough sleep and generally balance out our sleep patterns. While many people ingest valerian root in tea or supplement form to help promote restful sleep as needed, you can employ the flower essence to help you find your own natural rhythm and most beneficial sleep habits. For this purpose, try taking four drops of the essence at the same time each evening until your sleep patterns reach and maintain a desirable balance for at least one month.

Soothing Grief

At one time or another, we all experience grief. And since times of grief can be characterized by depression, stress, and the disruption of sleep patterns, valerian can help support and balance us as we weather these periods.

Wealth

Because wealth is our natural state, subtracting stress, tension, and limiting beliefs (and getting into our most natural and harmonious life flow) can sometimes be a much more powerful wealth-drawing endeavor than adding anything else. This is why valerian can help us attract wealth—she gets us into a receptive state and clears the way for the blessings to flow.

WEALTH-DRAWING CHARM

On the evening of the full moon, tie a few valerian blossoms (not the whole head, just a few of the tiny blossoms) into a piece of blue flannel, along with a moonstone and a clean silver dollar or other silver coin. Hold the charm in both hands and say: "I now relax and allow good fortune to come to me. Wealth is my natural state." Anoint with lemon essential oil. Keep the charm in a place that feels powerful to you, such as your wallet or near your checkbook and banking information.

Wisdom

Just like wealth, wisdom naturally desires to flow to everyone in abundance. It's the stripping away of ego, stress, and limiting beliefs that allows its simple beauty to shine forth in the most helpful way. And since valerian is all about calming us down and getting us into the flow, she can help us tap into that vast, divine wisdom that is our birthright.

Magical Correspondences

Elements: Air, Water
Gender: Female
Planets: Moon, Jupiter

Vervain (*Verbena*)

ike cool springtime dew shimmering in a just-before-sunrise glow, delicate vervain blossoms possess a gentle, faerylike energy and a palpable magical gleam. In many cultures, religions, and ancient medicine systems (both Eastern and Western), many (not all!) species of vervain were—and *are*—recognized as good magic and powerful medicine.

While vervain generally includes members of the *Verbena* species, this entry does not include members of the genus *Lantana*, which have a notably different vibration. (For the magical properties of this genus, see the entry entitled "Lantana.")

Also, note that not all flowers in the verbena family are safely edible or medicinal, and some are even toxic, so please be very careful.

Magical Uses

Connection with the Faery Realm

The faery realm invites you in with the scent of fresh blossoms, the sound of wind in the trees, and the flittering butterflies. And it's beckoning you toward a whole layer of reality where time is fluid and you can easily perceive that all is one. Here it's easier to sense the aliveness of everything, and the little beings we call the fey share their wisdom, help, and magical companionship.

If you're ready to enter this realm, you might spend some time with live, growing, blossoming vervain. Simply relax and gaze at it. Begin with the clear intention to visit the faery kingdom, but then let everything go (except your gaze) and let your mind relax or wander or do whatever it wants to do. You'll soon notice that your senses and intuition are heightened and that everything takes on an otherworldly glow. This is the doorway to the realm of faery!

To enter even more fully, relax on your back near the blossom, close your eyes, and let your inner awareness enter deeply into the faery realm. Let yourself see what you see. Notice who you meet and what you say or do. You might receive gifts or guidance or healing. Just be sure not to eat or drink anything during your stay, and to go back the way you came before you open your eyes and return to the everyday realm. (But even though you'll be back, the doorway will still be open to you, and it will be easier for you to naturally sense the proximity of the two realms.)

One more thing: after your visit to the faery realm, place a gift for the faeries in the physical realm, near the flower. This might be something shiny or colorful like a small crystal or coin, something sweet and tasty like a few grapes or raisins, or a celebratory beverage (like champagne, beer, or sparkling cider) in a walnut shell.

Eternal Love

In truth, all love is eternal. Love is more than just an emotion; it is divine energy and, as such, is beyond time. All of vervain's considerable magical power derives from its energetic alignment with the eternal nature of love. As such, vervain blossoms can be very useful in magic related to healing or supporting romantic relationships and relationships of all kinds.

Good Luck

It's said that in the Middle Ages vervain was carried to attract good luck. This is not surprising, as vervain blossoms can be magically employed to align us with our most ideal life flow, which of course attracts our most ideal life conditions. They also lend themselves to luckiness by helping us curry the favor of the faeries.

....

Good Luck Cocktail

When celebrating a new project or endeavor, float one fresh vervain blossom (please be 100 percent positive that it's a nontoxic, safely consumable variety) in a glass of champagne or sparkling cider. Make a cocktail for everyone at the celebration, and make a simple and positive toast, such as: "This project is blessed with luck and is perfectly unfolding in all ways!" (You don't have to swallow the blossom—its energy will be in the beverage.) Alternatively, you might float a few edible vervain blossoms in the punch bowl or substitute the blossoms with a few drops of vervain flower essence.

Healthy Balance of Work and Play

Being passionate about your work is one thing; working so obsessively that every other aspect of your life suffers is another thing entirely. And what the workaholic usually doesn't realize is that their work actually suffers as well! When we're in balance and in touch with our playful side, we're ten times more creative and effective at work.

If workaholism is an issue for you, vervain flower essence—one of the thirty-eight Bach essences—can help. Simply put four drops in a large water bottle and drink it throughout the day. Repeat every day until balance prevails.

If your partner is a workaholic and won't admit it, you might sneak a few drops of vervain essence in the pasta during dinner or coffeepot in the morning every day until balance is established. While it might seem like you're breaching magical ethics by interfering with your partner's free will, the essence will access and only work with the part of your partner that genuinely craves balance, so their free will will not be violated at all. Of course, having a talk with them about it might be a good idea too.

....

Heart Healing

Because of its steadfast and nurturing qualities, and its alignment with the energy of eternal love, vervain is also really helpful for healing a broken heart. For this purpose, you might spend time with the flower, take the essence, or safety-pin a sachet of dried vervain (just blossoms or aerial parts) to the inside of your clothes, near your heart.

Joy

Put all of vervain's unique spiritual wisdom and many magical qualities together, and what do you get? Joy! If your soul feels mired in the mundane and is crying out to experience more joy, vervain might be just the magical ingredient for you. Try taking vervain essence under the tongue, spending time with blossoming vervain, making an infusion of dried vervain, or all of the above. You might also try whipping up a batch of the illustrious…

MIST POTION FOR HAPPINESS AND JOY

Into a mister of spring water, add six drops peppermint essential oil, ten drops lavender essential oil, and five drops vervain essence. Shake well, and mist your entire body and aura at least once per day until joy returns. You can also mist your home or workspace to lift the vibration and establish a joyful ambiance. This potion is also excellent for helping heal a broken heart and supporting physical healing.

Lightening Up

If you're tired of reading classic Russian novels, frowning incessantly, and blogging about the dire state of the world—or even if you simply feel that a slightly brighter perspective and lighter heart might do you some good—vervain can help. To put a skip in your step and help you finally unburden yourself of that pendulous knapsack holding all the world's troubles, work with the essence or try drinking the following potion. (Rest assured this will not hamper your ability to create positive change—quite the opposite, in fact!)

Lighten-Up Potion

On the night before a full moon, place two teaspoons dried blue vervain (available at some health food stores) and two teaspoons dried peppermint in a large jar. Pour spring water over the herbs until the jar is full. Cover and refrigerate. The next night (on the full moon), strain the herbs out of the water and add ten drops vervain essence. Pour into a wine glass (or more glasses if you're sharing—make extra if you're having a party) and drink as is or add ice and a shot of vodka or brandy. If you really want to get fancy, you might also add a fresh vervain blossom or two to each glass. Before you drink, hold the glass up to the heavens and chant:

> *The world will end but not today*
> *We need more joy, not more dismay!*
> *I now refuse to be dragged down*
> *And choose to laugh more than I frown.*
> *Our natural state is to be free*
> *And the healing of all begins with me.*

Take a moment to continue to hold your glass up toast-style to the Universe and/or your friend(s). Then merrily drink!

Magic

It's said that Druidic initiates wore crowns of vervain. Indeed, all its qualities lend themselves to supporting those of us on the magical path.

Physical Healing

By aligning us with the energies of joy, divine magic, inner balance, and eternal love, vervain's vibration can help us restore our natural state of physical health. Whether you're supporting your own healing or someone else's, you might place fresh vervain blossoms near the bed or add a couple drops of vervain essence to water or tea daily as needed. Or you might make the following charm.

HEALING SACHET

Pick nine fresh vervain blossoms and place them in a small muslin bag, along with a white quartz point that has been cleansed/empowered with bright sunlight for at least five minutes. Tie closed with a green ribbon or cord.

Hold in both hands and envision very bright green light coming down from above, entering the crown of your head, going down to your heart, down your arms, and out through the palms of your hands and into the bag. Visualize/imagine/feel it swirling and pulsating with this light. Say:

Archangel Raphael and spirit of vervain, I call on you!
Thank you for swirling your healing energy around (name).
Thank you for speeding her (his/my) healing and supporting her (his/my) vibrant health.
Thank you, thank you, thank you.
Blessed be! And so it is.

Hang the charm near the head of the healing person's bed.

Magical Correspondences

Element: Water
Gender: Female
Planet: Moon

Viola and Violet

*S*ee "pansy."

Water Lily

*T*he ancient Egyptians highly valued the alchemical properties of flowers and scents, and to them, the water lily was among the most magical of plants. While they referred to this particular flower as a lotus, according to author Scott Cunningham, "overwhelming evidence now indicates that the true lotus was unknown in Egypt until its fairly late introduction by the Persians. The flower that the Egyptians loved, treasured, and worshipped above all others was actually the water lily."

Like the bright sunlight that illuminates the moon, water lily has a cool brightness and a soothing, nourishing, balancing, and deeply healing spiritual wisdom.

Magical Uses

Clarity of Desire and Direction

Because water lily can help align us with our true emotions and the beauty of our emotional flow, her vibration can help us discover our true desires and most ideal direction. She can also give us the insights and courage necessary to take effective steps toward manifesting our dreams.

Cooling Passions

I am a big proponent of passion. But if you find that you repeatedly make rash or unwise decisions because of passionate feelings like anger or desire, water lily can help calm your emotions and clear your mind so that you can make decisions with a more balanced internal landscape. To name a few examples, water lily can be helpful if…

- you'd like to begin to make healthier decisions when it comes to romantic partners and situations
- you'd like to interact with challenging people and situations in a calmer, wiser, and more effective manner
- you'd like to bring the whole atmosphere in your home or a certain area down a notch so that everyone is kinder and more respectful of one another

For the first two examples, I suggest taking the essence regularly. Or, for the first example, you might like to visit a blossoming water lily and have a heart to heart with her. For the third example, I suggest creating the following mist potion and misting the room or area daily or as needed.

Water Lily "Down a Notch" Mist Potion

Add sixteen drops water lily essence to a mister of rose water, along with twenty drops lavender essential oil and ten drops neroli essential oil. Shake before misting. In addition to misting areas, you can employ this potion to lightly mist yourself or other people for a similar passion-cooling effect.

Creative Flow

We are like flames, rays, or sparkles of the one Divine Sun. The Divine Creator (God/dess) flows through us, animates us, and gives us form, so it follows that we are inherently creative. And when our creativity is flowing freely, we easily digest the process of life. In other words, when we encounter suffering of any kind, we have the capacity to transmute it into beauty and allow it to fuel our connection with others, ourselves, and the Divine.

Water lily helps us activate our natural creativity through helping us enter fully and bravely into our emotional flow. Once this happens, all we have to do is create the space for our creativity to flow through us. Our creative work feels like receiving divine dictation rather than struggling to prove our cleverness or demonstrate our skill.

Creative Juice

If you crave a deeper alignment with your natural creativity, you might like to drink this potion every morning until your creative juices are sufficiently flowing. Find or create a 100 percent juice blend containing blueberries. Fill a small juice or shot glass with it. Add a spray of rose water and six drops water lily essence. Hold it in both hands and visualize clear light with rainbow sparkles coming down from above, entering the crown of your head, moving down to your heart, through your arms, and out through the palms of your hands and into the juice. Say: "I am a clear channel of divine creativity." Drink. (Please note: when emotions come up, even if they feel unpleasant, don't suppress them or decide that they are indications that the potion isn't working. Allow them. Explore them. Let them flow through you.)

Healing Depression

Our emotions are the river of our life experience. When they stop flowing, our life experience becomes stagnant and we begin to feel depressed. Water lily can help heal depression by opening up the flow and realigning us with the beauty of the full spectrum of our emotional landscape. For this purpose, you might take the essence regularly until the cloud of depression has lifted. Also, at least once a week, try misting yourself with rose water into which you've added twenty-two drops water lily essence, or take a forty minute (or longer) bath into which you've added one cup of sea salt and twenty-two drops water lily essence.

Additionally or instead, if you have access to a blossoming water lily that you can get close enough to smell, inhale the fragrance with the intention to realign with your most ideal emotional flow.

Heart Healing

What we call "having a broken heart" is actually a natural aspect of the human experience. At one time or another, because of death or some other form of ending, we all experience the loss of people and animals that we have deeply loved. And there is no way to get around the pain. In fact, the only way to get to the other side is to go straight through it. This is a specialty of water lily: she helps us open our heart to grief so that we can feel it fully and consequently begin to heal. She even helps us to see the beauty that resides within the pain.

This aspect of water lily's magic brings to mind author Kahlil Gibran's famous quote: "The deeper that sorrow carves into your being, the more joy you can contain."

If you can get close enough to a blossoming water lily to inhale its scent, do so with the intention to feel your grief fully and speed the healing of your heart. Alternatively, spend time gazing at the blossom or take the essence.

Purification

Water lily purifies the spirit by healing the heart and breaking down our defenses so that a clear stream of life-force energy flows through our being as a matter of course. Over time, this energy helps us let go of old hurts, limiting beliefs, harsh emotions, and anything else that may be holding us back from possessing a clear and positive self-image and sparkly-fresh state of mind.

Spiritual Nourishment

What is spiritual nourishment? It's that feeling that we all crave: the feeling that we are a part of something bigger than our little egos, and the feeling that at the base of everything is the profound energy of pure and transcendent love. When we don't feel spiritually nourished, we feel depressed and empty. We feel unsafe and unsettled. And we gravitate toward addictive behaviors to try filling the empty hole in our hearts.

To help yourself discover the spiritual nourishment that you crave, you might employ water lily in any of the ways suggested in this entry or as you feel guided.

Transmutation

Every challenge holds an important key for our spiritual unfolding. Sometimes when we encounter a particularly stubborn challenge, rather than working *against* it, the best way to magically deal with it is to work *with* it and gently transmute its negative aspects into positive ones. For example, say you've got a phobia or there's a particularly challenging person in your life. And the more you resist the phobia or person, the worse the situation seems to get. You might try working with water lily's energy to flow with the situation, rather than against it, so that you can begin to transmute the challenging energies associated with it. Taking the essence would be one way to facilitate this dynamic. Another way would be the following exercise.

TRANSMUTATION EXERCISE

Sit comfortably near a blossoming water lily. Relax and take some deep breaths. Connect with the water lily and silently request her help. Let her know that you're going to send some energy her way and that you'd like her to transmute it into positivity and to help you see the blessings contained within the challenges. When you get the okay from the flower and when you feel ready, gently bring the situation to mind.

Imagine it fully. Don't fight it. Let it get really bad in your imagination, and feel all the feelings that go along with it to the very best of your ability. Feel this in your energy field as a glowing red light. Now send all that light into the center of the blossom. Feel all your resistance and unhappiness draining out of you and going straight into the center of the flower. Know that the flower is completely equipped to field this negativity and will even receive nourishment from it. It's in her nature to see challenging energy as fuel for exuding her natural spiritual beauty. In your mind's eye or with your feelings, notice all this unwanted energy shifting into something cool, nourishing, and useful. When this process feels complete, express your heartfelt thanks to the flower and feel her heartfelt thanks in return.

The water lily will almost definitely be willing to help. But if for any reason you don't get the inner okay from the flower, just thank her and try again later.

Magical Correspondences

Element: Water
Gender: Female
Planets: Moon, Sun

Wisteria

While many flowers reach exclusively upward toward the sun, wisteria, after her vines spiral upward, falls gracefully downward like a fragrant waterfall. Although she's technically named after the botanist Caspar Wistar, her name is evocative of her energetic nature, which is nothing if not *wist*ful.

Magical Uses
Beauty That Increases with Age

Yoga teaches that we each possess a "radiant body," which—as yoga teachers Ana Brett and Ravi Singh describe it—is "a level of beauty that increases with time." In other words, it's the divine light that shines from within, resulting in a potent spiritual power and graceful beauty. And it is this brand of beauty that wisteria magically supports.

This can be especially helpful for times when we might feel down on ourselves about our age or our changing appearance. For example, taking wisteria essence under the tongue first thing in the morning and last thing before bed can help us to love and approve of ourselves deeply, exactly as we are, while reminding us that divine beauty is infinite and that we are channels for that beauty.

You might also receive these benefits by placing wisteria essence in your beauty products or bath water, planting wisteria in your garden, spending time in quiet contemplation with blossoming wisteria, or employing wisteria blossoms in charms or rituals.

Divine Blessings, Comfort, and Love

Simply spending time with a blossoming wisteria gives you the feeling that divine blessings, comfort, and love are cascading down from above, surrounding you and swirling into your life—which, of course, they are.

This can be especially helpful if you seem to have found yourself in a negative holding pattern or if any of the following thoughts seem to be running through your inner dialogue or characterizing the narration of your life:

- "Everyone's out to get me."
- "Nothing seems to be working."
- "No one's on my side."
- "Why do I have such bad luck?"
- "I'm stuck."
- "Why can't I get a break?"
- "Isn't that always the way?"

To short-circuit these thoughts and disrupt the external conditions they're holding in place, you might spend time with the blossom or work with the essence.

Healing Grief

While grief and other "negative" emotions often get a bad rap, the truth is that great amounts of grief have the potential to instill us with a great amount of inspiration. Why? Because nothing reminds us of the following things more than grief:

- the depth of our love
- the impermanence of the appearance of things
- the eternal, timeless nature of the Divine

And while there's no cure for grief (whether it comes from a divorce, a death, or any other kind of loss), the secret to healing it is to go straight into it: to feel it fully and to give it all the time and space it needs. This takes the poison out while leaving our hearts wide open so our wounds can heal and our hearts can grow even stronger than they were before.

Like a gentle hand on our shoulder in our time of need, wisteria helps us do this by infusing us with the feeling that we are not alone; by softening the harsh energies of guilt, blame, anger, and remorse; and by giving our emotions the space they need to flow.

GRIEF TREATMENT

To support the grieving process and help transmute painful emotions into inspiration and love, put six drops wisteria essence in a sixty-four-ounce bottle of pure water and drink the entire bottle throughout the day. Additionally, put six drops wisteria essence in a mister of rose water and mist your entire body and aura before going to bed at night. Repeat every day for at least one month or until you intuitively feel like the treatment is complete. (Alternatively or additionally, spend at least a few moments in quiet contemplation with a blossoming wisteria daily for the same period of time.)

Softness, Soothing, and Stress Relief

Wisteria's gentle and cloudlike energy soothes and softens harsh energies and instills a sense of luxurious calm. This can be especially useful for times when we feel all caught up in the hustle and bustle of things; when we work in environments beset by hostility, greed, or other poisonous vibes; when we're too hard on ourselves; or when we're just generally frazzled, overworked, or stressed out. For example, you might try:

Floral Armor

For isolated incursions into the realm of the harsh (such as jury duty, a trip to the DMV, or going to the pound to adopt an animal), or if you traverse harsh conditions on a regular basis (such as for a job), you might try surrounding yourself with this armor of softness before you leave the house and refreshing it as needed.

Add four drops wisteria essence to a mister of rose water, along with ten drops lavender essential oil and six drops ylang ylang or neroli essential oil. Shake well and mist your entire body and aura. (For situations where fragrance is not permitted, just add twelve drops wisteria essence to a mister of pure spring water instead.)

Wisdom

Wisteria possesses a quiet spiritual wisdom that she is happy to share with anyone who will quiet her mind and heart long enough to listen. This wisdom is beyond words and must be experienced firsthand to get the full effect. Still, if I were to attempt verbally relating it, I might include kernels such as:

- You are so much more than just a body: you are a soul, and your soul is eternal.
- Nothing is as important as you think it is.
- There is no need to force anything to happen.
- Everything is occurring in perfect timing.
- The bitter comes along with the sweet, and it is better that way.
- There is a time for everything, though everything eventually dissolves into the nothing from which it came.
- Shh, shh, shh. There is nothing to worry about.

Magical Correspondences

Element: Water

Gender: Female

Planet: Saturn

Yarrow

A revered and much-used ingredient in Western and Eastern magical traditions alike, the potent yarrow blossom is exceptionally useful for magic related to protection, healing, and banishing.

Magical Uses

Banishing and Exorcism

Just as Chinese medicine suggests employing yarrow essential oil to remove blocks and stimulate ideal chi (energy) flow throughout the body, the magic of the yarrow flower can help dissuade unwanted energetic patterns, conditions, or entities from lingering around a person or place so that energy is free to flow in the most harmonious possible way. Here are some suggestions for how to employ yarrow for banishment or exorcism:

- Bless and empower a bowl of dried yarrow in bright sunlight. Then sprinkle the herb around the perimeter of the outside of your home.

- Add yarrow essential oil to a mister of spring water, along with a clove of garlic cut into four pieces. Shake well and mist your space.

- Diffuse yarrow essential oil as an accompaniment to banishment or exorcism rituals.

- Add a pinch of dried yarrow to a metal salt and pepper shaker, along with a handful of dried beans and a clove of garlic cut into eight pieces. Close and use as a space-clearing rattle.

Divination

Although many of us flip three coins for the purpose nowadays, yarrow stalks were employed in some of the more traditional methods of I Ching divination. Additionally, author Scott Cunningham recommends drinking yarrow tea to strengthen one's psychic abilities; inhaling or diffusing the essential oil or taking the essence can have a similar effect. Incidentally, because of yarrow's fortifying and shielding dynamics, he can be an excellent flower to work with when you want to enhance your psychic powers while simultaneously fortifying your courage and shielding yourself from negative energy (two important concerns for sensitive intuitive folk everywhere).

Healing

Chiron, the legendary "wounded healer" in Greek mythology, reportedly taught Achilles to carry yarrow with him in battle to heal potential injuries (hence the first part of yarrow's botanical name *Achillea millefolium*). Interestingly, Civil War soldiers followed Achilles' lead, using the dried herb to help staunch blood flow. Even today, holistic healers employ yarrow (in herb or essential oil form) to treat a variety of issues, including wounds, menstrual conditions, colds, flu, fever, headaches, and circulation. To employ yarrow's healing abilities, consult an herbal healer or herbal healing manual, diffuse the essential oil in your space to support physical healing, or work with the essence.

Releasing Negative Emotions

In the Victorian language of flowers, yarrow was given as a gift to help heal heartbreak. Interestingly, this is mirrored in the way that yarrow essential oil is sometimes employed by aromatherapists such as Gabriel Mojay, who writes in *Aromatherapy for Healing the Spirit*:

> Yarrow's "visionary" effect on an emotional level is one that
> helps those in depression release the bitterness of hidden

*rage; while in those who are habitually defensive and
severe, it allows them to tap and relinquish their tears.*

For help releasing negative emotions, spend time in quiet contemplation with yarrow blossoms and have a silent heart to heart about what you'd like help with. Or diffuse the essential oil in your space, add a pinch of dried yarrow or forty drops yarrow essence to your bath water, or take the essence as needed.

Protection

Some etymologists believe that the word *yarrow* comes from an Anglo-Saxon word meaning "to be ready" or "to prepare." Considering yarrow's extensive history as a protective talisman, this is not surprising. Indeed, many magical practitioners (myself included) consider his blossoms to be an old standby ingredient for all forms of protective magic. For example, you might try:

- creating a protective charm by empowering dried yarrow, a clove of garlic, and a white quartz crystal point in sunlight and tying them all into a piece of red cotton cloth

- hanging a pouch of yarrow on the outside of your front door and on any other door that borders to the outside

- adding ten drops yarrow essential oil to a small bottle of sunflower oil and lightly anointing yourself, another person, an object, or the outside of your doors and windows

Magical Correspondences

Element: Air
Gender: Male
Planet: Sun

Ylang Ylang

Ylang ylang, whose name is sometimes translated as "flower of flowers," is unmistakably a representative of the heavenly realm. If you're wondering what I could possibly mean, simply open up a bottle of the essential oil and inhale. The scent, which is one of the most popular notes in perfumery and an aromatherapy essential, in addition to evoking the essence of nirvana itself, is evocative of custard, banana, vanilla, and jasmine. As you might expect, this exotic, sensual flower flourishes in the exotic, sensual (and heavenly) climates of the Phillipines and Indonesia.

Magical Uses

Joy

If I were to summarize ylang ylang's magical gifts, I might say that she brings us to our senses, reminds us of the sweetness of life, and helps us to dwell simultaneously in the heavenly eternal realm and the realm of the finite/physical. Another way to put this would be she reminds us that heaven is not an unreachable place in the sky but is here, on earth, in this very moment. And if that doesn't sound like a recipe for joy, I don't know what does.

To employ ylang ylang to call more joy into your life, spend time with the blossoming plant (if you are lucky enough to be in her vicinity) or inhale the essential oil through diffusing it, anointing yourself with it (be sure to dilute with a carrier oil if your skin is sensitive), adding it to a mist potion, or simply wafting a bottle under your nose. Be sure to set the intention as you consciously inhale, making the inhaling process into an active, magical meditation. The flower essence may also be used for this purpose.

Healing

Ylang ylang flowers (and the essential oil they yield) have been employed by traditional, holistic, and conventional healers to treat a number of health challenges, including fevers, infections, skin disorders, impotence, shock, stomach issues, mild food poisoning, high blood pressure, malaria, typhus, and intestinal issues. I do not suggest ingesting the essential oil or any part of the plant internally, but ylang ylang essential oil is generally safe to employ aromatherapeutically (by diffusing or simply inhaling the scent) or topically when diluted with a carrier oil such as sweet almond or jojoba. For example, authors and aromatherapists P. J. Pierson and Mary Shipley suggest mixing two to three drops in a carrier oil and massaging onto the stomach to treat mild stomach upsets.

Love

The feeling of falling in love with someone who is simultaneously falling in love with you is quite similar to the swirling, spinning combo of euphoria and sensual pleasure that the scent of ylang ylang tends to arouse. This makes ylang ylang a very useful magical ingredient when it comes to manifesting exactly that situation. If falling in love with someone who is also falling in love with you is your magical goal, you might seriously consider employing essential oil of ylang ylang (or actual ylang ylang flowers). For example:

MAGICAL AROMATHERAPY FOR TRUE LOVE

The night before the new moon, place a bottle of ylang ylang essential oil next to your bed. Immediately upon awakening, sit up and waft the bottle under your nose. Allow the scent to go deep into your body and awareness. When you feel you have merged with the scent, as you continue to inhale, think, "I am in love with someone who is also in love with me. I love to love! I love to be loved!" Stay with this feeling/affirmation for as long as you like. Repeat until the full moon or until the next new moon, as you feel guided. (Please note: do your best not to think of anyone specific for this ritual, as this will severely inhibit your degree of success and may eventually create a sticky situation. If someone specific does seem to appear in your mind, remain as unattached as possible to this outcome and consciously think something like "I am open to manifesting the perfect situation with the perfect partner, whomever that may be!")

Peace and Relaxation

By aligning us with the divine realm and getting us out of our heads and into our bodies, ylang ylang can dissolve anger, stress, and harsh vibrations in general and transmute the energies associated with these conditions into peace, relaxation, and holistic well-being. For this purpose, diffuse the essential oil in your space, inhale, or add a few drops to a lotion or carrier oil and apply topically. If your skin isn't too sensitive, you can apply it neat (or undiluted) to your nostrils, wrists, or temples. You might also add it to a stress-relief mist such as the following.

....

MIST POTION FOR PEACE AND RELAXATION

Add ten drops ylang ylang essential oil to a mister of rose water, along with eight drops lavender or chamomile essential oil. Shake and mist yourself and your space to dissolve stress and promote peace and relaxation.

Sex and Sensuality

Aromatherapists often recommend ylang ylang as an aphrodesiac, to treat impotence, and to soothe sexual fears and inhibitions. In fact, ylang ylang's sexually soothing properties are probably the reason for the Indonesian tradition of spreading fresh ylang ylang flowers on the bed of a newly married couple. For any of the abovementioned purposes, try diffusing the essential oil in the space with an aromatherapy diffuser or mister or adding a few drops to a carrier oil and using it as a massage oil or lotion. You might also try misting the bed sheets, simply wafting the oil under your nose, or employing the oil into charms or rituals designed for the purpose.

Weight Loss and Body Image

Weight and food issues often stem from some form of sexual inhibition or past abuse, or simply from being so caught up in our heads that we are out of touch with the simple pleasure of being in our bodies. In either case, we compensate by finding sensual pleasure through food or, on the flipside, deny ourselves this pleasure despite the fact that we seem to find ourselves obsessed with it. This is why ylang ylang can be helpful for any sort of body-image challenge or eating disorder, by helping us to balance out and find a healthy relationship with our bodies and the foods we choose to eat (or not eat). For this purpose, I suggest diffusing the essential oil in your space, adding it to your bath water, wafting it under your nose as desired, or adding a few drops to your body lotion and applying it on a daily basis, perhaps before bed or first thing in the morning. You might also keep a bottle of the oil by your bed and inhale it immediately upon awakening or just before falling asleep (whichever feels right), bringing the scent deeply into your body and awareness as you think, "I love my body. I love being in my body. I treat my body well."

Magical Correspondences

Element: Water
Gender: Female
Planet: Venus

How to Make a Flower Essence

While there are a number of variations on the theme, below you'll find a simplified two-part method for creating your own flower essence. While you might choose to add other aspects to your flower essence creation process (such as prayer, chanting, placing the bowl on the ground instead of on a table, or surrounding the dish with white quartz crystals points), for safety reasons, please be sure to hit all the main points in the following directions.

Part 1: The Mother Essence

1. Obtain the following tools: a medium or average-sized plain glass bowl, a large or average-sized glass jar with lid, and a small (1 ounce) glass bottle with a dropper lid. Sterilize each object by placing in cold water, gradually bringing it to a boil, and boiling for at least twenty minutes. Then dry each tool with a clean cloth.

2. Fill the glass jar with spring water. Also gather a bottle of brandy, a small stool or table, a large organic nontoxic leaf or bed of leaves such as lettuce or chard placed on a plate, and some garden shears.

3. In the morning or midday, on a sunny day without a cloud in the sky, take all ingredients to a serene natural or botanical setting where the flower of your choice is growing. Place the bowl on the stool or table in a place where no shadows will fall on the bowl for three to four hours. Fill the bowl with the water, being careful not to allow any part of your shadow to cross over it.

4. Shears and plate (with leaf or leaves) in hand, locate the flower you would like to make an essence from. Sit or stand comfortably near the plant as you relax and take some deep breaths. Come fully into the moment.

5. When you feel centered, silently tune in to the flower and request that she assist you with your essence creation. Honor her, respect her, and simply be with her for a moment.

6. As you feel intuitively guided, snip between three and six blossoms, allowing them to fall onto the leaf.

7. Lovingly take the flowers to the bowl of water and, without touching them, spill them in so that they float on the surface. Place the leaf or leaves near the base of a tree.

8. Allow the flowers to merge with the energy of the water by leaving them undisturbed for three to four hours.

9. Fill the dropper bottle with brandy. With the dropper cap, add two drops of the water from the flower bowl. Snugly replace the cap.

10. Pour the remaining water from the bowl, along with the blossoms, near the base of the flowers.

You now have what is known as "the mother essence." This is not the essence and *should not be consumed or magically employed*. Rather, it is the concentrated stock for creating the flower essence, which brings us to part 2.

Part 2: The Flower Essence

This portion of the process may be repeated with the same mother essence until the mother essence bottle is empty, provided you use the mother essence within two years after it is created (after that, the mother essence may begin to lose its potency). You may do this anywhere that feels right: in your kitchen, near your altar, or out in nature.

1. Sterilize an additional small bottle and dropper (as above).

2. Fill the bottle halfway with brandy and the rest of the way with spring water.

3. Add two drops of the mother essence.

4. Replace the cap.

Appendix B

Magical Uses Overview

Abundance/Prosperity/Wealth
Camellia
Chamomile
Citrus
Clover
Crocus
Daisy
Honeysuckle
Hyacinth
Jasmine
Oak
Orchid
Peony
Pittosporum
Rose
Tuberose
Tulip
Valerian

Abuse, Healing From
Crabapple
Freesia

Activation
Black-Eyed Susan
Hibiscus

Addictions, Healing From
Lavender
Poppy

Adolescents, Support For (Including Inner Adolescents)
Plumeria

Ancestors / Heritage
Heather
Hollyhock
Hydrangea

Angelic Alignment / Assistance
Citrus
Lily
Narcissus

Animals, Support or Protection of
Chamomile
Dandelion
Lupine

Astral Travel
Datura

Astrological Wisdom
Aster

Authenticity
Allysum
Camellia
Geranium
Orchid
Snapdragon

Authority
Agapanthus
Snapdragon
Sunflower

Balance, General
Chamomile
Dandelion
Iris
Lavender
Manuka
Pittosporum
Rhododendron
Vervain
Water Lily

Balance, Masculine / Feminine
Dandelion
Forget-Me-Not
Rhododendron
Snapdragon

Beauty
Baby Blue Eyes
Bougainvillea
Carnation
Cherry Plum
Citrus
Clover
Dahlia
Foxglove
Jasmine

Lily
Orchid
Petunia
Rose
Tulip
Wisteria

Beginnings
Aster
Narcissus

Blessing
Rose
Vervain

Boundaries, Establishing / Maintaining
Hydrangea
Lantana
Marigold (*Tagetes*)
Sage

Chakras
Cherry
Cherry Plum
Freesia
Lantana
Lilac
Morning Glory
Rose
Tuberose

Charm/Attractiveness/Irresistibility
Hyacinth
Jasmine
Rhododendron
Sweet Pea
Tulip

Children, Support Of
Baby Blue Eyes
Chamomile
Citrus
Geranium
Lupine

Clarity/Focus
Chrysanthemum
Citrus
Forget-Me-Not
Freesia
Lantana
Lavender
Morning Glory
Oak
Pansy
Sage
Sunflower
Water Lily

Cleansing/Clearing/Detoxification/Purification/Release
Aster
Baby Blue Eyes

Black-Eyed Susan
Bougainvillea
Cherry Plum
Clover
Crabapple
Daisy
Freesia
Geranium
Holly
Iris
Lantana
Lavender
Lily
Manuka
Marigold (*Calendula*)
Oleander
Pansy
Peony
Rose
Sage
Tuberose
Water Lily

Clearing Blocks
Geranium
Honeysuckle
Lantana
Manuka
Marigold (*Calendula*)
Nasturtium
Oleander
Primrose
Sage

Clutter Clearing
Cherry Plum
Honeysuckle
Lily

Comfort
Allysum
Citrus
Sweet Pea
Wisteria

Concealment/Secrecy
Datura
Poppy
Rose

Confidence
Agapanthus
Camellia
Hollyhock
Peony
Rhododendron
Snapdragon

Courage
Cherry Plum
Foxglove
Freesia
Geranium
Lavender
Nasturtium
Rhododendron
Snapdragon

Creativity/Imagination
Amaryllidaceae
Cinquefoil
Iris
Lupine
Magnolia
Nasturtium
Petunia
Plumeria
Sunflower
Water Lily

Curse/Hex Breaking
Chamomile
Holly
Hydrangea
Lantana
Yarrow

Curse/Hex Reversal
Hydrangea
Snapdragon

Death, Support During/After
Calla Lily
Carnation
Marigold (*Tagetes*)
Poppy
Tuberose

Decisions
Camellia
Chrysanthemum

Freesia
Pansy
Water Lily

Depression, Healing From
Bleeding Heart
Freesia
Lantana
Lavender
Marigold (*Calendula*)
Poppy
Primrose
Valerian
Water Lily

Digestion
Chamomile
Cherry Plum
Lavender
Ylang Ylang

Discernment/Truth Discovery
Datura
Geranium
Pansy
Sunflower

Divination
Dandelion
Datura
Iris
Lupine

Pansy
Tuberose
Yarrow

Divine Alignment/Divine Love
African Daisy
Agapanthus
Amaryllidaceae
Aster
Calla Lily
Cherry
Citrus
Holly
Iris
Lavender
Lily
Morning Glory
Pansy
Poppy
Rose
Vervain
Water Lily
Wisteria
Ylang Ylang

Divine Mother/Goddess Alignment
Camellia
Geranium
Lily
Magnolia
Orchid

Rose
Tulip

Divine Timing
Impatiens
Vervain

Dreams
Chrysanthemum
Cinquefoil
Crocus
Dahlia
Rose
Valerian

Elegance
Agapanthus
Orchid

Emotional Balance
Citrus
Crocus
Dahlia
Oleander
Peony
Pittosporum
Primrose
Rose
Water Lily
Yarrow

Employment
Oak

Enchantment
Datura

Energetic Fine-tuning
African Daisy
Iris

Energy Healing
African Daisy
Hollyhock
Hydrangea
Iris
Sage

Energy
Camellia
Narcissus
Nasturtium
Oak
Poppy
Sunflower

Excellence
Agapanthus

Exorcism/Banishing
Aster
Geranium
Lantana
Lilac
Lily
Peony
Sage
Yarrow

**Faeries, Alignment/
Communication With**
Clover

Foxglove
Lupine
Narcissus
Vervain

**Femininity/Feminine
Healing**
Aster
Camellia
Freesia
Geranium
Lavender
Magnolia
Marigold (*Calendula*)
Sage Blossom
Sweet Pea
Yarrow

Fertility
Orchid
Sunflower

Fidelity
Magnolia

Forgiveness
Cherry

Freedom/Liberation
Cinquefoil
Hibiscus
Narcissus
Nasturtium
Petunia
Plumeria

Friendship
- Camellia
- Crepe Myrtle
- Rose
- Sweet Pea

Gentleness
- Alyssum
- Aster
- Baby Blue Eyes
- Cherry
- Citrus
- Clover
- Crocus
- Pansy
- Rhododendron
- Wisteria

Geometry, Sacred
- Bird of Paradise

Gifts, Attracting
- Hyacinth

Glamour/Radiance
- Hyacinth
- Rhododendron

Grief, Soothing
- Calla Lily
- Carnation
- Chamomile
- Chrysanthemum
- Marigold (*Tagetes*)
- Poppy
- Primrose
- Valerian
- Wisteria

Grounding
- Alyssum
- Black-Eyed Susan
- Dandelion
- Geranium
- Impatiens
- Jasmine
- Kalanchoe
- Tuberose
- Tulip
- Ylang Ylang

Guilt, Banishing
- Calla Lily
- Cherry
- Lavender

Happiness
- Chamomile
- Citrus
- Crocus
- Dandelion
- Marigold (*Calendula*)
- Marigold (*Tagetes*)
- Morning Glory
- Sunflower

Harmony
- Chamomile
- Citrus
- Hibiscus
- Kalanchoe
- Lavender
- Lily
- Morning Glory
- Orchid
- Valerian

Headaches
- Lavender
- Yarrow

Healers, Support for
- Echinacea
- Lavender
- Yarrow

Healing/Health/ Immunity
- Alyssum
- Cherry Plum
- Cinquefoil
- Clover
- Daisy
- Dandelion
- Echinacea
- Forget-Me-Not
- Geranium
- Heather
- Lavender
- Manuka
- Marigold (*Calendula*)
- Pansy
- Peony

Sunflower

Vervain

Yarrow

Healing/Releasing, Emotional

Baby Blue Eyes

Crabapple

Heather

Hollyhock

Lantana

Lavender

Narcissus

Oleander

Pansy

Peony

Poppy

Primrose

Rose

Sage

Yarrow

Heart Healing/ Strengthening

Carnation

Foxglove

Geranium

Lavender

Marigold (*Tagetes*)

Primrose

Rose

Tulip

Vervain

Water Lily

Yarrow

Heart Opening

Camellia

Cherry

Rose

Valerian

Home, Happy

Citrus

Crepe Myrtle

Geranium

Lavender

Marigold (*Calendula*)

Orchid

Petunia

Hope

Primrose

Humility

Camellia

Independence

Hibiscus

Magnolia

Nasturtium

Influence

Hyacinth

Valerian

Innocence

Baby Blue Eyes

Calla Lily

Cherry

Pansy

Inspiration

Cherry Plum

Crepe Myrtle

Pansy

Petunia

Integration

Black-Eyed Susan

Intelligence

Agapanthus

Interconnectedness, Awareness Of

Bird of Paradise

Intuition/Psychic Abilities

African Daisy

Agapanthus

Aster

Bird of Paradise

Dandelion

Honeysuckle

Iris

Lilac

Morning Glory

Orchid

Tuberose

Invisibility

Datura

Poppy

Invisible Reality, Awareness Of
Bird of Paradise

Joy
Amaryllidaceae
Cinquefoil
Cherry Plum
Jasmine
Lavender
Petunia
Vervain
Ylang Ylang

Karma Clearing
Hydrangea
Lantana
Primrose

Land, Healing
Hollyhock

Legal Success
Lily
Marigold (*Tagetes*)

Life Path, Alignment With
Echinacea
Orchid

Longevity
Carnation
Chrysanthemum
Crepe Myrtle
Marigold (*Tagetes*)

Love/Romance
Aster
Bleeding Heart
Carnation
Cherry
Citrus
Crepe Myrtle
Forget-Me-Not
Geranium
Hibiscus
Iris
Lilac
Narcissus
Orchid
Pansy
Pittosporum
Plumeria
Rose
Tulip
Vervain
Ylang Ylang

Luck
Chamomile
Cinquefoil
Heather
Honeysuckle
Oak
Vervain

Luxury
Citrus
Hyacinth

Orchid
Peony
Sweet Pea

Magical Abilities, Enhancing
Cinquefoil
Datura
Iris
Lilac
Magnolia
Morning Glory
Narcissus
Vervain

Marriage
Citrus
Crepe Myrtle
Marigold (*Calendula*)
Orchid
Petunia
Ylang Ylang

Mathematical Prowess
Bird of Paradise

Meditation, Support For
Sage

Mediumship/Spirit Communication
Black-Eyed Susan
Lilac
Lupine
Marigold (*Tagetes*)

Memory
Forget-Me-Not
Heather
Hollyhock

Mysteries, Solving
Chrysanthemum

Mystique
African Daisy
Dahlia
Rhododendron

Nightmares, Banishing
Chrysanthemum
Crocus
Peony

Organization
Forget-Me-Not

Pain, Beauty In
Bleeding Heart

Partnership
Crepe Myrtle

Passion
Bougainvillea
Cherry Plum
Hibiscus

Past Lives
Hollyhock

Peace
Alyssum

Calla Lily
Chamomile
Crocus
Lilac
Pansy
Poppy
Tuberose
Valerian
Ylang Ylang

Perspective
Carnation
Citrus
Forget-Me-Not
Pansy
Petunia
Poppy
Wisteria

Playfulness
Amaryllidaceae
Cinquefoil
Vervain

Positivity
Chamomile
Chrysanthemum
Citrus
Geranium
Lavender

Prejudice, Banishing
Nasturtium

**Present Moment
Awareness**
Impatiens
Narcissus
Sage
Vervain
Wisteria

Productivity
Echinacea
Oak

Protection/Shielding
African Daisy
Aster
Bird of Paradise
Chrysanthemum
Clover
Foxglove
Geranium
Heather
Holly
Hydrangea
Iris
Kalanchoe
Lavender
Marigold (*Tagetes*)
Nasturtium
Oleander
Peony
Rose
Sage
Snapdragon

Tuberose
Yarrow

**Psychic Attacks,
Protecting From**
Hydrangea
Sage
Tuberose
Yarrow

Radiance
Bougainvillea
Sunflower
Wisteria

Rebirth
Carnation
Marigold (*Tagetes*)
Narcissus

Receptivity
Camellia
Morning Glory

**Relationship Healing/
Blessing**
Baby Blue Eyes
Bleeding Heart
Lavender
Orchid
Petunia
Plumeria
Primrose
Tulip

Vervain
Ylang Ylang

**Relationships,
Long-Distance**
Plumeria

Relaxation
Chamomile
Hibiscus
Jasmine
Lavender
Morning Glory
Poppy
Valerian
Ylang Ylang

Resilience
Echinacea
Geranium
Kalanchoe
Yarrow

Sacred Space, Creating
Holly
Lantana
Sage

**Self-Acceptance/
Self-Esteem/Self-Love**
Amaryllidaceae
Crabapple
Freesia
Honeysuckle
Lavender

Narcissus
Pansy
Pittosporum
Rose
Sage

Self-Mastery
Agapanthus

Sensuality
Citrus
Geranium
Jasmine
Pittosporum
Tuberose
Tulip
Ylang Ylang

Serenity/Stillness
Crepe Myrtle
Pansy
Poppy
Sage

**Sexuality, Healing/
Activating**
Hibiscus
Honeysuckle
Jasmine
Orchid
Pittosporum
Tuberose
Ylang Ylang

Simplicity
Clover
Daisy
Echinacea
Morning Glory
Tulip

Skin
Crabapple
Marigold (*Calendula*)
Pansy
Rose
Ylang Ylang

Sleep
Calla Lily
Chamomile
Lavender
Morning Glory
Poppy
Sage
Valerian

Strength
Carnation
Cherry Plum
Clover
Echinacea
Geranium
Lantana
Oleander
Sunflower
Yarrow

Stress, Relief From
Chamomile
Citrus
Lavender
Morning Glory
Pansy
Valerian
Wisteria
Ylang Ylang

Success
Cherry Plum
Echinacea
Forget-Me-Not
Marigold (*Tagetes*)
Oak
Peony
Sunflower

Sustenance
Sunflower

Synchronicity
Citrus
Wisteria

Transitions/Change
Aster
Calla Lily
Carnation
Crepe Myrtle
Freesia
Honeysuckle
Marigold (*Tagetes*)

Nasturtium
Poppy
Tuberose

Transmutation
Dahlia
Freesia
Heather
Hollyhock
Oleander
Primrose
Water Lily
Ylang Ylang

Travel
Heather
Lily

Trust
Baby Blue Eyes
Citrus

**Truth, Speaking/
Aligning With**
Allysum
Geranium
Iris
Lantana
Snapdragon

Uniqueness, Expressing
Amaryllidaceae
Nasturtium
Orchid

Vitality
Echinacea
Marigold (*Tagetes*)
Sunflower

**Weight Loss/
Body Image**
Cherry
Citrus
Honeysuckle
Pittosporum
Ylang Ylang

Wildness
Baby Blue Eyes
Cinquefoil
Foxglove

**Wisdom, Ancient
(Accessing)**
Magnolia

Wisdom, Occult
Dahlia

Wishes
Dandelion

Womb Healing
Freesia

**Workaholism,
Support For**
Vervain

Youthfulness
Cherry Plum
Crepe Myrtle
Plumeria
Rose
Wisteria

Appendix C

Elemental Correspondences

Earth
Allysum
Bird of Paradise
Camellia
Citrus
Crepe Myrtle
Dandelion
Geranium
Heather
Hollyhock
Honeysuckle
Kalanchoe
Magnolia
Oak
Petunia
Pittosporum
Primrose
Tuberose
Tulip

Air
African Daisy
Agapanthus
Aster
Baby Blue Eyes
Cherry
Cinquefoil
Clover
Crabapple
Crocus
Daisy
Dandelion
Forget-Me-Not
Holly

Honeysuckle
Lantana
Manuka
Narcissus
Orchid
Poppy
Rhododendron
Sage
Valerian
Yarrow

Fire

Bougainvillea
Carnation
Cherry Plum
Chrysanthemum
Dandelion
Echinacea
Hibiscus
Marigold (*Calendula*)
Marigold (*Tagetes*)
Oleander
Peony
Snapdragon
Sunflower

Water

African Daisy
Agapanthus
Amaryllidaceae
Aster
Baby Blue Eyes
Bleeding Heart
Calla Lily
Chamomile
Cherry
Cinquefoil
Citrus
Crocus
Dahlia
Datura
Foxglove
Freesia
Honeysuckle
Hyacinth
Hydrangea
Iris
Jasmine
Lilac
Lily

Lupine
Morning Glory
Nasturtium
Orchid
Pansy
Peony
Plumeria
Rose
Sweet Pea
Tuberose
Valerian
Vervain
Water Lily
Wisteria
Ylang Ylang

Appendix D

Planetary Correspondences

Jupiter
Agapanthus
Camellia
Carnation
Cinquefoil
Echinacea
Hollyhock
Honeysuckle
Pittosporum
Sage
Valerian

Mars
Cherry Plum
Foxglove
Hibiscus
Holly

Oleander
Snapdragon

Mercury
Clover
Hydrangea
Lantana
Manuka

Moon
African Daisy
Camellia
Chamomile
Crocus
Dahlia
Daisy
Dandelion

Datura
Jasmine
Morning Glory
Peony
Rhododendron
Tuberose
Valerian
Vervain
Water Lily

Neptune
Amaryllidaceae
Narcissus
Nasturtium
Orchid
Pansy
Poppy

Pluto
Bird of Paradise
Heather

Saturn
Agapanthus
Allysum
Carnation
Crepe Myrtle
Geranium
Kalanchoe

Marigold (*Tagetes*)
Oleander
Primrose
Wisteria

Sun
Chamomile
Chrysanthemum
Crocus
Daisy
Dandelion
Lupine
Marigold (*Calendula*)
Marigold (*Tagetes*)
Oak
Peony
Sunflower
Water Lily
Yarrow

Uranus
African Daisy
Cinquefoil

Venus
Allysum
Aster
Baby Blue Eyes
Bleeding Heart

Bougainvillea
Calla Lily
Cherry
Citrus
Crabapple
Forget-Me-Not
Freesia
Geranium, Rose
Hibiscus
Hyacinth
Iris
Jasmine
Lilac
Lily
Magnolia
Narcissus
Orchid
Petunia
Plumeria
Primrose
Rose
Sweet Pea
Tuberose
Tulip
Ylang Ylang

Acknowledgments

I would like to thank Elysia Gallo, Rebecca Zins, Bill Krause, Sandra Weschcke, Amy Glaser, Anna Levine, and everyone at Llewellyn. Next, great big thank-yous to Ted Bruner, Aron Whitehurst, Joel Whitehurst, Brandi Palachek, Annie Wilder, Allie Chee, Jonathan Kirsch, Descanso Gardens, and the Northern California Women's Herbal Symposium. I would also like to offer my deepest gratitude for the writings and wisdom of Ellen Dugan, Scott Cunningham, Judika Illes, Gretchen Scoble, Ann Field, Gabriel Mojay, P. J. Pierson, Mary Shipley, Mechthild Scheffer, James Green, and Diana Wells. And finally, an infinite thank-you to the flower spirits, who are, of course, the true authors of this book.

Bibliography

Bartholomew, Terese Tse. *Hidden Meanings in Chinese Art*. San Francisco: Asian Art Museum, 2006.

Baum, L. Frank, and Michael Patrick Hearn. *Annotated Wizard of Oz (Centennial Edition)*. New York: W. W. Norton & Company, 2000.

Beckman, Wendy. "Ancient Sunflower Fuels Debate About Agriculture in the Americas." *UC Magazine*. University of Cincinatti, 29 April 2008.

Beer, Robert. *Encyclopedia of Tibetan Symbols and Motifs*. Chicago: Serindia Publications, 2004.

Bradler, Christine M., and Joachim Alfred P. Scheiner. *Feng Shui Symbols*. New York: Sterling, 2001.

Brett, Ana, and Ravi Singh. *Yoga Beauty Body*. Raviana Productions, 2007.

Chevallier, Andrew. *Encyclopedia of Herbal Medicine*. London: Dorling Kindersley, 1996.

Cunningham, Scott. *Cunningham's Encyclopedia of Magical Herbs*. St. Paul, MN: Llewellyn, 1985.

————. *Magical Aromatherapy: The Power of Scent*. St. Paul, MN: Llewellyn, 1989.

Dass, Ram. *Remember, Be Here Now*. Santa Fe, NM: Hanuman Foundation, 1971.

Davidow, Joie. *Infusions of Healing: A Treasury of Mexican-American Herbal Remedies*. New York: Fireside, 1999.

Department of the Army. *The Complete Guide to Edible Wild Plants*. New York: Skyhorse, 2009.

Dugan, Ellen. *Garden Witch's Herbal: Green Magick, Herbalism & Spirituality*. Woodbury, MN: Llewellyn, 2009.

―――――. *Garden Witchery: Magick from the Ground Up*. Woodbury, MN: Llewellyn, 2003.

Ewing, Jim PathFinder. *Clearing: A Guide to Liberating Energies Trapped in Buildings and Lands*. Findhorn, Scotland: Findhorn Press, 2006.

Fritz, Thomas, et al. "Universal Recognition of Three Basic Emotions in Music." *Current Biology* 19 (14 April 2009), 573–576.

Gibran, Kahlil. *The Prophet*. New York: Alfred A. Knopf, 1923.

Green, James. *The Herbal Medicine-Maker's Handbook: A Home Manual*. Freedom, CA: Crossing Press, 2000.

Grey, Alex. *Sacred Mirrors: The Visionary Art of Alex Grey*. Rochester, VT: Inner Traditions, 1990.

Hardie, Titania. *Hocus Pocus: Titania's Book of Spells*. London: Quadrille Publishing Limited, 1996.

Hay, Louise L. *You Can Heal Your Life*. Santa Monica, CA: Hay House, 1987.

Hou, Joseph P., and Youyu Jin. *The Healing Power of Chinese Herbs and Medicinal Recipes*. New York: Haworth, 2005.

Illes, Judika. *The Element Encyclopedia of 5000 Spells: The Ultimate Reference Book for the Magical Arts*. London: HarperElement, 2004.

―――――. *The Element Encyclopedia of Witchcraft: The Complete A–Z for the Magical World*. London: HarperElement, 2005.

―――――. *Encyclopedia of Mystics, Saints, and Sages*. New York: HarperCollins, 2011.

―――――. *Encyclopedia of Spirits: The Ultimate Guide to the Magic of Faeries, Demons, Ghosts, Gods & Goddesses*. New York: HarperCollins, 2009.

Kaminsky, Patricia, and Richard Katz. *Flower Essence Repertory: A Comprehensive Guide to North American and English Flower Essences for Emotional and Spiritual Well-Being*. Nevada City, CA: Flower Essence Society, 1994.

Medici, Marina. *Good Magic*. New York: Fireside, 1988.

Miller, Iona, and Richard Alan Miller. *The Magical and Ritual Uses of Perfumes.* Rochester, VT: Destiny Books, 1990.

Mojay, Gabriel. *Aromatherapy for Healing the Spirit: Restoring Emotional and Mental Balance with Essential Oils.* Rochester, VT: Healing Arts Press, 1997.

Myers, Luke A. *Gnostic Visions: Uncovering the Greatest Secret of the Ancient World.* Bloomington, IN: iUniverse, 2011.

Nozedar, Adele. *The Element Encyclopedia of Secret Signs and Symbols: The Ultimate A–Z Guide from Alchemy to the Zodiac.* London: HarperElement, 2007.

Pierson, P. J., and Mary Shipley. *Aromatherapy for Everyone: Discover the Scents of Health and Happiness with Essential Oils.* Garden City Park, NJ: Square One Publishers, 2004.

Pomeroy, Sarah B. *Goddesses, Whores, Wives, and Slaves: Women in Classical Antiquity.* New York: Pantheon, 1995.

Richardson, David Lester. *Flowers and Flower-Gardens.* Calcutta: D'Rosario and Co., 1855.

Rose, Jeanne. *Jeanne Rose's Herbal Body Book: The Herbal Way to Natural Beauty and Health for Men and Women.* New York: Grosset & Dunlap, 1979.

Rost, Amy, ed. *Natural Healing Wisdom & Know-How: Useful Practices, Recipes, and Formulas for a Lifetime of Health.* New York: Black Dog & Leventhal, 2009.

Royce, Anya Peterson. *Becoming an Ancestor: The Isthmus Zapotec Way of Death.* New York: State University of New York Press, 2011.

Scheffer, Mechthild. *Bach Flower Therapy: Theory and Practice.* Rochester, VT: Healing Arts Press, 1988.

———. *The Encyclopedia of Bach Flower Therapy.* Rochester, VT: Healing Arts Press, 1999.

Schiller, Carol, and David Schiller. *The Aromatherapy Encyclopedia: A Concise Guide to Over 385 Plant Oils*. Laguna Beach, CA: Basic Health Publications, 2008.

Scoble, Gretchen, and Ann Field. *The Meaning of Flowers: Myth, Language, and Lore*. San Francisco, CA: Chronicle Books, 1998.

Shroder, Tom. *Old Souls: Compelling Evidence from Children Who Remember Past Lives*. New York: Fireside, 2001.

Sunset Editors. *Sunset Western Garden Book*. Menlo Park, CA: Sunset Publishing Company, 2005.

Virtue, Doreen. *Archangels and Ascended Masters: A Guide to Working and Healing with Divinities and Deities*. Carlsbad, CA: Hay House, 2003.

Wells, Diana. *100 Flowers and How They Got Their Names*. Chapel Hill, NC: Algonquin Books, 1997.

Whale, Winifred Stevens. *Tremoille Family*. Boston: Houghton Miffin, 1914.

Whitehurst, Tess. *The Good Energy Book: Creating Harmony and Balance for Yourself and Your Home*. Woodbury, MN: Llewellyn, 2012.

————. *Magical Housekeeping: Simple Charms and Practical Tips for Creating a Harmonious Home*. Woodbury, MN: Llewellyn, 2010.

Woolfolk, Joanna Martine. *The Only Astrology Book You'll Ever Need*. New York: Madison Books, 2001.

Index